PRAGMATICS
OF
CHINESE
AS
NATIVE
AND
TARGET
LANGUAGE

TECHNICAL REPORT #5

PRAGMATICS OF CHINESE AS NATIVE AND TARGET LANGUAGE

edited by GABRIELE KASPER

SECOND LANGUAGE TEACHING & CURRICULUM CENTER
University of Hawai'i at Mānoa

© 1995 Second Language Teaching & Curriculum Center
University of Hawai'i
All rights reserved
Manufactured in the United States of America

Funds for the publication of this technical report were provided in part by a grant to the University of Hawai'i under the Language Resource Centers Program of the U. S. Department of Education.

ISBN 0–8248–1733–8

∞ ™ The paper used in this publication meets the minimum requirements of American National Standard for Information Sciences–Permanence of Paper for Printed Library Materials.

ANSI Z39.48–1984

Distributed by
University of Hawai'i Press
Order Department
2840 Kolowalu Street
Honolulu, Hawai'i 96822

CONTENTS

Preface...........vii

'It's Good to be a Bit Chinese':
Foreign Students' Experience of Chinese Pragmatics
Gabriele Kasper & Yanyin Zhang..............1

Strategies in Chinese Requesting
Yanyin Zhang...........23

Indirectness in Chinese Requesting
Yanyin Zhang...........69

Refusing in Chinese
Xing Chen, Lei Ye, and Yanyin Zhang.........119

Performance of Face-Threatening Acts in Chinese:
Complaining, Giving Bad News, and Disagreeing
Jinwen Steinberg Du.........165

Complimenting in Mandarin Chinese
Lei Ye........207

References.........297

ABOUT THE NATIONAL FOREIGN LANGUAGE RESOURCE CENTER

THE SECOND LANGUAGE TEACHING AND CURRICULUM CENTER of the University of Hawai'i is a unit of the College of Languages, Linguistics, and Literature. Under a grant from the U.S. Department of Education, the Center has since 1990 served as a National Foreign Language Resource Center (NFLRC). The general direction of the Resource Center is set by a national advisory board. The Center conducts research, develops materials, and trains language professionals with the goal of improving foreign language instruction in the United States. The Center publishes research reports and teaching materials; it also sponsors a fellows program for senior scholars, an internship program, and a summer intensive teacher training institute. For additional information about Center programs, write:

> Dr. Richard Schmidt, Director
> National Foreign Language Resource Center
> East-West Road, Bldg. 1, Rm. 6A
> University of Hawai'i
> Honolulu, HI 96822

NFLRC ADVISORY BOARD

Kathleen Bardovi-Harlig
Center for English Language Teaching
Indiana University

Claire Kramsch
German Department
University of California, Berkeley

Ronald Walton
National Foreign Language Center
Johns Hopkins University

John Clark
Defense Language Institute
Monterey, California

James Pusack
Project for International
Communication Studies (PICS)
University of Iowa

Representatives of
other funded NFLRCs

PREFACE

THIS TECHNICAL REPORT INCLUDES SIX DATA-BASED STUDIES on different aspects of Chinese pragmatics: an interview study exploring nonnative speakers' experience as learners and communicators in a Chinese environment, and five studies on the realization of different speech acts by native speakers of Mandarin Chinese.

Acquiring communicative ability in Chinese is said to be difficult for adult nonnative speakers, yet to date there are no studies identifying what exactly learners' problems are. Kasper and Zhang's paper examines how nonnative speakers, most of them native speakers of American English, experienced Chinese communication practices, how they saw themselves as foreigners in a Chinese environment, the strategies they developed in their interaction with Chinese interlocutors, and the learning opportunities they encountered to improve their Chinese. Data for this study were collected through semi-structured interviews. One important outcome of this study is that total convergence to Chinese communication practices seems neither necessary nor desirable (nor, in fact, possible for most adult learners of Chinese). 'Optimal convergence' is context-specific and in no small part dependent on the foreign participants' own goals and perceptions of their roles in a Chinese environment.

In two studies, Zhang explores different aspects of requesting. The first study identifies the strategies used for requesting in Mandarin, and some of the context variables that influence their selection. The second study examines how requests are performed indirectly. Using roleplays as a data collection technique, Zhang demonstrates that in Chinese, indirectness operates at the level of discourse rather than at utterance level. Interlocutors' concerns are for face support communication patterns which mutually protect and enhance their 面子 *miànzi*. This is achieved by delaying or avoiding on-record requests when compliance is problematic. In order to decrease the possibility that their request might be refused, speakers carefully test the ground for indications of compliance or refusal, and modify their conversational goals accordingly.

Refusing an interlocutor's initiation effectively and politely can be a trying task even for native speakers. Cheng, Ye, and Zhang investigate how Chinese speakers refuse requests, suggestions, offers, and invitations in different social contexts. In analogy to Goffman's (1967) distinction between substantive and ritual apology, the authors distinguish substantive from ritual refusals. In substantive refusal, the speaker's goal is to convey non-compliance; in ritual refusal, the speaker's goal is to accept the hearer's proposition (an offer or invitation, for instance) but to refuse initially in order not to appear greedy or immodest. Unlike substantive refusal, ritual refusal is not a face-threatening act but a politeness strategy because it enhances participants' 面子 *miànzi*. The authors identify distinct features which index a strategy as ritual or substantive refusal.

Du investigates the realization of three face-threatening acts: complaining, giving bad news, and disagreeing. Complaining about someone else's behavior seems to be viewed as a socially risky business, as indicated by the many subjects who decided not to complain when a particular offense had occurred. When deciding whether or not to deliver bad news, on the other hand, most subjects felt that they should inform their interlocutor about an undesirable aspect in her or his appearance or performance because such information was in the other person's best interest. In order to deflect embarrassment, the bad news was often delivered in a joking manner, although joking was not seen as appropriate in status-low to status-high interlocutor relationships. Expressing disagreement, too, depended on the relationship between the interlocutors: in low-to-high interactions at the work place, disagreement was avoided or expressed indirectly, whereas disagreement with a friend in matters of personal taste was expressed quite openly. As expected, the face-threatening acts examined by Du are highly context-sensitive, as evident not only from the context-dependent preferences for realization options but also from whether such an act is performed at all, and whether it is indeed perceived as 'face-threat'.

Turning from face-threat to face-support, Ye explores compliments and compliment responses. Against stereotypical beliefs about Chinese reactions to compliments, Ye found that the preferred response was 'acceptance with amendment' rather than rejection of the compliment. Just as in previous studies of compliment events among native speakers of English, Ye also found gender-related variation in giving and receiving compliments.

It is the authors' and editor's hope that the papers in this volume will be useful to students and teachers of Chinese. They can be no more than a first step into exploring the intricate patterns of Chinese communication practices, and have to be followed up by studies examining how native speakers perform linguistic action in a variety of communicative encounters, how nonnative speakers interact with Chinese interlocutors in different contexts and for different purposes, and how learners develop their pragmatic competence in Chinese. These are a few urgent issues for a research agenda on the pragmatics of Chinese as a second or foreign language.

Gabriele Kasper and Yanyin Zhang

'IT'S GOOD TO BE A BIT CHINESE': FOREIGN STUDENTS' EXPERIENCE OF CHINESE PRAGMATICS

INTRODUCTION

IN ORDER TO DESIGN THE PRAGMATIC COMPONENT of a curriculum for Chinese as a foreign language, it has to be decided which aspects of Chinese pragmatics to include, which of these aspects to emphasize more or emphasize less, and how to sequence the chosen information. Observation of communicative practices in the target community is an essential part of an input component to such a curriculum. Yet the research available on Chinese pragmatics to date is still minimal. There are virtually no studies available on the acquisition and use of Chinese pragmatics by non-native speakers. In order to establish a research agenda and prioritize research tasks, criteria are needed on which such decisions can be based.

One source of information for the preparation of a research agenda are experienced foreign language users. Their experience as learners and users of Chinese and as outsider participants in interaction with Chinese people can serve to highlight problem areas for learners of Chinese, and give us clues about the patterns of communication in Chinese culture — from the perspective of the foreigner. The information provided by these experienced non-native speakers can thus indicate where to concentrate research efforts on Chinese pragmatics in the broader context of cross-cultural communication. At the same time, systematically gathered information about students' learning and communication experience can function as part of a needs analysis on which curricular decisions for the teaching of Chinese pragmatics can be based. With these two goals in mind, we conducted the study reported on below.

Kasper, G., & Zhang, Y. (1995). 'It's good to be a bit Chinese': Foreign students' experience of Chinese Pragmatics. In G. Kasper (Ed.), *Pragmatics of Chinese as native and target language* (Technical Report #5, pp. 1–22). Honolulu, Hawai'i: University of Hawai'i, Second Language Teaching & Curriculum Center.

INFORMANTS

The participants in the study consisted of twenty-one advanced learners of Chinese at the University of Hawai'i. At the time of the interview, ten of them were attending 300 level Chinese language classes, and nine were attending 400 level Chinese classes. About eleven of them were graduate students and two were University faculty. Seventeen of the interviewees had been to China, Taiwan, or Hong Kong. The length of stay in the Chinese-speaking community ranged from between four weeks to six years. Eleven of them were female and ten, male.

METHOD

Each of the students participated in an interview session of 30 to 50 minutes in length, conducted by both a Chinese and a Western interviewer working in collaboration. Students were interviewed either individually or in pairs. The interviews were semi-structured in that each informant was asked the same series of questions, however, depending on students' answers and follow-up questions, additional topics were sometimes introduced. In fact, students were encouraged to talk about any of their experiences as foreigners in China and as learners of Chinese as these came to their minds during the session. In addition providing information about the common topics covered, the interviews thus supplied a variety of personalized accounts. Even though the students knew that they were being interviewed as part of a research project on Chinese as a foreign language, the sessions evolved much like informal "talk story" events, and were greatly enjoyed by interviewees and interviewers alike.

ANALYSIS AND RESULTS

The interviews were transcribed. Information about recurrent themes was extracted from the material and organized according to the topics presented below.

Complimenting

This was one of the recurring themes in the interview. All the learners reported that they had received a great many compliments while in China. Compliments focused on their appearance, achievements, skills, but most of all, on their Chinese language, regardless of how fragmentary it was. They felt that people were being very polite in this respect.

Learners in general knew that in Chinese culture, the receiver of the compliment is supposed to deny the praise and denigrate him/herself instead of saying "thank you". However, they found it difficult to respond appropriately since, according to their observation, there is no definite set of formulaic expressions of compliment response in Chinese. Limited in Chinese proficiency as well as in cultural knowledge and uneasy about using the same expressions all the time, they were nevertheless unable to vary their linguistic choices at will. Attempts, however, were made. One highly advanced student tried several what he thought were "formal and nice" expressions of denial only to find they were rude and meant "Nonsense!" in Chinese. He told the following story, "One day I was at a formal dinner with professors from University in Taiwan. Everything was proper. I wanted to do my best and do everything correct. They praised my Chinese, as usual, and I thought of a phrase which sounded to me like classic Chinese because it has four characters, 豈有此理 qǐyǒucǐlǐ. It means literally 'there's no such a thing', but it actually means 'Stop your bullshit!' The professors almost dropped their chopsticks and said to me immediately 'You can't say that'. Inspired by the expression 過獎 guòjiǎng 'you praise me too much', he also tried the expression 亂講 luàn jiǎng 'nonsense', thinking it meant "what you've said is not true/nonsense" and thus humbling himself to the praise. In retrospect, the learner said that it took him some time to realize that it was not proper to question or deny what complimenters asserted but to say that he was not good enough to deserve such praise.

Many learners felt uncomfortable to denigrate themselves in compliment situations. A female student thought it was not so much a cultural but a political position that she prevented her from self-denigration, especially in response to a compliment to or about her children. In English, she would respond "I'm proud of them myself". She was aware that her reaction was highly culturally offensive in a Chinese context, but to her, it was a very normal response.

Misunderstandings did occur. An American Chinese student was puzzled at her neighbor, a girl whom she honestly thought was very pretty but who always returned her compliment with "no, no, no, you look better". "What's the matter with her? Did she like my compliment or not?", the American Chinese student wondered. Another student observed that one must be careful when complimenting objects in the homes of Chinese. They may think the guest is making a request to be given the objects.

Refusal to invitation/offer

Most of the learners knew that in Chinese culture, one is not supposed to accept an invitation or an offer right away. They commented that one should refuse several times before accepting, i.e., the students realized that ritual refusal is almost obligatory in an invitation/offer event. However, the result of their ritual refusals was sometimes less successful than expected. During his first short study trip to China, one learner tried it every time in acceptance, and the anticipated insistence on the part of the inviter did not follow. He was wondering even at the time of the interview if it was because the Chinese did not expect him, a foreigner, to perform ritual refusal, or whether he did it inappropriately, i.e., too sincerely, using the wrong expressions, body language, or other cues. To explain the Chinese ritual refusal behavior, one learner commented that the invitation-refusal sequence was a strategy for the invitee to assess the sincerity of the invitation, i.e., how firm was the invitation and if the invitation was not a ritual one or a matter of "face". To play it safe, the learner said, he always refused an invitation the first time it was issued. If the inviting-refusing sequence went on several times, he could figure out that the invitation was probably meant sincerely. (For further discussion of refusal and ritual refusal in Chinese culture, see Chen, Ye, and Zhang, this volume). Another learner observed that whether or not ritual refusal was performed also depended on the relationship between the two parties. If the interlocutors were good friends, probably it was not necessary to "put on such a big show". One would be safe to accept at first offer when invited by a friend.

Many learners reported the difficulty they had to refuse the Chinese, who always offered help, for example, offering seats on buses, taking them around to places, etc. They found that it is almost impossible to refuse offers of food, cigarettes, etc. One student reported that he finally ended up smoking in China because when offering cigarettes, no one would take his "no" for an answer. Several students related their experience of dealing with coffee or tea offers when with a Chinese either in cafeterias or at his/her home. The coffee or tea would invariably be served whether they said "yes" or "no" to the offer. "The tea would just come closer and closer," one student said.

Refusal to request

One learner, who had worked in China for several years, warned that one should avoid saying "no" abruptly. There were certain Chinese expressions which meant "no" and everyone reads them that way. For example, when a Chinese says 我有事 wǒ yǒu shì 'I have something planned', one should not ask "what is it you are going to do?", because that expression is a "conventional mask" that says "don't bother me". Maybe nothing is going on. It means "no" and no possible negotiations.

Several learners observed that Chinese would sometimes say "yes" when really mean "no". The evidence for the intended "no" is that they would not follow up expressed compliance with action. It took one learner quite a while to find out that her Chinese supervisor in Taiwan meant "no" in response to her request without saying the word. When she confronted the supervisor with her request without saying the word. When she confronted the supervisor with the problem, the supervisor appeared surprised and puzzled. Apparently, she did not expect her responses to be understood any other way. Based on this kind of experience, one learner who was well-versed in Chinese culture behavior suggested that since Chinese would not say "no" directly due to 面子 *miànzi* considerations, it is crucial to observe how they say "yes" and how they follow it up. "面子 *miànzi*" refers to "the need of an individual to conform to social conventions and express one's desire to be part of this community" (Hu, 1944; Mao, 1994).

The other side of the coin was that many learners found it hard to refuse a request. For example, one learner was once asked to give a lecture while in China. To a Chinese, it was more of an invitation, a compliment, an honor, to the person invited. However, the learner did not feel up to it and repeatedly declined the request by saying that he did not know what to talk about, that he was not good enough, etc., etc. To a Chinese, it sounded like compliment-response situation: a purely ritual process of self-denigration. The more he declined in this way, the more escalated became the request. Eventually, the student became upset and remembered the experience with an uneasy feeling.

Thanking/appreciation

Several learners had problems identifying Chinese ways of expressing gratitude and appreciation while in China. They found it hard to understand situations where, according to their expectations, explicit verbal thanking was in order but none occurred. A Japanese native speaker reported that she once did a favor for a Chinese woman at her request and bought her some imported cigarettes. Upon receiving them, the woman did not say "thank you", as she had been expected to do, especially since the Japanese student had paid for the commodities. What was more, the woman did not even show any signs of happiness, excitement or appreciation, according to the student. The Japanese student did not, and still does not know, whether the woman was happy or not, or whether she had bought her the wrong brand. A similar experience was shared by an American student who was told one day, during his study in China, to bring some fruit to his teacher, who was sick, to show his concern, something the student would never do in the U.S. When he went to the teacher's home, the teacher took the fruit at the door and did not express any (overt) signs of gratitude. This left the student wondering ever since whether he had done the right thing.

Another student who used to teach at a joint-venture hotel in Beijing told a story which took place at the hotel. The foreign management there decided to give every Chinese employee a cash bonus before a major holiday.

you", and the foreign management personnel were secretly grudging and called the Chinese employees "ungrateful". However, the next day, they saw a drastic improvement of performance: the Chinese employees worked harder. This student remarked that it was not so much words like "thank you", but action, that Chinese people often use to express their gratitude and appreciation. This experience was confirmed by another incident, more personal in nature. This time, the learner gave a birthday gift to a good friend of his. No thanking was mentioned upon receiving the gift. However, the learner saw later that his friend was happy about it and showed gratitude non-verbally.

Several students also mentioned that the Chinese do not thank each other in the family or between close friends. In fact the students respond that Chinese people always scold their foreign friends for saying "thank you" and "sorry" too often. "Don't say that", one learner was told by his Chinese friends, "It sounds too American." Some learners found it hard to understand while others regarded it as a Chinese way of exhibiting social proximity. Even for those who did understand it and strove to behave like a Chinese person, it was psychologically frustrating not to say "thank you", when they really wanted to.

Requests

The students noted that Chinese requests can be both direct and indirect. As an example of direct requesting, exchanging money was mentioned. Several learners reported that their Chinese friends asked them to exchange money for them and were very direct about it, so much so that they started to wonder if they became friends simply because the Chinese saw this potential benefit for themselves. About indirect requests, one subject had the following story to tell. During her stay in China, she was being tutored informally by a Chinese teacher. After meeting several times, her tutor started to say something like "I also have time next Tuesday", something which did not make sense to the student. It took her a while to figure out that the tutor would have liked her to pay in the future, but just would not say it in so many words. Another subject said that one must be roundabout in requesting when encountering possible reluctance, because the Chinese would not use the word "no" in refusal. Expressions of reluctance indicate refusal.

To make a request in bureaucratic settings is not an easy thing. One student reported an incident in which she had to act as an interpreter on behalf of two foreign students who did not speak Chinese. These students had been involved in a traffic accident and their damaged bikes were taken away by security officers. They wanted them back. The girl went to the local security bureau frequently over a period of several months, each time asking for the return of the bikes and each time being turned over to another section.

Although she finally succeeded in getting the bikes back, she did not know why it took so long: whether it was because she did not address the security office staff correctly or whether other aspects of the language she used were not appropriate. In general, several people reported that in order to get what you want, a forceful and pushy manner does not work.

One learner related an incidence in which he was trying to help the Chinese instructor out by demanding right in front of the whole class that the principal leave the test room. Not only did he fail in his attempt, but learned later from the Chinese instructor that he actually made her lose face in front of her superior.

"When making a request in Chinese," one student observed, "it is important to be self effacing and act in a calculated way to get what you want. Use expressions that the other person likes to hear, e.g., acknowledging the trouble they are taking even if it's their duty."

Terms of address

This is one of the few areas which elicited a wide range of reactions. Quite a few students did not feel they had problems with choosing the right terms of address. They had a few expressions at hand for people they most often encountered, e.g., peers, teachers, and total strangers. By using the appropriate address terms, they did not experience major problems getting around. However, most of the students interviewed agreed that terms of address were a tricky thing for learners of Chinese since there are so many relations in Chinese culture and the Chinese "are very sensitive about generation", an issue embedded in address terms. One student once asked a child to call him 爷爷 *yéye* 'grandfather' in front of the child's father. He was warned not to do that because, by being addressed by this term, he put himself above the father in the family system.

Terms of address encode not only information about relations between interlocutors, but also information about social distance and hierarchy. One Australian professor said that during a group tour in China, she was treated differently from the students in the same group. One of the indications of this differential treatment was that she could use certain term of address to talk to the guide. She was allowed to call him 小李 *xiǎo Lǐ* 'Little Li'. When one of the students once attempted to do the same, out of ignorance, he was immediately reminded by the guide that 李先生 *Lǐ xiānsheng* 'Mr. Li' was what he should have used.

Errors in the choice of address terms were causally related to the students' limited knowledge of Chinese cultural customs, terms of address and their specific, sometimes highly emotionally charged semantics as well as the desire to try and manipulate the language. Such errors were found to have positive and negative effects. One American female student, who worked at an American University office together with several Chinese students from China, was told by a male Chinese office-mate not to call him "Lao Tian" (old + family name) because, as he explained, "we are equal and I am not that much older than you." To respect his request as well as keep their social distance unchanged, she chose the term for older male sibling with the Chinese student's family name attached, 田哥哥 *Tián gēge*, 'Older Brother Tian'. Little did she know that this kind of usage carries a high degree of intimacy, usually reserved for (potential) lovers (i.e., "sweetheart").[1] This was a "happy mistake", which all the Chinese in the office enjoyed hilariously, hearing her call the Chinese guy "my sweetheart" everyday. The American girl, however, took the merriment as confirmatory and congratulated herself to her choice.

Conscientious choice of address terms can also produce less than "sweet" effects. One American woman in her early 40's felt uncomfortable about being called 小姐 *xiǎojiě* 'Miss', a term traditionally used for unmarried women up to their 40's (or even older). She was "so startled" the first few times she heard it, because in America, "We seldom call someone 'miss' who is over 25 years old unless in a formal setting. I thought being called and being considered younger is not advantageous in Chinese culture, which reveres seniority and where wisdom is associated with age. I assume that if you call someone younger than they are, then you are not implying something good about her." She herself chose the term 大娘 *dàniáng* 'old lady' which she thought meant "Auntie" but, which in fact is a "folksy" term for older women.

Feelings of discomfort are not uncommon even when learners are told what address terms to use. One American girl had a neighbor in Taiwan who was a doctor. People there called him "uncle" and his daughter told her to also call him "uncle". But she could not. She did not feel comfortable using a kinship term to address a non-family member. She continued to call him "doctor", fully aware that it was not as nice and sounded very distant.

A few learners found certain Chinese terms of address offensive. Usually these terms referred to women. For example, "grandma" in Chinese is 外婆 *wàipó* in which 外 *wài* literally means 'outside'. They felt that these address terms reflected the political and social bias against women in Chinese history and tradition. Although they saw no connections between the literal meaning and the use of these address terms today, these expressions were still quite difficult for them to accept.

---

[1] Family name + *mèimei* (younger sister) used by male, and family name + *gēge* (older brother) used by female, are signs of a potentially intimate relationship or intention.

Topics for conversation

Many learners were uncomfortable with the kinds of small talk Chinese people usually engaged in, especially in casual encounters such as on a train. The topics were invariably "personal" — age, marital status, salary, family members and background, children, etc. Some learners were repulsed, particularly at the beginning, and many still did not understand why it is the case that the Chinese talk about personal matters the way the Westerners talk about the weather. Quite a few, mostly females, had the attitude "it's none of your business", while the majority realized over time that talking about personal topics was the Chinese way of establishing some kind of common ground for further conversation, and the Chinese did not really expect to be given accurate information. The ways of getting to know somebody in China are simply different from American ways. One could say something which satisfied the convention without going into much detail.

The topic of obesity is a taboo topic for conversation in western culture, certainly in American culture. However, the learners found that it is not at all taboo in Chinese conversation. Almost all the learners were surprised that Chinese would openly and without embarrassed comment on them or each other for being "fat". In looking for an explanation to this drastic difference in these "taboo" topics, one student commented that the Chinese hold a rather "pragmatic" and "realistic" attitude toward certain limitations they are born with. "Young girls have no problems admitting to the whole world that 'I'm fat, I'm not beautiful, but I have nice skin'. They just take their strong points and run as far as they can and be realistic about that. Being fat can be said in front of a thousand people but that doesn't devaluate a person as a whole. Having that attitude, you are not being slapped." Most students did not comment on different expressions used to refer to body weight, moreover, the native speaker of Japanese recalled that what the Chinese usually said was 你胖了 *nǐ pàng le* 'you've put on some weight' or 'you look a bit heavier now', which was extremely different from 你眞胖 *nǐ zhēn pàng* 'you are fat' although the latter is not necessarily an insult when said to relatively familiar interlocutors. The former, on the other hand, is a compliment, based on the Chinese value that being fat is a sign of happiness, good fortune, and no worries.

Learning and communication strategies

For these advanced learners of Chinese, the problems they encountered, according to their own analysis, were not so much linguistic but cultural background knowledge and culturally based linguistic schemata and choices. They felt a certain void in their repertoire of Mandarin, which did not provide them with a base to fall back on in their daily functioning in the target culture.

Various strategies were used to compensate for this lack of relevant knowledge. Some learners would ask people for specific language expressions for certain situations. For example, one student knew that, as a general rule, Chinese people deny a compliment they receive, and that he was proficient enough to use denial expressions in compliment situations. However, since, as he also found out, there does not seem to be a definite set of formulaic expressions for compliment responses, it was somewhat hard for him to determine which were most appropriate expressions and to vary the linguistic forms in each specific case, if he did not want to repeat himself all the time. What he did was ask his teachers for specific expressions, such as 我還差得遠 *wǒ hái chà de yuǎn* 'I still have a long way to go'. Quite a few learners used avoidance strategies. They would not say anything unless they were absolutely sure how; or they would only speak English to avoid misunderstanding. They would avoid using specific terms of address in service encounters and to strangers, instead, they frequently used 對不起 *dùibuqǐ* 'excuse me', to get attention, a formula the Chinese do not use in this function.

Many learners focused their attention on the specific behaviors of Chinese, using these as short cuts to cultural learning and to make life easier, instead of trying out complicated" and intriguing linguistic work. One example is that a learner, who after trying unsuccessfully to refuse repeated offers of cigarettes each time he met people in China, simply gave in and ended up smoking. Since it was almost impossible to stop Chinese hosts from putting food on the plates of their guests, some learners observed how Chinese guests dealt with the situation and followed suit, e.g., eating slowly, saying certain things, stopping eating even though the plate was full and the hosts kept putting food on the plate.

As a piece of "advice", one student said that based on his own experience in Taiwan, one had better make friends with the boss or the brother of the boss, etc. if one wanted to function smoothly in a Chinese company. Knowing people and having connections were very important to get things done in China.

Pragmatic transfer was another strategy which many learners relied on. Positive transfer can make things easier. The Japanese native student was the only one among the interviewees who did not feel frustrated or strange in compliment situations since, according to her, the Japanese behave culturally the same way in this aspect as the Chinese. A few learners reported that a lot of times they did not know what to say and thought about American ways but never actually use a transfer strategy for fear of being rude. However, one girl felt it was so hard to respond to compliment that she simply did it the American way by saying 謝謝 *xièxie* 'thank you' and dismissing it. To play it safe, many learners preferred to be "overpolite" in situations where they were uncertain. For example, they noted that Chinese people do not say "thank you" as frequently as Americans do, but the learners did not mind saying "thank you" more often than necessary or when they were not sure whether they should say it or not.

Some learners would switch their pragmatic behavior according to cultural context and their interlocutor: they would do things in the Chinese way when in China or when talking with Chinese, and the American way when in the U.S. or talking to the westerners.

Learning sources

Most learners reported that they had not received adequate, if any, culture training in class before going to China. Those who had had training felt that it was not enough to prepare them for what happened to them in China. Only two learners had received systematic training and briefing in these matters. For half a year or so, they had Chinese teachers from China in their respective programs, preparing them for situations like those aforementioned. Roleplays and demonstrations were sometimes conducted, and discussions on specific cultural differences were held.

Some of the learners picked up the behavior of their Chinese instructors. For example, the first professor of Chinese one learner had was, according to her, very traditional. Through his words, attitude and general behavior, he instilled a feeling of humbleness in the students. One Chinese American student picked things up from his parents as part of his socialization e.g., ritual refusal. Some students asked their Chinese tutors and friends explicitly about matters of Chinese culture and behavior. Others took courses in Chinese history, philosophy, religion, etc. and tried to learn the fundamental principles which underlie daily cultural behavior. They found it important to know why the Chinese say and do things certain ways. Many of them watched Chinese movies and TV, and read books in or about China in order to get an idea of Chinese culture.

Many students learned Chinese everyday culture from their observation of Chinese people in China, e.g., at the dinner table, getting on the bus, buying train tickets, addressing people. They learned what works in actual encounters. As one learner observed, what one learned in class very often did not correspond to what happened "out there". However, through attentive and purposeful observations of how people reacted to his invitation, he learned the schemata for different situations. "You pick up those little conventions, the set of exchanges and finally you pick that up as a whole entity and use it. As you use it, you get a lot of feedback and feel it so smooth. If you have ways of refusing, etc., you are better accepted because people think you are very Chinese. You cannot go beyond your face but having ways of talking makes social relationships go smoothly. In fact," he stressed, "there is a lot of emphasis on it in traditional Chinese culture: saying what you should, responding in certain ways, etc. If you master those little patterns, you just feel great, although that takes a while to learn."

Suggestions for teaching

About one third of the students expressed skepticism about whether these patterns of everyday culture can be taught and learned in the classroom. Some thought that books and classes were useless and teaching culture out of context was no good. Others felt that this cultural information is good to teach but hard to learn. One has to go into the culture to observe what is going on and how to deal with each situation. Everyday life in China provides a vast amount of input, and the best way to learn is to ask people what things mean and the ways to do things.

Another group of students thought that training in Chinese pragmatics would certainly be helpful. It would at least build some kind of supportive knowledge which one can fall back on when the occasion arises. Given the fact that many linguistic expressions for specific situations are formulaic, one could pull out those conventionalized blocks and teach them in the classroom. On the other hand, more students feel that being taught culture-specific behavior in certain situations would help tremendously even if no appropriate linguistic tool is provided. They felt that they would not freeze and give wrong responses.

Cultural comments about the teaching of Chinese as a foreign language in the American universities pointed to a number of problem areas:

1. The amount of Chinese spoken in the classroom is less than sufficient.
2. Language taught in the classroom is unnatural in comparison to language use outside the institutional setting. It is less casual, slower in speed, including obsolete words and usage.
3. Taiwan Mandarin is better represented than PRC Mandarin.
4. Too little culture information is provided.

One student compared two types of Chinese classes at the 200 level: one was taught with traditional methods, focusing on grammar, reading, vocabulary, etc.; the other one used a communicative approach, emphasizing specific functions of language use. Once in China, the students in the communicative class were immediately better at getting around. But the traditional class, to which this student belonged, picked things up quickly. In specific functions of language use. Once in China, the students in the communicative class were immediately better at getting around. But the traditional class, to which this student belonged, picked things up quickly. In reflection, the student commented "In the first two years, people shouldn't concentrate on specific functions. While that gets you around, there is always a hole there. Grammar, tones, vocabulary, etc. should be emphasized, because, after all, it is not hard to function and get around." A few students also expressed their confusion as to the goal of the first two years of instruction — "to prepare students to go to China or to help students get some Chinese sentences out?"

Almost all the students offered suggestions of how to incorporate cultural information in the classroom teaching of Chinese. The following is a summary of these points.

1. Classroom teaching of Chinese should include, on a regular basis, relevant situations and things people say/do in these situations. This is to prepare the students for effective communication in the future. Communication itself can only happen in the target culture.

2. Teaching should also include the underlying cultural principles which motivate the specific cultural behaviors. Culture with a "capital C", such as Confucius, Taoism, etc. should be taught because it helps explain the things Chinese people do and the ways in which they behave. Although many specific practices can be picked up along the way or learned in class, that does not provide the students with the knowledge why things are done the way they are.

3. A course in Chinese should be designed around culture instead of grammar. Linguistic information in such a course would serve to support cultural events. In addition, most of the relevant cultural knowledge can be taught through discussion and reading in English or other native languages of the learners.

4. Roleplay should be used as an instrument of culture training in the classroom. Two learners who had benefited from such training in their respective countries felt strongly that it was helpful to put students in a simulated situation and observe how they reacted to it. Similarly, it was found useful to contrast video recordings of parallel social situations in China and America, and talk about the differences and similarities of meaning and appropriateness in these scenarios.

Chinese, I tried to add some culture element and give them some language to bridge the gap. For instance, I taught them to say 辛苦了 xīnkǔ le 'you work very hard'. They used it and received positive feedback. Chinese people find it funny if foreigners can say a few slang expressions. I tried to teach them some harmless ones. They liked it and remembered it. When they used it, there was contact there and both parties felt good."

Being a foreigner in China

The majority of the students agreed that in being conspicuously non-Chinese a foreigner in China enjoys many privileges and latitudes which are denied to the Chinese. They can get away with misdemeanors, minor mistakes, etc. Miscommunication happens but can often be laughed off. Some students felt that one has to accept the fact of being a foreigner and prepare oneself for being treated in certain ways. It is not appropriate for foreigners to behave like a Chinese person, some of students observed, at least not in the beginning. However, it is important to take care not to give offense.

Their obvious foreign role notwithstanding, quite a number of students thought that it would be useful to adopt Chinese linguistic behavior in some ways and to be a bit of a Chinese. For one thing, this makes social interaction smoother and more comfortable for both the Chinese and foreign interactants, for example, by providing ritual refusal to invitations, knowing ways of responding to Chinese hosts' pleading to eat more, etc. Furthermore, these students felt that the linguistic expressions used on these occasions were more or less conventionalized and all one needs to learn (and to teach) is to know when to use which expressions in which slot in the discourse. Once learners have mastered this, the Chinese would sometimes read them in the Chinese way; thus social encounters proceed smoothly and both sides feel at ease. Along this line, it was advised that one must not say "thank you" and "I'm sorry" too often because that would remind the Chinese participant of the cultural gap between themselves and the foreigner, especially after one has become friends with a Chinese person. The students also observed a relationship between language proficiency and expectations of cultural adaptation — the better one's language skill is, the higher the Chinese participants' expectations of cultural conformity.

Some subjects reported that the Chinese treated foreigners differently from the way they treated each other. According to their experience, the Chinese seldom complimented or commented each other on appearance, but they often did so with foreigners. Due to such differences in treatment, many learners found it difficult to observe how Chinese dealt with such situations.

The students unanimously commented that in China, everyone was friendly and many people would "bend over backwards" to help a foreigner. Several students said that they tried to show respect and found that a respectful attitude helpful in order to get along. In fact, linguistic skills became secondary to a respectful attitude. In the midst of the hospitality and latitude she enjoyed in China, one student said she was being especially careful not to abuse it.

Culture-specific practices

Two outstanding situations were mentioned many times by the students. The first of these was paying the bill in a restaurant. It seems to be the usual practice for the Chinese that one person pays for all present at a meal and people take turns. "Going Dutch" is not a familiar concept in China. However, it was noted as a problem knowing when to volunteer to take care of the bill and when to hold back. In fact, many students found that they never had the chance to pay since they were unlikely to belong to the circle of people who would hang out together and thus have the opportunity to take turns, and furthermore, they were "guests" among the Chinese and thus were not allowed to pay. It was noted that it is very important for the Chinese to treat their guests well and take care of them in every respect. Chinese hosts do not seem to have financial concerns when their hospitality is called upon. A student who used to teach in China said that one of her students who would not pay for a seating ticket on the train would nevertheless insist on paying for the teacher's dinner.

The second situation had to do with classroom behavior. Chinese classrooms are very quiet. Students must request to speak by raising hands. Many learners have had the experience of being either a teacher or a student in China. As a student, one learner felt it frustrating not to be able to ask as many questions as he had. He got the feeling that the teacher just wanted him to shut up.

As teachers, several learners found that the students in China were very respectful of teachers and highly motivated to study. However, they could not get their students to discuss things or answer questions. Teachers were expected to do most of the talking. Classroom discourse in China was mostly conducted as one-way traffic originating from the teacher.

Language, directness, and politeness

At various times during their experience as learners of the Chinese language, the learners were told, either by their instructors, or in readings, that Chinese society was very polite. "In German Sinology," one learner said, "there is this conception that the Chinese are sages made up of thousands of little

Confuciuses." Once in China or having contacts with the Chinese people, learners found that average people on the street are not like that. Much of the "disillusionment" occurred during culture-specific language practice. As one learner commented "I'm sure Chinese society is polite, but our definition of politeness is not the same as theirs. We always say 'thank you' and 'I'm sorry' to be polite, even among family members, but they don't and still regard themselves as polite."

It was noted that linguistic means used to perform certain speech acts, when translated literally from one language to another, may alter their original meaning and instead, perform a different speech act. For example, one student perceived her Chinese friend's way of giving advice or making suggestions almost like a command. "[In China,] there seems nothing wrong to tell people 'you should do such and such'. To Americans, nobody, not even your parents, will tell you what to do after you reach a certain age. I expect people who are going to give me advice to couch it in a gentler wording like 'If I were you, I would'. You have to be very close friends to say it so directly." She was referring to her Hong Kong friend, who switched linguistically but not conceptually and culturally when talking to her in English. Finally the American student came to understand her friend in his own cultural context, i.e., that giving advice or making suggestions very directly is the Chinese way and that he did not expect her to always follow his ideas, as a command would require.

Many learners observed that the Chinese are quite direct on certain topics, e.g., age, salary, obesity, but indirect on others, e.g., response to invitations, offering criticism, and talking about intimate relationships. Uncomfortable feelings usually stemmed from the directly addressed topics. As some students noted, it was not so much these that constituted sources of discomfort, for Americans also talk about these themselves. Rather, it was the direct way in which these topics were introduced by the Chinese that made the American learners uncomfortable. As examples, "you are really fat", "you have a big nose", or "My niece is an American but she didn't speak good Chinese. Her Chinese is really bad, like yours." Some students experienced these comments as "kind of brutal in a way". A few of them were able to recognize that this kind of language use does not bother the Chinese and is not impolite to them. One student commented, "If you get into that language, you know it is different and there is no connection [between the language they use and politeness intentions]."

CONCLUSION

THE STUDENTS' COMMENTS SUGGEST that for the population they represent, explicit teaching of Chinese pragmatics is advisable. In order to enable students to better understand their Chinese interlocutors and make appropriate choices for their production of linguistic action, focus should be given to increasing students' awareness about Chinese cultural practices as parts of a changing socio-historic context. Background information about cultural beliefs and values is more valuable than piecemeal information such as 'Chinese people request indirectly' or 'don't say thank you when you receive a compliment' because such generalizations are more likely to promote half-truths and stereotypes than foster understanding and successful communication. A course in Chinese history and philosophy, including recent socio-economic changes and their impact on cultural members' rights and obligations, may in fact contribute more to students' appreciation of Chinese ways than lists of useful phrases.

On the other hand, given the complexity and foreignness of the Chinese language, explicit instruction in the sociopragmatics and pragmalinguistics of Chinese communication needs to be emphasized. Listening comprehension activities should make use of audiovisual material such as video productions of Chinese everyday life, including study and work situations as appropriate for the targeted student population. Such material should not only be used for students to extract referential meaning but also social, relational, and affective information. Particular emphasis should be given to the linguistic material used to convey such information. Obviously, it would be unrealistic to expect students to master the complexity of pragmalinguistic conventions productively.

What then should be the goal for students' productive pragmatic ability? Considering that a recurrent theme in the interviews is the students' role as foreigners in the Chinese community, full convergence to the pragmatic norms observed by native speakers seems not only unrealistic but undesirable.

As one student commented, 'being a bit Chinese' seems be the appropriate line to take on most occasions. Just what this 'bit' entails is difficult to define, however. Obviously, foreigners in China place themselves on a continuum between foreigness and cultural adaptation. Just where exactly an individual student will be located on this continuum at a given moment, and the degree of convergence desirable for that person as a future goal, will greatly vary individually. And even for the individual student, there will be variation in the desirable approximation to Chinese pragmatic norms depending on different discourse domains and current communicative goals.

What is needed, then, are two kinds of research on Chinese pragmatics:

1. studies of the linguistic action and interaction among Chinese native speakers (because this is the kind of input foreign students will have to make sense of, even if contributions addressed to them may be somewhat different)
2. studies of interactions between foreigners and their Chinese interlocutors in a variety of discourse domains.

The second type of study will have to pay particular attention to the relationship between accommodation and context and its impact on relative communicative success and failure. A cumulative body of such interlanguage pragmatics research will help define what 'a bit Chinese' may entail for different non-native users in different contexts, and shed light on the pragmatic principles and practices which foreign speakers of Chinese and their Chinese interlocutors are most comfortable with ◆

APPENDIX A

INTERVIEW QUESTIONS

Stimuli

Instances of invitation and refusal in Chinese were supplied.

Miscommunications and their causes (pragmalinguistic & sociopragmatic)

Have you encountered any situations where communications break down or misunderstanding occurred when you acted according to your own cultural norms?
If yes,

— is it because you did not know the Chinese cultural norms?
— is it because you had problems with appropriate linguistic expressions?
— is it because you chose to behave the way you did?

Situation types

Are there any particular situations which you find more difficult to handle?

— professional: work, study, teachers, fellow-students
— private: friends, acquaintances
— service encounters: shopping, buying ticket, cafeteria/restaurant
— bureaucracy: residence, work, travel requirements
— any other situations in which you must function

Social variables

Are there any contrasts in communication behavior in terms of gender, age, status, or familiarity between Chinese and your native culture?

If yes,
— what are the situations in which these contrasts present themselves most sharply?

Transfer

To what extent do you rely on your own language and cultural patterns when you communicate in Chinese (successfully)?

Learning

In your learning experience, how do you make systematic progress in this area (pragmatic ability)?

— explicitly taught
— through observation and mimicking
— figure it out yourself
— through reading (references)

What pragmatic skills in your opinion are relatively easier/more difficult to learn and master?

— linguistic means
— pragmatic knowledge
— appropriateness

Teaching

Would explicit teaching of cultural knowledge of this kind helpful and necessary?

If yes,
— supply your suggestions about what would be helpful (or not helpful) in teaching and learning pragmatic skills

Yanyin Zhang

STRATEGIES IN
CHINESE REQUESTING

THE SPEECH ACT OF REQUESTING

THE PERFORMATIVE VERBS which denote requestive action directly in Chinese all encode the literal meaning of 'beg' (求 qiú): 請求 qǐngqiú, 懇求 kěnqiú; 要求 yāoqiú. This notion of 'begging' in a requestive action reflects the humble position in which the speaker (S), i.e., the person who issues the request, perceives him/herself to be in the interactive event in relation to the hearer (H), the person who receives the request. However, the actual meanings of these verbs do not necessarily all connote the meaning of 'begging'. The requestive force being equal, these verbs differ in their range of politeness force. While 請求 qǐngqiú and 懇求 kěnqiú express humbleness and self-denigration of S's attitude, an important component in Chinese polite behavior (Gu, 1990), 要求 yāoqiú, on the other hand, appears more assertive and denotes certain perceived rights of S to request and obligations of H to comply.

DEFINITION

In the Western literature, requests have been defined as acts by means of which S attempts to get H to do something. This "something" is usually seen as being "costly" to H, i.e., requiring of H some expenditure of time, energy, or material resources (Leech, 1983; Blum-Kulka, House & Kasper, 1989). The imposition involved in a request constitutes a threat to H's negative face (Brown & Levinson, 1987). Unless, for some reason, S does not mind to cause offense, or decides to give up the request altogether, S's task is to mitigate threat to H's negative face while at the same time pursuing the requestive goal.

Zhang, Y. (1995). Learning Chinese pragmatic skills. In G. Kasper (Ed.), *Pragmatics of Chinese as native and target language* (Technical Report #5, pp. 23–67). Honolulu, Hawai'i: University of Hawai'i, Second Language Teaching & Curriculum Center.

The universal validity of this conceptualization of requests has been challenged from various angles. Wierzbicka (1985) argues that including impositiveness as a definitional criterion of requests betrays an anglocentric bias because asking somebody to do something does not need to be perceived as an infringement of H's space. Indeed the very concept of privacy as personal space has been seen as closely tied to an individualistic view of person and hence of limited applicability to more interdependence-oriented communities (Matsumoto, 1988). Even in an anglo context, requests are not always viewed as positing risk to H's face. When the requested activity provides for H an occasion for displaying socially valued abilities or attributes, its function is face-enhancing rather than face-threatening (Fraser, 1990). The same could be said about Chinese culture, where requests are often regarded as signs of a good relationship and even respect. A person who has never been asked to do something for others is generally perceived as lacking "friends" or other social relationships.

REQUEST STRATEGIES

Requests can be performed at different degrees of directness. For instance, in order to get her roommate to clean up, S might say 把房間打掃干淨 *bǎ fángjiān dǎsǎo gānjing* 'Clean up the room', which is a *direct* expression of a request because the syntactic and semantic structure of the utterance convey both that the utterance is a request and what the request is about. On the other hand, in the same context, S might say 房間真髒 *fángjiān zhēn zāng* 'This room is in a mess'. Here, it is not obvious from the utterance structure that a request is being made, nor what it is about. In order to understand the utterance as a request to clean up the room, H has to interpret the utterance in its context and thereby hypothesize (or guess, if you like) what it is S means by what she says. This kind of request is called *indirect*. The two examples represent opposite ends of a directness continuum. A third way of requesting takes a middle position on this continuum. S might choose to say to her roommate 把房間打掃打掃怎麼樣？ *bǎ fángjiān dǎsao dǎsao zěnmoyàng?* 'How about cleaning the room?' or 你能把房間打掃打掃嗎？ *nǐ néng bǎ fángjiān dǎsao dǎsao ma?? '*Could* you tidy up the room?' In this case, the formulae 怎麼樣 *zěnmoyàng* 'how about' and 你能...嗎 *nǐ néng...ma* 'could you...' represent conventionalized forms to convey requestive force. Therefore, even though the semantic and syntactic utterance structure does not indicate that a request is being made, the use of conventionalized forms of requesting allow H to immediately determine its pragmatic meaning.

DIRECTNESS AND POLITENESS

The scale of directness-indirectness is closely related to the degree of politeness. It has been claimed (Searle, 1975; Brown & Levinson, 1987; Leech, 1983) that as a general rule, the more directly a request is realized, the less polite it is. However, empirical studies have found that the scale of directness and the degree of politeness are not perceived to have a one-to-one relationship. For instance, "Conventional Indirectness" was rated by Israelis and Americans as the most polite request strategy (Blum-Kulka, 1987). In addition, the interaction between directness and politeness in a request utterance is influenced by factors such as power and familiarity between interactants, the degree of imposition in a given request (Brown & Levinson, 1987), personal factors such as age and gender (Fraser, Rintell & Walters, 1980), directive goals, the requester's right and estimated difficulty to request, the requester's obligation to carry out the request, and likelihood of compliance (Blum-Kulka, Danet & Gerson, 1985; Blum-Kulka & House, 1989).

THE STUDY

METHOD

IN ORDER TO INVESTIGATE the realization patterns of requesting in Chinese, data were collected by means of a production questionnaire, which included the following contexts:

S1	*Loan*	Student A wants to borrow $100 from fellow student B to buy a TV.
S2	*Roommates*	Student A comes to visit his friend B and would like to stay at B's place for two weeks. B has three roommates.
S3	*Paper*	Student wants professor to change the length requirement for a term paper.
S4	*Editing*	Editor wants professor to revise his book for publication.
S5	*Restaurant*	Customer wants to change his order.
S6	*Leave*	Lecturer wants the Chair to grant her one year leave of absence to study abroad.
S7	*Room*	Student A wants roommate B to clean up the room after B's party.
S8	*Notes*	Student A wants to borrow student B's lecture notes.
S9	*Ride*	A wants to catch a ride home with her neighbor.

S10 Police   Police officer wants driver to move her car away from the driveway.
S11 Deadline   Student wants professor to extend the deadline for a term paper.
S12 Lecturer   Lecturer wants student to give a class report a week before the scheduled date.

Sample Situation: S10 Police:

黃玲把車停在了一所剛剛著過火的房前的人行道上。執勤的警察發現后，請黃玲把車移開。如果您是警察，您會怎樣對黃玲講，讓她把車移開？

Huáng Líng bǎ chē tíng zài le yī suǒ gānggāng zhāo guò huǒ de fáng qián de rénxíngdào shang. Zhíqín de jǐngchá fāxiàn hòu, qǐng Huáng Líng bǎ chē yíkāi. Rúguǒ nín shì jǐngchá, nín huì zěnyàng duì Huáng Líng jiǎng, ràng tā bǎ chē yíkāi?

Huang Ling parked her car on the sidewalk in front of a house where there had been a recent fire. The police officer on duty saw it and asked Huang Ling to move the car away. If you were the police officer, what would you say to Huang Ling to make her move her car?

The questionnaire was completed by 30 native speakers of Mandarin from the People's Republic of China who were students at various universities in the U.S. Their ages ranged between 22 and 35. About half of them were female.

ANALYSIS AND RESULTS

Data were analyzed following an adapted version of the coding manual for requests developed by the Cross-Cultural Speech Act Realization Project (Blum-Kulka, House, & Kasper, 1989). Care was taken not to impose coding categories on the material which are inadequate to capture forms and functions of request realizations in Chinese. However, all major coding categories proved to be applicable to the Chinese data. Realization forms not found in the data but commonly used by Chinese speakers were added and indicated by a cross (†).

In the analysis of request responses, a distinction is made between the Head Act of the request and the strategies by which it can be modified. Such strategies can be applied internally or externally to the Head Act. For instance,

王教授，有件事想和您說一下。我這幾天特別忙，有好幾件事必須做。所以可能要晚幾天才能交論文。如果可能的話，您能不能稍微寬容兩天？

Wáng jiàoshòu, yǒu jiàn shì xiǎng hé nín shuō yī xia. Wǒ zhè jǐ tiān tèbié máng, yǒu hǎo jǐ jiàn shì bìxū zuò. Suǒyǐ kěnéng yào wǎn jǐ tiān cái néng jiāo lùnwén. Rúguǒ kěnéng de huà, nín néng bù néng shāowēi kuānróng liǎng tiān?

Professor Wang, I have something to talk to you about. I have been extremely busy these days because of a few urgent matters I had to attend to. Therefore, I might have to turn in my paper a few days late. Could you give me a couple of days leeway?

(S3 Paper)

The Head Act in the above passage, i.e., the request utterance proper, occurs at the end of the passage 您能不能稍微寬容兩天？ *nín néng bù néng shāowēi kuānróng liǎng tiān?* 'Could you give me a couple of days leeway?'. It is a *Conventionally Indirect* request featuring modal verb 能不能 *néng bù néng* 'can' to inquire about preparatory conditions. The 如果 *rúguǒ* clause within the utterance is an internal syntactic downgrader, while the second person pronominal 您 *nín* (V-form) and 稍微 *shāowēi* 'kind of' are *Politeness Marker* and *Downtoner* respectively, in the catalog of lexical and phrasal *Downtoners*. Except for the term of address at the beginning 王教授 *Wáng jiàoshòu* 'Professor Wang' and the Head Act, the rest of the utterances are supportive moves of various kinds. These modification strategies will be commented on in detail below.

Alerters

Alerters function to alert the Hearer's attention to the ensuing speech act. Most of the alerters in Chinese are realized as terms of address.

Title/Role

服務員，對不起，我忘了自己不能吃雞。
Fúwùyuán, duìbuqǐ, wǒ wàng le zìjǐ bù néng chī jī.
Attendant, I am sorry, I forgot I myself cannot eat chicken.
(S5 Restaurant)

主任，英國一所學校已錄取我。我想在那里進修一年。
Zhǔrèn, Yīngguó yī suǒ xuéxiào yǐ lùqù wǒ. Wǒ xiǎng zài nàlǐ jìnxiū yī nián.
Director, I have been accepted by a British university. I would like to study there for a year. *(S6 Leave)*

同志，能不能換一盤菜？
Tóngzhì, néng bù néng huàn yī pán cài?
Comrade, could I change a dish? *(S5 Restaurant)*

小姐，請把車移開。
Xiǎojiě, qǐng bǎ chē yíkāi.
Miss, please move the car. *(S10 Police)*

女士，此地不能停車。
Nǚshì, cǐdì bù néng tíng chē.
Madam, you are not allowed to park here. *(S10 Police)*

教授,您的書真不錯。只是第四章在某些地方做些修改就更完美了。

Jiàoshòu, nín de shū zhēn búcuò. Zhǐshì dìsì zhāng zài mǒu xiē dìfang zuò xiē xiūgǎi jiù gèng wánměi le.

Professor, your book is really not bad, It's just that in Chapter 4 a few changes in certain places would make it perfect.　　(S4 *Editing*)

Surname + Title/Role

徐教授,我覺得二十頁論文不好寫。我可不可以只寫十至十五頁?

Xú jiàoshòu, wǒ juéde èrshí yè lùnwén bù hǎo xiě. Wǒ kě bù kěyǐ zhǐ xiě shí zhì shíwǔ yè?

Professor Xu, I think it is hard to write a 20-page paper. Can I write only 10 to 15 pages?　　(S3 *Paper*)

高主任,我請一年假去英國教書行不行?

Gāo zhǔrèn, wǒ qǐng yīnián jià qù Yīngguó jiāoshū xíng bù xíng?

Director Gao, can I have a one-year leave to teach in Britain?　　(S6 *Leave*)

王老師,我的論文可以晚幾天交嗎?

Wáng lǎoshī, wǒ de lùnwén kěyǐ wǎn jǐ tiān jiāo ma?

Professor Wang, can I turn in my paper a few days late?　　(S11 *Deadline*)

鄧先生,您的初稿我都看過了。其它都好,只是⋯

Dèng xiānsheng, nín de chūgǎo wǒ dōu kàn guò le. Qítā dōu hǎo, zhǐshì....

Mr. Deng, I have read the draft of your book. Everything else is fine except...　　(S4 *Editing*)

Full Name (surname + first name)

王平,我想買一架電視機,但還缺一百元。不知你有沒有?
Wáng Píng, wǒ xiǎng mǎi yī jià diànshìjī, dàn hái quē yībǎi yuán. Bù zhī nǐ yǒu méi yǒu?
Wang Ping, I'd like to buy a TV but I'm short 100 yuán. Do you happen to have it? (S1 Loan)

Prefix + Surname

小王,我今天有許多朋友要來。我們是否把房間整理一下?
Xiǎo Wáng, wǒ jīntiān yǒu xǔduō péngyou yào lái. Wǒmen shìfǒu bǎ fángjiān zhěnglǐ yīxià?
Wang, I'm having many friends over today. Shall we clean up the room? (S7 Room)

老李,你看第四章是不是可以改動一下?
Lǎo Lǐ, nǐ kàn dìsì zhāng shìbùshì kěyǐ gǎidòng yīxià?
Li, do you think you can revise Chapter 4? (S4 Editing)

Familiar/Casual Terms

哥們兒,借我一百塊錢。
Gēmer, jiè wǒ yībǎi kuài qián.
Buddy, lend me 100 dollars. (S1 Loan)

伙計,車不能停在這兒。得趕快開走。
Huǒji, chē bù néng tíng zài zhèr. Děi gǎnkuài kāizǒu.
Buddy, you can't park the car here. Move it away now. (S10 Police)

二位，讓我和你們擠兩個星期怎麼樣？

Èrwèi, ràng wǒ hé nǐmen jǐ liǎng ge xīngqī zěnmeyàng?

Guys, how about letting me cram in here with you for two weeks? (S2 Roommates)

師傅，對不起，能不能把我要的炒雞丁改成蔥爆肉片兒？

Shīfu, duìbuqǐ, néng bù néng bǎ wǒ yào de chǎojīdīng gǎichéng cōngbào ròupiànr?

Waiter, I am sorry, can you change my order from chicken to stir-fried pork? (S5 Restaurant)

Honorifics

黃老，能不能把論文縮短一些？

Huáng lǎo, néng bu néng bǎ lùnwén suō duǎn yīxiē?

Honorable Huang, could you shorten the length requirement of the paper? (S3 Paper)

Attention Getter

嘿，你現在是回校園嗎？能不能搭個便車？

Hei, nǐ xiànzài shì huí xiàoyuán ma? Néng bù néng dā ge biànchē?

Hey, are you going back to campus now? Can I catch a ride? (S9 Ride)

喂，我把炒雞丁換成蔥爆牛肉行嗎？

Wei, wǒ bǎ chǎojīdīng huànchéng cōngbào niúròu xíng ma?

Hey, can I change the chicken to beef? (S5 Restaurant)

對不起，請幫忙打掃一下房間。我的朋友要來。

Duìbuqǐ, qǐng bāngmáng dǎsǎo yīxià fángjiān. Wǒ de péngyou yào lái.

Excuse me, please help clean the room. My friends are coming. (S7 Room)

Combination

服務員同志，能不能把這個雞丁換成蔥爆牛肉？
Fúwùyuán tóngzhì, néng bù néng bǎ zhèi ge jīdīng huàngchéng cōngbào niúròu?
Comrade Attendant, could you change this chicken to beef?
(*S5 Restaurant*)

趙軍同學，我考慮一下後，覺得你的課堂報告還是提前一周做比較好。
Zhào Jūn tóngxué, wǒ kǎolù yīxià hòu, juéde nǐ de kètáng bàogào háishì tíqián yīzhōu zuò bǐjiao hǎo.
Mr. Zhao Jun, I have been thinking that it would be better to make your class presentation a week earlier. (*S12 Lecturer*)

小同志，剛才我菜單沒看清楚。點了菜再換還行嗎？
Xiǎo tóngzhì, gāngcái wǒ càidǎn méi kàn qīngchu. Diǎn le cài zài huàn hái xíng ma?
Little Comrade, I didn't look at the menu carefully enough just now. Could I change my order? (*S5 Restaurant*)

老同學，幫幫忙。借我筆記看看。
Lǎo tóngxué, bāngbang máng. Jiè wǒ bǐjì kànkan.
Old Classmate, please help me out. Lend me your notes. (*S8 Notes*)

Table 1 below represents the distribution of alerters in the data set. The contextual distribution of alerters suggests that their function goes beyond getting the Hearer's attention to the ensuing speech act. It is a reflection of the type of social relationship which is either in existence or which S tries to create. Therefore, address terms can be strategically manipulated. For example, unlike the *S3 Paper* and *S11 Deadline* situations where the standard, unmarked term of address *Surname + Title/Role* is invariably used by a student to a professor, the student-student encounters employ various address terms to create a positive politeness context prior to the request. Thus, not only are normal full names used in *S1 Loan* and *S2 Roommates* situations, but also *Familiar/Casual Terms* such as 哥們兒 *gēmer* 'Buddy', and 二位 *èr wèi* 'Guys', when interactants do not know each other (e.g., *S2 Roommates*). The familiarity and closeness projected this way creates an amiable atmosphere which is more likely to increase the likelihood of success in a request (Ju, 1991). The following are some of the general social customs and practices associated with the use of Chinese address terms.

Table 1. Distribution of alerters (%)

None	38.1
Surname + Title/Role	16.1
Full Name	12.5
Prefix + Surname	8.9
Attention Getter	7.5
Title + Role	5.3
Familiar/Casual Terms	3.3
Missing Data	3.1
Combination	2.4
Opt Out	2.2
Honorifics	0.6

The most commonly used address terms to a stranger are 同志 *tóngzhì* 'Comrade' (formal, impersonal, neutral in tone), 服務員 *fúwùyuán* 'Comrade Attendant', 司機同志 *sījī tóngzhì* 'Comrade Driver' (formal, impersonal, polite in tone), and 師傅 *shīfu* 'Master' (informal, casual). However, 師傅 *shīfu* 'Master' is not used to address professionals such as teachers, doctors, etc.

Certain kinship terms are commonly used as address terms and are perceived to be polite and respectful. It is almost an unwritten rule of politeness for people of younger age (relative to their interlocutors) to address their interlocutors by appropriate kinship terms. Such practice is not confined to familiar relations, but is common in interactions between strangers, e.g., 叔叔 *shūshu* 'Uncle', 爺爺 *yéye* 'Grandpa' 奶奶 *nǎinai* 'Grandma', etc. Kinship terms are not used in work and professional settings. A slightly modified version of kinship terms is most often used in interactions among neighbors, strangers, etc. Usually, a prefix such as 大 *dà* 'big' or 老 *lǎo* 'old' is added to the kinship terms, for example, 大爺 *dàyé* 'Grandpa', 大叔 *dàshū* 'Uncle', 大姐 *dàjiě*

'Sister', 老奶奶 *lǎo nǎinai* 'Grandma', etc. They are polite and less intimate in tone.

Chinese surnames, monosyllabic in most cases, cannot be used alone as address terms (Chao, 1968). When surnames are used as address terms, as is quite often the case, titles or prefixes such as 小 *xiǎo* 'little', 老 *lǎo* 'old', sometimes 大 *dà* 'big', etc. are added, depending normally, but not exclusively, on the age, gender, and appearance of "maturity" of the addressee. Middle-aged women are less likely to be called 老 *lǎo* 'old' than middle aged men. Once a particular prefix is chosen for a person, it stays with him/her regardless of the advancement of age.

Full names are preferred by youngsters and students when addressing each other. Prefixes plus surnames (e.g., 小王 *xiǎo Wáng*, 老李 *lǎo Lǐ*) are perhaps the most commonly used way of addressing (as well as referring to) each other in work places. Endearment terms (i.e., given names in Chinese) are avoided between peers and colleagues. They are not used between intimates in public, either. Nicknames are often used in familiar relationships. Neither endearment terms nor nicknames appeared in the data.

Honorifics are reserved for people who are both senior in age and experience and high in status. Only old top Party officials and senior, famous scholars are addressed with honorifics.

Terms of address in China have been and will always be associated with political situations, social and economic changes and cultural values (Ju, 1991). Due to the economic reform and open policy of China in the last decade or so, traditional address terms such as 小姐 *xiǎojiě* 'Miss', 女士 *nǔshì* 'Madam', 先生 *xiānsheng* 'Sir/Mr.', etc. have gained values whereas the once popular, politically connotated 同志 *tóngzhì* 'Comrade' and the casual 師傅 *shīfu* 'Master' are becoming depreciated. This phenomenon is especially strong in business domains. It also shows a tendency to spread to other domains.

Request perspective

Request perspective refers to the viewpoint from which a request is realized. A request utterance can take as its agent the Speaker, the Hearer, or both participants. Explicit mentioning of the agents can be (deliberately) avoided (Blum-Kulka, et al., 1989, p. 278). In Chinese, the subject, i.e., the agent, is frequently omitted from the surface structure, when the agent's role is clear from the context to all present, for example, 做了嗎 *zuò le ma?* 'Have (you) done it?'. However, ambiguity exists sometimes, as in 能換一個嗎 *néng huàn yīge ma?* 'Can (I/we/you) change it?'. This phenomenon is referred to as *implicit* perspective in the present analysis.

Hearer Dominance

您能不能準許我只寫十到十五頁？
Nín néng bù néng zhǔnxǔ wǒ zhǐ xiě shí dào shíwǔ yè?
Could you allow me to write only 10 to 15 pages? (S3 Paper)

你有沒有時間和我一起打掃房間？
Nǐ yǒu méi yǒu shíjiān hé wǒ yīqǐ dǎsǎo fángjiān?
Do you have time to clean up the room with me? (S7 Room)

你們不在意多一個人聊天吧？
Nǐmen bù zàiyì duō yī ge rén liáotiān ba?
You wouldn't mind one more person chatting with you, would you? (S2 Roommates)

請您馬上把車開走。
Qǐng nín mǎshàng bǎ chē kāizǒu.
Please move the car immediately. (S10 Police)

Speaker Dominance

我能不能晚幾天交論文？
Wǒ néng bù néng wǎn jǐ tiān jiāo lùnwén?
Can I hand in my paper a few days late? (S11 Deadline)

我搭你的車回家吧。
Wǒ dā nǐ de chē huíjiā ba.
Let me have a ride home with you. (S9 Ride)

我想換換，可以嗎？
Wǒ xiǎng huànhuan, kěyǐ ma?
I'd like to change it, may I? (S5 Restaurant)

Speaker and Hearer Dominance

我們是不是把房間整理一下？
Wǒmen shì bù shì bǎ fángjiān zhěnglǐ yīxià?
Shall we clean up the room? (S7 Room)

咱們一起走吧。
Zánmen yīqǐ zǒu ba.
Let's go together. (S9 Ride)

Implicit

能不能把辣子雞丁換成蔥爆牛肉？
Néng bù néng bǎ làzǐjīdīng huànchéng cōngbàoniúròu?
Can (you/I) change the spicy chicken to stir fried onion beef?
(S5 Restaurant)

好不好把你的筆記借給我看看？
Hǎo bù hǎo bǎ nǐde bǐjì jiè gěi wǒ kànkan?
Is it alright (for you) to lend your notes to me? (S8 Notes)

是不是把房間打掃打掃？
Shì bù shì bǎ fángjiān dǎsǎo dǎsǎo?
Shall (we/you) clean up the room? (S7 Room)

應該把房間打掃乾淨。
Yīnggāi bǎ fángjiān dǎsǎo gānjìng.
(You/we/I) should clean up the room. (S7 Room)

車得趕快開走。
Chē děi gǎnkuài kāizǒu.
(You) must move the car immediately.   (S10 Police)

Table 2. Distribution of perspectives (%)

Hearer Dominance	40.6
Implicit	29.4
Speaker Dominance	14.4
None	8.1
Missing Data	3.6
Opt Out	2.2
Hearer and Speaker Dominance	1.7

The contextual distribution of request perspectives is shown in Table 2. Table 2 shows that Hearer perspective is the preferred request perspective adopted, followed by implicit perspective. While no ambiguity exists about the requestive intent in implicit perspective, agentless request utterances can be manipulated for politeness reasons. For example, in the *S5 Restaurant* situation, the use of agentless request realizations such as 能換一個嗎？ *néng huàn yī ge ma?* 'Can (you/I) change it?' avoids naming both H (you) and S (I), for the mention of the former may give the request utterance the touch of a command or order, and the mention of the latter could be perceived as being too coercive and thus inconsiderate of others. The *Implicit* perspective is used perhaps most often when the request is perceived to be rather face-threatening.

Request strategies

As mentioned initially, requests can be performed at different degrees of directness. The major directness levels — *Direct, Conventionally Indirect*, and *Indirect* — can be subdivided into nine requestive strategies. The choice of one or more of these strategies is obligatory in request performance. Below, the nine strategies in the Chinese data are organized in the order of decreasing degree of directness.

Request strategies: Direct

Mood Derivable
The prototypical form of this strategy is the imperative.

借我一百塊錢。
Jiè wǒ yībǎi kuài qián.
Lend me 100 dollars. (S1 Loan)

把車開走。
Bǎ chē kāizǒu.
Move the car. (S10 Police)

勞駕把車停到別的地方去。
Láojià bǎ chē tíng dào bié de dìfang qu.
Please move the car to another parking spot. (S10 Police)

請給我換成蔥爆牛肉。
Qǐng gěi wǒ huànchéng cōngbàoniúròu.
Please change it to stir fried beef for me. (S5 Restaurant)

Explicit Performative
The illocutionary intent is explicitly named by the speaker by using a relevant illocutionary verb.

請您趕快把車開走。
Qǐng nín gǎnkuài bǎ chē kāizǒu.
Drive the car away immediately, please. (S10 Police)

麻煩您幫我換一個。
Máfan nín bāng wǒ huàn yī ge.
I'd like you to change it for me, please. (S5 Restaurant)

In Chinese, 請 *qǐng*, 麻煩 *máfan*, and 勞駕 *láojià* (please) are all directive verbs encoding certain politeness values. They soften the tone of an otherwise direct, imperative request utterance, giving due recognition to the rights and the troubles a requestee must go through in order to comply to the request.

Hedged Performative
The illocutionary verb denoting the requestive intent is modified, e.g., by modal verbs or verbs expressing intention.

> 我想讓你提前一週做課堂報告，行嗎？
> *Wǒ xiǎng ràng nǐ tíqián yī zhōu zuò kètáng bàogào, xíng ma?*
> I'd like to ask you to do your presentation a week earlier, is that all right? (S12 *Lecturer*)

> 我得勞駕您批我一年假到國外去學習。
> *Wǒ děi láojià nín pī wǒ yī nián jià dào guówài qu xuéxí.*
> I must ask you to give me a one-year leave to study abroad. (S6 *Leave*)

Locution Derivable
The use of this strategy, which is also called "obligation statement", enables the listener to directly derive the illocutionary intent from the semantic meaning of the utterance (locution).

> 你務必要把我們提到的地方再修改一下。
> *Nǐ wùbì yào bǎ wǒmen tí dào de dìfang xiūgǎi yīxià.*
> You must revise those places we have mentioned. (S4 *Editing*)

> 車得馬上開走。
> *Chē děi mǎshang kāizǒu.*
> The car must be moved immediately. (S10 *Police*)

> 最好把你的筆記借我看看。
> *Zuìhǎo bǎ nǐ de bǐjì jiè wǒ kànkan.*
> (You)'d better lend your notes to me a while. (S8 *Notes*)

你的第四章需要修改。
Nǐ de dìsì zhāng xūyào xiūgǎi.
Your Chapter 4 needs revising.   (S4 Editing)

Want Statement
The utterance expresses the speaker's desire that the event denoted in the proposition come about.

我想換換，行嗎？
Wǒ xiǎng huànhuan, xíng ma?
I'd like to change, may I?   (S5 Restaurant)

我想在這兒住兩個星期，你們不反對吧？
Wǒ xiǎng zài zhèr zhù liǎng ge xīngqī, nǐmen bù fǎnduì ba?
You don't object to my staying here for two weeks, do you?
                                          (S2 Roommates)

他們希望您能把第四章修改一下。
Tāmen xīwàng nín néng bǎ dìsì zhāng zài xiūgǎi yīxià.
They hope you can revise Chapter 4 again.   (S4 Editing)

Request strategies: Conventionally indirect

Suggestory Formula
The illocutionary intent is phrased as a suggestion by means of a framing routine formula.

二位幫幫忙怎麼樣？
Èrwèi bāngbang máng zěnmeyàng?
How about the two of you lending a hand?   (S2 Roommates)

減到十頁怎麼樣？
Jiǎn dào shí yè zěnmeyàng?
How about reducing the paper to 10 pages?   (S3 Paper)

讓我和你們擠兩個星期怎麼樣？
Ràng wǒ hé nǐmen jǐ liǎng ge xīngqī zěnmeyàng?
How about letting me cram in with you for two weeks?
(S2 Roommates)

Query Preparatory
The utterance contains queries about the conditions for request compliance, such as the hearer's ability, willingness, or possibility to carry out the requested act, or whether the speaker has permission to act according to her wishes. In Chinese, the conventionalized forms by which *Query Preparatory* requests are carried out are 能 *néng* 'can', 可以 *kěyǐ* 'may' and sentence-final 怎麼樣 *zěngmoyàng* 'how about'.

能否晚几天交論文？
Néng fǒu wǎn jǐ tiān jiāo lùnwén?
Can I turn in my paper a few days late?   (S11 Deadline)

你能借我一百塊錢嗎？
Nǐ néng jiè wǒ yībǎi kuài qián ma?
Can you lend me 100 dollars?   (S1 Loan)

我的論文可以晚几天交嗎？
Wǒ de lùnwén kěyǐ wǎn jǐ tiǎn jiāo ma?
May I turn in my paper a few days late?   (S11 Deadline)

我可不可以就寫十到十五頁？
Wǒ kě bù kěyǐ jiù xiě shí dào shíwǔ yè?
May I write 10 to 15 pages?   (S3 Paper)

Request strategies: Indirect

Strong Hint
The requestive intent is not immediately derivable from the utterance; however, the utterance refers to relevant elements of the intended requestive act. Such elements often relate to preconditions of the feasibility of the request. Unlike the *Preparatory* strategy, hints are not conventionalized in any way and thus require more inferencing activity on the part of the hearer.

今天輪到你值日。請認眞點兒。
Jīntiān lún dào ní zhírì. Qǐng rènzhēn diǎnr.
Today is your duty day. Please do the job well. (S7 Room)

論文要求的頁數太多了。十五頁比較合適。
Lùnwén yāoqiú de yèshù tài duō le. Shíwǔ yè bǐjiào héshì.
The length requirement for the paper is too much. 15 pages would be more appropriate. (S3 Paper)

我認爲這本書的美中不足是第四章。
Wǒ rènwéi zhè běn shū de měizhōngbùzú shì dìsì zhāng.
I think the only weakness in this excellent book is Chapter 4. (S4 Editing)

你還沒打掃房間呢。
Nǐ hái méi dǎsǎo fángjiān ne.
You haven't cleaned up the room yet. (S7 Room)

你沒長眼？怎麼到處停車？
Nǐ méi zhǎng yǎn? Zěnme dàochù tíng chē?
Don't you have eyes? How can you park the car just anywhere? (S10 Police)

Mild Hint
The utterance contains no elements which are of immediate relevance to the intended request. The hearer has to combine information from the context and the utterance to infer the speaker's intended meaning.

> 小王，你的女朋友剛才來找你。她說半小時以後再到宿舍來找你，讓你在這兒等她。
>
> *Xiǎo Wáng, nǐ de nǚ péngyou gāngcái lái zhǎo nǐ. Tā shuō bàn xiǎoshí yǐhòu zài dào sùshè lái zhǎo nǐ, ràng nǐ zài zhèr děng ta.*
>
> Xiao Wang, your girlfriend came to see you just now. She said that she would be back in half an hour. She asked you to wait for her here.   (S7 Room)

Table 3. Distribution of strategies (%)

Strategy	%
Query Preparatory	54.2
Mood Derivable	11.4
Want Statement	8.3
Suggestory Formula	7.2
Locution Derivable	5.8
Strong Hint	5.6
Missing Data	3.1
Opt Out	2.2
Mild Hint	1.4
Hedged Performative	0.6
Explicit Performative	0.3

Table 3 depicts the distribution of request strategies. The distribution of the nine requestive strategies suggests that *Query Preparatory* is by far the most preferred choice, accounting for more than half of the possible cases. Collapsing the nine strategies into three levels of levels of directness, the distribution shown in Table 4 below is obtained.

As in Table 3, *Conventional Indirectness*, which features *Preparatory* and *Suggestory* strategies, is by far the leading choice for making a request. Chinese requesters share their preference for *Conventional Indirectness* with a variety of western speech communities (Blum-Kulka & House, 1989). *Conventional Indirectness* allows speakers to express their requestive intent unambiguously while being polite at the same time. Illocutionary, referential and relational goals can thus be achieved with maximum efficiency. The preference for *Conventional Indirectness* does not hold true for the *S10 Police* situation, however. Due to the institutionalized asymmetrical power relationship between the interlocutors in this context, information flows mostly in one direction (from policeman to driver), and interactional outcomes are seldom open to negotiation (House, 1989). The *Conventionally Indirect* routines 怎麼樣 *zěnmeyàng* 'how about' and 能 *néng*, 'can' on the other hand, indicate a possibility for negotiation which a police officer on duty hardly needs to offer. In fact, the distribution of request strategies in this situation shows that *Mood Derivable* requests are overwhelmingly favored (92%) (Zhang, 1990).

Table 4. Distribution of strategies in three levels of directness (%)

Conventionally Indirect	59.2
Direct	26.4
Indirect	9.5
Missing Data	3.1
Opt Out	2.2

In addition to the power relationship between the interlocutors, social distance is another important variable which affects the choice of directness levels. As Wolfson pointed out (1989), people tend to be more direct in close and intimate relationships and with strangers than with friends, colleagues and other acquaintances. This holds true for Chinese, as can be seen by the preference for *Conventionally Indirect* strategies in this study: most of the relationships depicted in the request contexts involve people who know each other at work or are friends without being intimates.

Syntactic downgraders

Syntactic downgraders are those devices which modify the Head Act internally by mitigating the impositive force of a request by means of syntactic choices. In Chinese, the major set of syntactic downgraders includes the *Interrogative, Interrogative + Negation,* and *Conditional Clause.*

Interrogative

> 在你這兒住兩個星期行嗎？
> *Zài nǐ zhèr zhù liǎng ge xīngqī xíng ma?*
> Is it possible for me to stay at your place for two weeks?
>
> (S2 Roommates)

> 我在這兒呆幾天你們不在意吧？
> *Wǒ zài zhèr dāi jǐtiān nǐmen bù zàiyì ba?*
> You wouldn't mind my staying here for a few days, would you?
>
> (S2 Roommates)

Interrogative + Negation
A rhetorical type of interrogative which asks for permission and agreement.

> 我在這兒呆幾天你們不在意吧？
> *Wǒ zài zhèr dāi jǐtiān nǐmen bù zàiyì ba?*
> You wouldn't mind my staying here for a few days, would you?
>
> (S2 Roommates)

> 我想你們不會反對我在這兒住一夜吧？
> *Wǒ xiǎng nǐmen bù huì fǎnduì wǒ zài zhèr zhù yī yè ba?*
> I don't think you will object to my staying here tonight, will you?
>
> (S2 Roommates)

Conditional Clause
The speaker mitigates the requestive force by providing the hearer with an option to opt out.

> 你手頭要是有一百塊錢的話，借我用用。
> *Nǐ shǒutóu yàoshi yǒu yībǎi kuài qián de huà, jiè wǒ yòngyong.*
> Can you lend me 100 dollars if you happen to have it now?
>
> (S1 Loan)

我能用十到十五頁把問題說清楚的話,就不必寫二十頁了吧?
Wǒ néng yòng shí dào shíwǔ yè bǎ wèntí shuō qīngchu de huà, jiù bùbì xiě èrshí yè le ba?

Is it still necessary to write 20 pages if I can discuss the issue clearly in 10 to 15 pages? (S3 *Paper*)

Table 5. Distribution of syntactic downgraders

None	74.4
Interrogatives	13.3
Conditional Clause	3.1
Interrogative + Negation	0.6
Other	3.0
Opt Out	2.2
Missing Data	3.1

Table 5 displays the distribution of syntactic downgraders. The low frequency of interrogative downgraders is due to the fact that both of the *Conventionally Indirect* requestive strategies favored by respondents, *Suggestory* and *Query Preparatory*, are inherently interrogative and thus not coded as such. The three syntactic downgraders above are the most often used devices to soften the tone of a requestive utterance. In the interrogative and interrogative plus negation, the question form is often achieved through a "tag", which inquires about possibility and asks for permission, for example, 行不行 *xíng bu xíng*; 好嗎 *hǎo ma*; 可以嗎 *kěyǐ ma*; 不在意嗎 *bù zàiyì ba*; etc. They are suggestory in tone and equivalent in its social function — politeness — to *Conventional Indirectness*. The *Conditional Clause* is also one of the most frequently used devices to tone down the requestive force. Within the Head Act, it not only provides an opt-out option but also suggests the possibility of negotiation. Outside the Head Act, however, *Conditional Clauses* can function as aggravating devices to reinforce the request, as will be noted below.

Lexical and phrasal downgraders

Strategies of this category serve as optional additions to soften the impositive force of the Request by modifying the Head Act internally through specific lexical and phrasal choices.

Politeness Marker
A word or a formulaic phrase bidding for cooperative behavior.

> 勞駕您給換成蔥爆牛肉怎麼樣？
> *Láojià nín gěi huànchéng cōngbàoniúròu zěngmoyàng?*
> Could I please trouble you to change it to beef? (S5 Restaurant)

> 麻煩您幫我改一下。謝謝。
> *Máfan nín bāng wǒ gǎi yīxià. Xièxie.*
> May I impose on you to please help me change it? Thank you.
> (S5 Restaurant)

> 請把車移一下。
> *Qǐng bǎ chē yí yīxià.*
> Please move the car. (S10 Police)

> 拜託幫忙清掃一下房間。
> *Bàituō bāngmáng qīngsǎo yīxià fángjiān.*
> May I request that you please help clean the room? (S7 Room)

These phrases are at the same time directive verbs when used within requestive utterances. They are sentence-initial and do not appear to have the possibility of an aggravating function as the English 'Pul-eeeease!' The second person pronoun used with them is usually the V-form *nin* instead of the T-form *ni*. In terms of formality, 請 *qǐng* sounds more formal than 拜託 *bàituō*, 勞駕 *láojià*, and 麻煩 *máfán*.

Understater
Adverbial modifiers by means of which the speaker underrepresents the state of affairs referred to in the utterance.

> 只有一小部份需要修改。
> *Zhǐyǒu yīxiǎo bùfen xūyào xiūgǎi.*
> Only a small part needs revision. (S4 Editing)

Subjectivizer
Elements emphasizing that the speaker is voicing her subjective opinion about the state of affairs referred to in the utterance.

> 覺得你的課堂報告提前一週做比較好。
> *Juéde nǐde kètáng bàogào tíqián yīzhōu zuò bǐjiào hǎo.*
> I think it'd be better if you could do the presentation a week earlier. (S12 Lecturer)

> 我想您一定會支持我。
> *Wǒ xiǎng nín yīdìng huì zhīchí wǒ.*
> I am sure you will agree with me. (S3 Paper)

> 希望能在你這兒擠擠。
> *Xīwàng néng zài nǐ zhèr jǐjǐ.*
> I hope I can stay with you here. (S2 Roommates)

Downtoner
Modifiers which make the speaker sound less assertive and the request less coercive.

> 我大概會在這兒呆兩個星期。
> *Wǒ dàgài huì zài zhèr dāi liǎng ge xīngqī.*
> I will probably stay here for two weeks. (S2 Roommates)

> 咱們一起打掃吧。
> *Zánmen yīqǐ dǎsǎo ba.*
> Let's clean up the room together. (S7 Room)

> 我們一起走吧。
> *Wǒmen yīqǐ zǒu ba.*
> Let's go together. (S9 Ride)

The most commonly used *Downtoners* are particles. There are a fair number of particles in the Chinese language (e.g., *ba, ne, ah, le*). They serve grammatical as well as pragmatic functions. In terms of the latter, they give utterances a soft touch, indicating tentativeness and possibility of negotiation. Compare 快吃 *kuài chī* and 快吃吧 *kuài chī ba*. The referential meaning of both is 'eat quickly'. However, the first utterance is a prototypical *Mood Derivable* request (or order), leaving no room for H to argue. The second utterance, with particle 吧 *ba*, softens the request/order considerably by adding to it the flavor of imploring.

Appealer
Sentence-final question markers, or tags, which refer to possibility and permission, e.g., 行嗎 *xíng ma*, 行不行 *xíng bu xíng*, 可以嗎 *kěyǐ ma*, 可不可以 *kě bù kěyǐ*, 好嗎 *hǎo ma*, and 好不好 *hǎo bù hǎo*.

> 我想換一個，行不行？
> *Wǒ xiǎng huàn yī ge, xíng bù xíng?*
> May/Can I change it? / I'd like to change it, may/can I?
> (S5 Restaurant)

> 我想讓你提前一週做課堂報告，可以嗎？
> *Wǒ xiǎng ràng nǐ tíqián yīzhōu zuò kètáng bàogào, kěyǐ ma?*
> I'd like to ask you to do the presentation a week earlier, is that all right? (S12 Lecturer)

> 我想在這兒住兩個星期，不會影響你們吧？
> *Wǒ xiǎng zài zhèr zhù liǎng ge xīngqī, bù huì yǐngxiǎng nǐmen ba?*
> I'd like to stay here for two weeks. I hope that won't disturb you.
> (S2 Roommates)

> †借我一百塊錢，好嗎？
> †*Jiè wǒ yībǎi kuài qián, hǎo ma?*
> †Could you lend me 100 dollars? (S1 Loan)

One of the functions of this structure is similar to the agentless request perspective: the overt expression of personal desire, as for instance in a *Want Statement*, often connotes selfishness, egocentrism, and insensitivity. By inquiring about possibility and asking permission, such undesirable qualities are glossed over and politeness in the sense of other-orientedness (Mao, 1994) is achieved. The request intention is specified in the main clause. In this way, efficient transmission of information, maximum clarity and a high degree of politeness are achieved all at once.

V-form
"Honorifics" here refers solely to the second person pronominals 您 *nín* 'you'.

> 您，†您老
> *nín,* †*nín lao*
> you, †Your Honor

Realization forms not found in the data but commonly used by Chinese speakers were added and indicated by a cross (†). *V-form* are often used in combination with *Politeness Markers*, as in

> 麻煩您幫我改一下，謝謝。
> *Máfan nín bāng wǒ gǎi yīxià, xièxie.*
> Could you please help me change it? Thank you.   (S5 Restaurant)

Table 6 shows the distribution of lexical and phrasal downgraders. As can be seen, politeness devices such as *Politeness Markers* (請 *qǐng,* 勞駕 *láojià,* 麻煩 *máfán* 'please') and the honorific pronominal (您 *nín* 'you') and the combination of the two are used more than any other lexical downgraders. This is especially true when imbalance of age, familiarity, and rank exists between S and H. The overriding factor here seems to be familiarity. In Chinese culture in general, family members and close friends rarely, if at all, use *Politeness Markers* in their request or other types of speech acts. In a way, *Politeness Markers* are signs of social distance. In the case of acquaintances and strangers, age and rank very often determine the direction of the *Politeness Markers* being used. In general, the younger ones use *Politeness Markers* and honorifics (e.g., 請 *qǐng*; 您 *nín*) more often when speaking to those older than them. However, if the younger ones are higher in rank, *Politeness Markers* are often used by both sides to acknowledge age and rank difference.

Table 6. Distribution of lexical downgraders

None	60.3
Politeness Marker	8.1
Understater	3.1
Subjectiviser	3.7
Downtoner	2.8
V-form	7.2
Politeness Marker+V-form	5.0
Other	4.5
Opt Out	2.2
Missing Data	3.1

Upgraders

Upgraders are elements whose function it is to increase the impact of the request.

Intensifier

Modifiers used to intensify certain elements of the request. They are usually adverbs and modals.

> 還得再修改。
> *Hái děi zài xiūgǎi.*
> You must revise it once more. (S4 *Editing*)

> 請您一定同意。
> *Qǐng nín yīdìng tóngyì.*
> You must give me permission, please. (S6 *Leave*)

Expletive

> 你長沒長眼？！
> *Nǐ zhǎng méi zhǎng yǎn?!*
> Are you blind?! (S10 *Police*)

Time Intensifier

請您馬上把車開走。

Qǐng nín mǎshang bǎ chē kāizǒu.

Please move the car immediately. (S10 Police)

Table 7. Distribution of intensifiers (%)

None	90.3
Missing Data	3.1
Time Intensifier	2.8
Opt Out	2.2
Intensifier	1.4
Expletive	0.3

Table 7 shows the distribution of upgraders. Upgraders are overt imposition devices and are not often used in prototypical request situations where the requester is usually in a "begging" position (a popular Chinese term for the act of requesting). Upgraders occur most often when a speaker is (institutionally) authorized to demand compliance such that a request is turned into a command, e.g., in the *S10 Police* situation. *Time Intensifiers* are preferred over other types of upgraders. In requestive situations among equals and family members, *Time Intensifiers* and other intensifiers are often used in requests whereas *Expletives* are not. In addition, downgraders such as particles are also used quite often to balance out the imposition effect. For example, 你趕快走吧 *nǐ gǎnkuài zuǒ ba* 'Do it quickly' + *ba* = 'Could you do it quickly?', 你一定要去啊 *nǐ yīdìng yào qù a* 'You must go' + *a* = 'Please go/attend'.

Supportive moves

Supportive moves are external to the Head Act, occurring either before or after it. They are optional and function as a mitigating or aggravating device for the Request.

Preparator

The speaker prepares the hearer for the ensuing request by announcing that she will make a request by asking about the potential availability of the hearer for carrying out the request, or by asking for the hearer's permission to make the request — without however giving away the nature or indeed the content of the request.

你是回家嗎？
Nǐ shì huíjiā ma?
Are you going home? (S9 Ride)

我有一件事想和系裡談談。
Wǒ yǒu yī jiàn shì xiǎng hé xìli tántan.
I have something to discuss with the department. (S6 Leave)

你車裡還有地兒嗎？
Nǐ chē li hái yǒu dìr ma?
Is there still any space in your car? (S9 Ride)

怎麼在這兒碰見你了，真巧。
Zěnme zài zhèr pèngjiàn nǐ le, zhēn qiǎo.
What a coincidence that I run into you here. (S9 Ride)

Getting a Pre-commitment
In checking on a potential refusal before making the request, a speaker tries to commit the hearer before informing her about the requestive goal.

你能不能幫幫忙？
Nǐ néng bù néng bāngbang máng?
Can you help me/Can you do me a favor? (S1 Loan)

Grounder
The speaker gives reason, explanations, or justifications for the request, which may either precede or follow it.

我想買台電視，可是我手頭的錢不夠。
Wǒ xiǎng mǎi tái diànshì, kěshi wǒ shǒutóu de qián bùgòu.
I'd like to buy a TV, but I don't have enough money. (S1 Loan)

我可以幫你們省點兒錢。
Wǒ kěyǐ bāng nǐmen shěng diǎnr qián.
I can help you save some money (by staying with you).
(S2 *Roommates*)

聽說雞丁是辣的。我不能吃辣的。
Tīngshuō jīdīng shì là de. Wǒ bù néng chī là de.
I've heard that the chicken is hot and I can't eat hot food.
(S5 *Restaurant*)

我上節課病了，沒來。
Wǒ shàng jié kè bìng le, méi lái.
I was sick last time and didn't attend the class. (S8 *Notes*)

這座房子剛著過火，很危險。
Zhè zuò fángzi gāng zháo guò huǒ, hěn wēixiǎn.
This house was on fire not long ago. It's very dangerous. (S10 *Police*)

我最近很忙。有兩篇文章要在下星期寫完。
Wǒ zuìjìn hěn máng. Yǒu liǎng piān wénzhāng yào zài xià xīngqī xiě wán.
I have been extremely busy recently, because I must finish two papers by next week. (S11 *Deadline*)

Sweetener
The speaker uses a solidarity strategy by complimenting or flattering the hearer on a request-related issue or object.

你們的蔥爆牛肉非常有名。第一次來吃，真想吃個名氣呢。
Nǐmen de cōngbàoniúròu fēicháng yǒumíng. Dìyī cì lái chī, zhēn xiǎng chī ge míngqì ne.
The stir fried beef in your restaurant is well known. This is my first time here and I come for the well-reputed dish.   (S5 Restaurant)

你們宿舍真不錯，安靜，離我辦公的地方近。
Nǐmen sùshè zhēn bùcuò, ānjìng, lí wǒ bàngōng de dìfang jìn.
Your dorm is so nice. It's quiet and close to my office.
(S2 Roommates)

你是我們中間的"闊老"。
Nǐ shì wǒmen zhōngjiān de "kuòlǎo".
You are the "millionaire" among us.   (S1 Loan)

想欣賞欣賞你記筆記的藝術。
Xiǎng xīnshǎng xīnshǎng nǐ jì bǐjì de yìshu.
I'd like to appreciate your art of note-taking.   (S8 Notes)

聽說你這兒的蔥爆牛肉特別好。
Tīngshuō nǐ zhèr de cōngbàoniúròu tèbié hǎo.
I've heard that you have very good stir fried beef here.
(S5 Restaurant)

您的大作我已經拜讀過了。總的感覺很好。您真不愧是個"天才"。
Nín de dàzuò wǒ yǐjing bàidú guo le. Zǒng de gǎnjué hěn hǎo. Nín zhēn bùkuì shì ge "tiāncái".
I've finished reading your wonderful book. It's very good on the whole. You are really a "genius".   (S4 Editing)

Sweeteners usually occur before the Head Act. The sequence is not strictly fixed but in a request event, Sweeteners appear rather early to pave the way for the request by establishing good feelings in H and cultivating an amiable atmosphere.

Cost Minimizing
A promise or statement which intends to reduce the imposition and burden on the hearer.

> 我下月還你。
> Wǒ xià yuè huán nǐ.
> I'll return it (money) to you next month. (S1 Loan)

> 趙軍和我睡,不會影響你們。
> Zhào Jūn hé wǒ shuì, bù huì yǐngxiǎng nǐmen.
> Zhao Jun will stay with me and he won't bother you guys.
> (S2 Roommates)

Promise of Reward
In order to increase the likelihood of the hearer's compliance with the speaker's request, a reward due on fulfillment of the request is announced.

> 改好第四章,要發表沒問題。
> Gǎi hǎo dìsì zhāng, yào fābiǎo méi wèntí.
> The book will surely be published once Chapter 4 is revised.
> (S4 Editing)

Promise
A promise not pertaining to reward for the hearer, but to speaker's own request goal.

> 我保證寫得好一點兒。
> Wǒ bǎozhèng xiě de hǎo yīdiǎnr.
> I promise to write a better paper. (S11 Deadline)

我去英國學習一年回來後，會更好地教書。
Wǒ qù Yīngguó xuéxí yī nián huílai hòu, huì gèng hǎo de jiāoshū.
I will teach better after studying in Britain for a year.　　(S6 *Leave*)

Threat
This is an aggravating move which a speaker uses to threaten the hearer with potential consequences arising out of noncompliance with the request.

否則要罰款。
Fǒuzé yào fákuǎn.
Otherwise you'll be fined.　　(S10 *Police*)

否則發表有困難。
Fǒuzé fābiǎo yǒu kùnnan.
Otherwise it is difficult to get published.　　(S4 *Editing*)

不然把你的車也給燒了。
Bùrán bǎ nǐ de chē yě gěi shāo le.
If not your car will be burned, too.　　(S10 *Police*)

Structurally, this strategy often appears as conditionals. However, it differs from the conditionals under Syntactic Downgrader in that it occurs outside the Head Act.

Direct Appeal
The speaker tries to elicit compliance by direct calling for the hearer's sympathy.

幫幫忙。
Bāngbang máng.
Help, please.　　(S1 *Loan*)

> 懇求您手下留情。
> *Kěnqiú nín shǒuxià-liúqíng.*
> Be kind/lenient, PLEASE. (S3 Paper)

Offer of Help
In order to compensate the hearer for the cost of the request, the speaker offers help or other means in return.

> 有問題你可隨時找我。
> *Yǒu wèntí nǐ kě suíshí zhǎo wǒ.*
> You may come to me any time you have a problem. (S12 Lecturer)

Reprimand
An aggravating device aiming at increasing the impositive force on the hearer.

> 沒見這兒著火了？！
> *Méi jiàn zhèr zháo huǒ le?!*
> Can't you see the fire here? (S10 Police)

Moralizing Statement
In order to lend additional credence to the request, a speaker invokes general moral maxims.

> 文章好壞看內容，不在長短。
> *Wénzhāng hǎohuài kàn nèiróng, bù zài chángduǎn.*
> The quality of the paper should depend on content, not on length. (S3 Paper)

Apologizing
The speaker apologizes for the trouble the request will cause to the hearer. Apology expressions are usually formulaic.

> 真抱歉／對不起。
> *Zhēn bàoqian / Duìbuqǐ.*
> I'm very sorry. (S5 Restaurant)

這是給您添了很多麻煩。
Zhè shì gěi nín tiān le hěnduō máfan.
This has given you much inconvenience. (S2 Roommates)

Self-criticism
The speaker takes the blame by denigrating herself so as to put the hearer in a position where compliance appears to be a benevolent deed.

我搞錯了。
Wǒ gǎo cuò le.
It's my fault/I made a mistake. (S5 Restaurant)

我把菜點錯了。
Wǒ bǎ cài diǎn cuò le.
I ordered the wrong dish. (S5 Restaurant)

Thanking
Expressions of gratitude offered for the anticipated compliance of the hearer.

謝謝您的合作。
Xièxie nín de hézuò.
Thank you for your cooperation. (S7 Room)

麻煩你／您了。
Máfan ní(n) le
Thank you. (S5 Restaurant)

真不好意思。
Zhēn bù hǎo yìsi.
I am so embarrassed /Thank you. (S5 Restaurant)

Similar to *Politeness Markers*, *Thanking* is rarely used among family members and close friends. In requestive situations involving acquaintances and strangers, *Thanking* usually comes at the end of the request and discourse event. In general, the Chinese do not thank each other as much as Americans or Australians (Cottrill, 1990).

Advice Seeking
Formulaic expressions positioned at the end of the request to seek the hearer's opinion, and essentially, compliance.

> 你看怎麼樣？／你看行嗎？
> *Nĭ kàn zěnmeyàng? /Nĭ kàn xíng ma?*
> What do you think?   (S2 Roommates)

Advice Seeking formulas serve as tags to request utterances. They are positive signs of non-imposition and politeness. Usually, but not exclusively, they are used between acquaintances or by seniors (in age or rank) to juniors.

Table 8. Distribution of supportive moves

Move	%
Grounder	36.1
None	19.7
Apologizing	8.3
Cost-minimizing	6.4
Sweetener	6.1
Self-criticism	5.7
Preparatory	3.3
Missing Data	3.1
Advice Seeking	2.7
Thanking	2.5
Opt Out	2.2
Pre-commitment	0.6
Promise	0.6
Direct Appeal	0.6
Offer of Help	0.6
Reprimanding	0.6
Moralizing Statement	0.3
Threat	0.3
Promise of Reward	0.3

Table 8 displays the distribution of supportive moves. Most of the requests are accompanied by supportive moves of some kind. Only 19.7% of the requests are realized without them. Of the 16 identified supportive moves, the *Grounder* is the one used most often (36.1%). This shows that when making a request, Chinese people feel obligated to explain the situation and the reason why they must ask another person to do something for them. Studies focusing on the information sequence in Chinese requests have found that *Grounders* occur most often before a request utterance, less frequently after the request has been made. They are rarely absent in non-routine types of requestive situations (Kirkpatrick, 1991; Zhang, this volume). Studies on Chinese information sequencing also found that the presence of a *Grounder* and its position in a requestive event is closely linked with the Chinese concepts of directness-indirectness, face, and politeness (Scollon & Wong-Scollon, 1991; Kirkpatrick, 1991; Zhang, this volume). Furthermore, *Grounders* alone are capable of conveying requestive intention and functions as "feelers", sounding out the possibility for compliance (Zhang, this volume).

Among the supportive moves, some are used indiscriminately of situation types, e.g., *Grounders*, while others are tied to specific situations, such as *Sweeteners* and *Apologies*.

More than other situations, the *S5 Restaurant* situation elicited the majority of *Sweeteners* and *Apologies*. Compared with the requestive strategies used by American subjects in this situation (Zhang, 1990), it is obvious that the type of linguistic behavior manifested by the Chinese subjects pertains to the sociocultural structure of Chinese service encounters. Unlike in the U.S., where service encounters such as the *S5 Restaurant* situation entail customers' rights to various kinds of relevant services, in the government owned service businesses in China, the exact relationship between customers and providers of services is not clearly defined. Customers are not "patrons". Consequently, a request from a customer to change the original order sounds like a demand for an extra favor. It is almost imperative to accompany the request with proper explanations, extravagant compliments, and humble apologies. Small surprise that the Chinese subjects used a lot of *Apologies* (50%) and *Sweeteners* (11.5%) along with other self-denigration devices in their requests in this situation (Zhang, 1990).

CONCLUSION

THIS PAPER PRESENTS AN INITIAL ATTEMPT to catalog Chinese requestive strategies. Far from exhaustive, the catalog and sample utterances can be used as reference for a (contrastive) analysis of learners' second language production. For example, it has come to our attention that the tag structure poses some difficulty for American students of Chinese. Since imperatives and *Want Statements* are perceived to be direct and often impolite in English (Blum-Kulka, 1987), speakers of English tend to avoid using them in many situations (Blum-Kulka & House, 1989) and to be reluctant to use the Chinese imperative/*Want Statement* + tag structure. On the other hand, Chinese learners of English tend to transfer the Chinese structure into English by using imperative/*Want Statement* plus 'OK/all right'. Although imperative/*Want Statement* + tag is structurally similar between English and Chinese, it encodes different tones, force, and politeness values. In Chinese, it is soft, tentative, and polite, while in English, it is quite direct and less polite.

Future studies are needed on two levels. On the pragmalinguistic level, the conventions of means and forms by which requests are realized in Chinese will have to be more carefully examined. Particular attention should be devoted to the pragmatic function of particles, the relationship between request internal modification and external modification by means of supportive moves, and the sequencing of request events (cf. Zhang, this volume; Yeh & Shih, 1993). On the sociopragmatic level, the contextual conditions which impact requesting need close scrutiny. Interlocutor variables such as status, age, and familiarity, as well as the rights and obligations arising from different institutional contexts will have to be explored in their effect on request performance. Finally, in order to understand Chinese requesting in its cultural presuppositions and its function in reproducing Chinese cultural beliefs and behavioral patterns, requesting should be analyzed in different contexts, and interpretations of requestive events by community members should be solicited. Such a research program will be useful in order to promote our understanding of the pragmatics of Chinese communication, and serve as input to curricula for the teaching of Chinese as a second or foreign language ◆

Yanyin Zhang

INDIRECTNESS
IN CHINESE REQUESTING

INTRODUCTION

IN THE LAST FEW YEARS, the stereotypical perception of "frank" and open westerners and "inscrutable" and enigmatic orientals has been systematically investigated with the goal to reveal culture-specific ways of speech behavior and patterns of communicative interaction. The studies have focused on linguistic realizations of indirectness, its social value, and motivation in various cultures in order to find ways of promoting cross-cultural communication as well as improving second language learning, where pragmatic skills are of prime importance for acquiring native speaker-like proficiency.

It is for the benefit of teaching and learning Chinese as a second or foreign language that the present paper was written. It presents an account of indirect speech behavior of Chinese people in requestive situations and analyzes the realization, use and cultural motivations behind it. The first part discusses the concept of indirectness and related issues such as measurements and functions, i.e., its relationship with politeness. Chinese indirectness and its motivations are dealt with in the second part. Finally, indirectness as an interactional and politeness strategy is illustrated through the analysis of two Chinese requestive roleplays.

Zhang, Y. (1995). Indirectness in Chinese requesting. In G. Kasper (Ed.), *Pragmatics of Chinese as native and target language* (Technical Report #5, pp 69–118). Honolulu, Hawai'i: University of Hawai'i, Second Language Teaching & Curriculum Center.

INDIRECT SPEECH ACTS
CONCEPTUALIZATIONS AND DEFINITIONS

THIS SECTION IS CONCERNED WITH THE EXISTING THEORIES on indirect speech acts (SA), primarily on requestive acts. Their definition, scale, and relationship with politeness will be discussed. Empirical evidence will be presented during the discussion.

DEFINITION

Indirect speech behavior has been studied primarily through the analysis of individual utterances (Searle, 1975; Leech, 1983; Blum-Kulka, 1989; Weizman, 1989). The theory of indirect SAs investigates mismatches between the locutionary sense and illocutionary force of an utterance, and between utterance meaning and the meaning intended by the speaker. In the classic example "Can you pass the salt?", for instance, the theory of indirect SAs asks how, in the face of an interrogative about one's ability, the utterance serves as a request, and systematically so. According to Searle (1975), indirectness is concerned with the phenomenon that "the speaker utters a sentence, means what he says, but also means something more" (p. 59). It is about the "cases in which one illocutionary act is performed indirectly by way of performing another" (p. 60). In the case of "Can you pass the salt?" the requestive act is performed by way of an interrogative act.

There are two types of indirectness: conventional indirectness (CID) and non-conventional indirectness (NCID). CID refers to those utterances which are standardized to perform only those acts conventionally designated for certain functional purposes which are not assigned to them in their grammatical forms (Searle, 1975). In the case of "Can you pass the salt?", both the means, i.e., the kind of ability question that is used as an indirect utterance, and the form, i.e., the exact wording (e.g., "can you" as opposed to "are you able to") are conventionalized to signal the illocutionary force.

The second type of indirectness, non-conventional indirectness, also referred to as *"Hints"*, comprises those utterances which are ambiguous in either propositional content or illocutionary force or both (Weizman, 1989, 1993). For example, by replying "I have to study for an exam" to an invitation to a movie, the literal meaning of the utterance and the intended meaning, i.e., refusal, do not match. There is no systematic relation between the utterance and rejecting a proposal as there is between "can you pass the salt" and its directive illocution. Its meaning is very much context embedded. NCIDs are pragmatically vague, heterogeneous in realization, high in deniability potential and infinite in number (Searle, 1975; Grice, 1975; Weizman, 1989, 1993).

The theoretical specifications of indirectness in English have been extended to cross-linguistic inquiries into requestive realization patterns in other languages. On the basis of encoding conventions and formal equivalent features, Blum-Kulka (1989) identified similar CID request strategies ("Can you do A?") in Australian English, Canadian French, Hebrew, and Argentinean Spanish. The Cross-Cultural Speech Act Realization Project (CCSARP) (Blum-Kulka, House, & Kasper, 1989) also looked into the request realizations of American English, British English, Danish, and German with the result that equivalent CID strategies were found in all these languages. In two graduate course research papers on the requestive behavior of Chinese learners of English, Zhang (1990) and Ye (1991) found identical CID requestive strategies in Mandarin Chinese (ni(n) neng...ma?). Few exceptions have been noted to date. In Tamil, the equivalent to English "Can you do A?" is not an idiomatic expression and does not carry the force of request (Brown & Levinson, 1987, p. 139). Likewise, Wierzbicka (1991, p. 32) asserts that formal equivalents of "Will/would/won't you/why don't you do A?" do not have requestive force in Polish. Empirical studies on requests also identified NCID strategies, but their frequency of occurrence is low. For example, the percentage of NCID requests in the CCSARP studies and the Mandarin data does not exceed 10%, compared with over 50% of CID (Blum-Kulka & House, 1989; House & Kasper, 1987; Kasper, 1989; Zhang, 1990; Ye, 1991).

A related issue in the discussion of indirectness has to do with the way such indirect utterances are processed during comprehension. When meaning conventions are no longer functioning as such, what do hearer (H) and speaker (S) rely on to construct and impart intent without causing communication breakdowns? Psycholinguists have focused on the actual processing route between linguistic input and the interpretive end of CID utterances. Theories about what is processed first, literal meaning or conventional meaning, or whether both types of meaning are processed simultaneously have all received support from empirical studies (for a review of these models, see Takahashi, 1990). These models presuppose that final comprehension has been achieved, and the focus of interest centers on the reconstruction of the stages involved.

In order to trace the interpretive process of indirect SAs including both CID and NCID requestive utterances, Searle's theory of speech acts (1975), Grice's "Conversational Maxims" (1975), and "Conversational Postulates" (Gordon & Lakoff, 1975, cf. Takahashi, 1990) postulate that H and S are "rational agents" who operate and abide by certain conversational rules during interactions. These rules allow them to match and check the linguistic information against contextual conditions for interpretation. Upon analyzing NCID data with respect to types and degrees of opacity, Weizman (1993) states that although the lack of anchor in conventional form deprives NCID from dependence on meaning conventions, NCID is not entirely convention-free. It seems that "the use of [NCID] obeys a certain order" in the sense that "in a given situation, a given set of semantic contents is more likely to be preferred, although an open-ended repertoire of potential candidates is available" (p. 7). Inquiries about preparatory conditions in certain situations (e.g., "Do you have any money with you?" as a request for a loan) are instances of conventional use of NCID and are often perceived as such. The interpretive process is triggered by a series of information, including referential information contained in the utterance, contextual information, Conversational Maxims, and conventions of use (Blum-Kulka, 1989; Weizman, 1989, 1993).

SCALE OF INDIRECTNESS

Defined as "those cases in which one illocutionary act is performed indirectly by way of performing another" (Searle, 1975, p. 60), indirectness is characterized chiefly by its inherent semantic ambiguity or opacity. With regard to indirect requests, the extent to which ambiguity varies can be posited along a continuum. At the one end of the continuum, no ambiguity exists between the locutionary sense and illocutionary force. At the other end, propositional as well as illocutionary opacity characterizes a given request utterance. To represent such a continuum, two scales have been constructed.

One such scale is found in the CCSARP (Blum-Kulka et al. 1989) which elicited request (and apology) realization patterns in seven languages for cross-cultural comparison. Nine requestive strategies were identified from the data corpus and were rank-ordered by increasing degrees of indirectness on the basis of their formal as well as their functional features (Blum-Kulka et al. 1989, p. 275; also Fraser, 1978):

#1 *Mood Derivable*   Clean up the kitchen!
#2 *Performative*   I ask/request you to clean up the kitchen.
#3 *Hedged Performative*   I'd like to ask you to clean up the kitchen.
#4 *Locution Derivable*   You should/have to clean up the kitchen.
#5 *Want Statement*   I'd like/want/wish you to clean up the kitchen.
#6 *Suggestory Formula*   How about cleaning up the kitchen?
#7 *Query Preparatory*   Can/Could you/we clean up the kitchen?
#8 *Strong Hint*   The kitchen is in a mess.
#9 *Mild Hint*   Whose duty is it today?

These nine strategies were grouped into three levels of directness: Direct strategies range from #1 to #5, CID includes strategies #6 and #7, and the last two strategies belong to NCID.

For the direct strategies, the requestive force is derived from the sense of the utterance. *Performative* verbs such as "ask", "request", "demand", etc. convey both the utterance and the speaker's meaning. In CID, as explained above, disparity exists between the locutionary sense and illocutionary force although the force has been conventionalized so that the meaning is no longer ambiguous. For NCID, where the sense cannot express the force without context, the utterances can be taken to perform a variety of SAs. Levels #8 and #9 were constructed on the basis of presence (#8) and absence (#9) of (relatively) explicit reference to the agent and the proposed action.

Brown and Levinson's (1987) approach to direct/indirect strategies by which face-threatening acts (FTAs) are carried out represents yet another "scale".

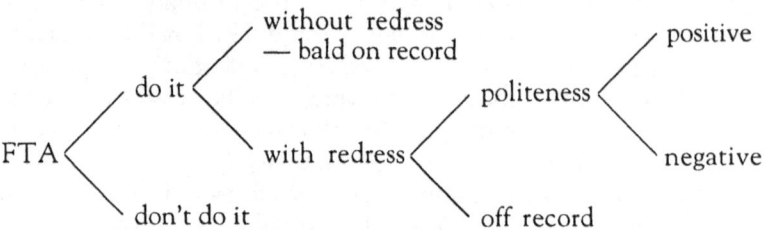

On the surface, "bald on record", "do it with redress", and "off record" correspond to the three levels of directness developed in CCSARP, yet the categorization principle is functional rather than linguistic. Centering on the strategic concerns for H's face, i.e., H's desire for approval (positive face) and freedom from imposition (negative face), "bald on record" is comprised of cases of either non-minimization of face-threat or FTA oriented usage. "Do it with redress", on the other hand, includes strategies which attend to either H's positive or negative face. "Off record" refers to strategies which invite conversational implicatures or violate Grice's Manner maxim by being vague or ambiguous. In this chart, the linguistic realizations within each level are not prescribed in terms of mutually exclusive syntactic markings, as in the CCSARP scale. Thus, particular linguistic realizations labelled as "direct, CID, NCID" in CCSARP appear in all three categories depending on context. As stated by Brown and Levinson, "it is not linguistic forms, but linguistic forms in context that distinguish on/off record" (p. 134).

INDIRECTNESS AND POLITENESS: THE RELATIONSHIP

The CCSARP scale of indirectness proves to be a ready instrument to investigate the relationship between indirectness and politeness. A number of people, Searle in particular, have repeatedly stated that politeness is the chief motivation behind indirect language use (Searle, 1975; Leech, 1983; Brown & Levinson, 1987). Disagreement exists and is supported by the studies of NCID which maintain that it is not so much an issue of politeness but high degree of deniability potential that underlies the use of indirectness (Weizman, 1989).

As regards the argument in favor of politeness-motivated indirect language use, it is proposed that the reason for indirect illocutions to be more polite is (a) because they increase the degree of optionality, and (b) because the more indirect an illocution is, the more diminished and tentative its force tends to be (Leech, 1983; p. 108). Degree of indirectness, according to this line of reasoning, is directly related to degree of politeness.

From a social and psychological perspective, it is argued by Brown and Levinson that the heavier the FTA, the greater the demand for linguistic politeness, hence, indirectness is preferred over directness. The weightiness of FTAs is computable by adding up the values of social power (P), social distance (D) and rating of imposition (R) involved in an FTA.

Viewing politeness from the perspective of its normative rather than strategic function, Leech formulated politeness maxims which suggest that certain acts are, depending on their benefit or cost to H, inherently polite and face giving (e.g., thanking, offering, inviting, congratulating, greeting), while others are inherently impolite and face-threatening (e.g., requesting, refusing). One of his pragmatic scales shows that the more beneficial an act is and the more polite it is for S to perform it, the more direct S will be in linguistic realizations, and vice versa.

The parallel relationship between politeness and indirectness, as maintained by Searle and others, has been empirically tested and proven to be not only non-linear, but also sensitive to more constraints than Brown and

Levinson's three predictive variables. Using the CCSARP scale, House (1986) found that native speakers of British English and German perceived NCID to be less polite than CID. In a study examining the politeness perceptions of speakers of American English and Israeli Hebrew, Blum-Kulka (1987) found that CID was rated as the most polite strategy by both American and Israeli subjects. While speakers of American English chose NCID as the second most polite strategy, speakers of Hebrew favored directness. The preference for CID as the most polite requestive strategy was also confirmed in a pilot judgement test on the relationship between indirectness and politeness in Chinese (Zhang, 1991).

Based on the findings from cross-cultural studies of compliments, invitations, leave-takings, disapproval, expression of gratitude, refusal, and apology, Wolfson (1989) formulated the "Bulge Theory" which accounts for a "qualitative difference in the speech behavior of middle-class Americans with intimates, status unequals, and strangers on the one hand, and with non-intimates, status-equal friends, co-workers, and acquaintances on the other" (1989, p. 137). Linguistic behavior with respect to the three types of relationships: intimates, acquaintances, and strangers, does not follow a linear pattern. Direct speech is more likely to occur with the two extremes on the social distance scale than with the middle section, creating a characteristic bulge shape. This demonstrates that social distance does not affect indirect speech behavior in a positively correlated manner.

Studies of family discourse suggest that the type of speech event affects the relationship between indirectness and politeness. American, American-Israeli and Israeli parents' speech to children at the dinner table shows a very high preference for the direct mode, which appears to encode for parents both power and intimacy, and functions as a neutral or unmarked expression in the politeness system of family discourse. In addition, a culture-specific preference for politeness realization is shown by the fact that while Israelis favor directness plus rich mitigation devices such as nicknames, Americans lean toward CID. A similar preference for mitigated directness has also been documented for Polish discourse practice (Blum-Kulka, 1990; Wierzbicka, 1985).

Not only is the relationship between indirectness and politeness non-parallel, it is affected by, in addition to P, D, R and domain of discourse, a variety of social and interpersonal factors such as age and gender (Fraser, Rintell, & Walters, 1981), the nature of the propositional content of the utterances (Brown & Levinson, 1987; Leech, 1983; Cottrill, 1990), directive goals, degrees of right and estimated difficulty to request, obligations to carry out the request, the likelihood of compliance, etc. (Blum-Kulka, Danet, & Gerson, 1985; Blum-Kulka & House, 1989). Finally, "relationship affect" is proposed to be a fourth parameter to Brown and Levinson's three predictive variables of politeness (Brown & Gilman, 1989; cf. Blum-Kulka, 1990).

In summary, studies on indirect speech behavior found cross-culturally similar linguistic forms of CID and semantic properties of NCID. The relationship between indirectness and politeness proved to be affected by various social and psycholinguistic factors. Within this framework, I will, in the following, examine the indirectness issue in Chinese culture, dealing specifically with the definition of indirectness in Chinese and its relationship with politeness. Culture-specific conceptions, perceptions, and linguistic manifestations will be illustrated through research findings and two roleplays.

CHINESE INDIRECTNESS

BOTH CID AND NCID EXIST IN CHINESE. Similar to its English counterpart, the Chinese CID request, 你／我能嗎？ *nǐ/wǒ néng... ma?* (you/I can...+ question marker), for example, is also characterized by two levels of meaning: the locutionary sense of ability 能 *néng* and the illocutionary force of request. In addition, both the means: an interrogative utterance questioning ability, and form — ability interrogative with modal *néng*, are conventionalized to pragmatically signal request. NCID, i.e., those utterances in which there is a gap between utterance meaning and speaker's meaning, are also present in Chinese. The meaning is context dependent instead of form-dependent.

In two empirical studies using discourse completion tests to investigate the requestive patterns of Chinese learners of English, a high preference for CID was manifested by learners (62%) and native speakers of English (71.9%). In addition, most of the CID was realized by the structure *nǐ néng...ma?*, the equivalent of English "Can you...?". NCID, on the other hand, appeared far less in the data and was realized either as inquiries about preparatory conditions or as other types of SAs (Zhang, 1990; Ye, 1991).

The realizations of Chinese requestive forms in individual utterances do not seem to diverge from the theoretical construct of requestive indirectness and empirical findings from other cultures. It is when the request utterances were studied to determine their level of indirectness that differences started to surface. The initial indication of the divergence appeared in a pilot replication of Blum-Kulka's study (1987) on the relationship between directness and politeness (Zhang, 1991). Six native speakers of American English and six native speakers of Chinese rated request utterances for directness and politeness. While the American subjects' ratings confirmed Blum-Kulka's findings, the Chinese subjects rated the utterances differentially only on the politeness scale. They strongly objected to there being a difference in terms of directness-indirectness (直接／直率 - 間接／婉轉 *zhíjiē/zhíshuài – jiànjiē/wǎnzhuǎn*). The Chinese subjects reported that all nine strategies were more or less equally direct the way they were presented, as single utterances, although those single utterances did differ with respect to their politeness degrees. Since the data base was very small, only a tentative conclusion was drawn, namely, that the rules operating on the directness-indirectness distinction were different in English and Chinese. The question then is how indirectness expresses itself in Chinese and how the Chinese perceive it.

Subsequent interviews with the subjects and other native speakers of Chinese revealed that the representation of Chinese indirectness occurs at the discourse level, realized either by "small talk", e.g., conversation on topics other than those related to the intended action, or "supportive moves", i.e., utterances which either inquire about preparatory conditions or goal-oriented NCID (*Hints*). Individual utterances, when used as requests, encode various degrees of politeness information with the presence or absence of mitigating devices such as pragmatic particles, politeness markers, terms of address, pronouns, etc. They modify the tone of the utterances, moving them along the politeness scale, but they do not change the illocutionary or propositional transparency or opacity to vary the degree of directness. Due to conventionalization, the propositional content is as clear in "Can you pass the salt?" or even in "The soup is bland" as it is in "Pass the salt", given an appropriate context. In Chinese, the distinction between directness and indirectness in individual utterances of these kinds seems to be overridden by the distinction in politeness.

Chinese indirectness, so it seems, is associated with information sequencing. Whether or not A's speech is more indirect than B's depends on first, whether A prefaces his/her intended proposition with any small talk or supportive moves, and second, how much of it A employs to convey his/her communicative intention before explicitly bringing it up. The degree of indirectness is determined by the length of the supportive moves which do not contain explicitly the intended proposition. The more one beats around the bush, the more indirect one's speech becomes (interview data). To define indirectness in Chinese, and to realize it in interaction, external modification of (request) utterances is mandatory, utterance internal modification is not.

Defined and realized this way, research findings on Chinese indirectness contrast with the findings on requesting in British English, German, and Danish. Upon analyzing internal and external request modifications in the above language groups, Faerch and Kasper (1989) reported that internal and external modification work independently. While internal modification is mandatory, external modification is optional. Indirectness obtains if the utterance is realized in CID. In Chinese, the opposite is true — while directness exists in interaction, indirectness is not perceived (or issued) without external modifications preceding the requestive utterance. The formulation of the utterance itself and its internal modification do not constitute indirectness.

On the basis of their one-year teaching experience in Taiwan and Korea, and a short sojourn in Japan, Scollon and Wong-Scollon (1991) found that "the Chinese and other Asians generally defer the introduction of the topic until after a considerable period of small talk." They labelled this speech behavior "inductive" as opposed to "deductive" style where topic precedes explanations (also Young, 1982). In contrast, Faerch and Kasper (1989) cited a request sample supplied by a Danish subject in response to a DCT situation where a lecturer asks a student to give a class presentation a week earlier than scheduled. In this "somewhat drastic example", where lengthy supportive moves were used, it is interesting to see how the request-related information is sequenced.

> I am calling to hear if you can perhaps do your presentation. It is not what we have agreed on but it will fit better into the course structure. Of course you do not have to do it if you cannot manage. Then I have to think of something else.
> (Translated version, p. 240)

The request proper is made at the beginning and supportive moves follow. Pre-supportive moves do occur in English and increase the degree of deference in the utterance (Rintell, 1981). Taking a response to the same situation from three "somewhat drastic" examples in the Chinese DCT corpus, we see a different order (translated version; see Appendix for the original Chinese):

> Is this Zhao Jun? This is Hu Yun. I'd like to talk with you about something. The school has recently required us to give the students one week for studies on society. So my teaching schedule has to be changed, which in turn, will affect your oral report on Whitman in class. Could you hurry up a bit and do the report one week earlier? This way, it will fit the changed schedule. If time is too short, you may turn in your reading report two weeks late. How about that? Do you think it's OK with you?   (#68)

All the three Chinese responses which feature long supportive moves are sequenced in the pattern: Supportive moves + Request + Supportive moves (Zhang, 1990).

Similar observations were made by Kirkpatrick (1991) after analyzing the structure of forty letters of request written by Mainland Chinese to the China Section of Radio Australia. He found that only three letters did not preface the request with some kind of "small talk". In fact, there was a distinctive structure in the remaining thirty-seven letters, a structure which he labelled as an "indirect way" of making a written request:

Salutation
Preamble (facework)
Reasons for request
Request

In the follow-up judgement interviews, six out of ten native speakers of Chinese found two of the three request-fronted letters "direct" and the remaining one "impolite". For explanations, Kirkpatrick resorted to a syntactic analysis of Chinese complex sentences with subordinate clauses, where the normal unmarked sequence is subordinate clause + main clause (Lin & Liu, 1955; Lin, 1983; cf. Kirkpatrick, 1991). The "because...therefore" sequence is the preferred unmarked order. He hypothesizes that "it is possible that this sequence is also the preferred sequence at discourse and text levels" (p. 77).

To summarize, for a Chinese, a single utterance, be it an "on record" impositive or a CID act, has as much direct force as an impositive in English, although it varies in politeness degree. Indirectness in Chinese is achieved mainly through utterance external linguistic build-ups, i.e., small talk or supportive moves, rather than utterance internal devices, e.g., modals, particles, pronouns, etc. In other words, how a particular speech act utterance is realized is unrelated to indirectness. It is in the way the utterance is framed in the larger discourse context that indirectness becomes relevant.

INDIRECTNESS AND POLITENESS: THE RELATIONSHIP

Linguistic indirectness in Chinese is also motivated by politeness concerns and functions as a face-redressive strategy. However, politeness values and face semantics in Chinese are different from those in Anglo-American culture (Hu, 1944; Gu, 1990; Kasper, 1990; Mao, 1994). The Chinese "face" has two aspects: one, "面子 *miànzi*", refers to "the need of an individual to conform to social conventions and express one's desire to be part of this community"; the other, 脸 *liǎn*, defines a need to show one's moral sense of place and role. Both roles revolve around "a recognition by others of one's desire for social prestige, reputation or sanction" (Hu, 1944; Mao, 1994).

The social orientation and public character of Chinese face converge with Goffman's idea of face as a public image that is on loan to the individual from society (Goffman, 1967, cf. Mao, 1994). It contrasts with Brown and Levinson's face theory, which evolves around an individual's private face "wants". Furthermore, the interactional dynamics of facework in Chinese is positively reciprocal with both parties engaged in mutually shared orientation to negotiate, elevate, and attend to each other's face as well as one's own face. The facework proposed in Brown and Levinson, on the other hand, is unidirectional with S taking redressive measures to address H's face. The three predicative variables, P, D, R, are indices by which S assesses situations for linguistic strategies to take care of the face wants of H. Finally, face-balance is central in Chinese facework — giving face simultaneously enhances one's own face; by the same token, depriving other's face damages one's own face. "To be polite (i.e., 有禮貌 *yǒu lǐmào*) in Chinese discourse," Mao observes, "is to know how to attend to each other's *lian* and *miànzi* and to perform speech acts appropriate to and worthy of such an image" (Mao, 1994, p. 19).

The character of Chinese face as a "public self-image", interactive and reciprocal in balance, motivates to a large extent the Chinese way of indirectness in interaction. As discussed in the previous section, Chinese indirectness is characterized most prominently by "supportive moves" or "small talk" preceding and oriented toward the proposed action. It is more of an utterance external phenomenon. In terms of information sequencing, Chinese indirectness is closer to a "because...therefore" structure than to "therefore...because" structure (Kirkpatrick, 1991). Utterance level indirectness by and of itself does not possess as much indirect force in Chinese as in English, although individual utterances do contain politeness information. In the context of face concerns and politeness, what roles do "small talk" and "supportive moves" play?

Since Chinese "face" is a "public self-image", interacting on every social, personal and interpersonal level (Hu, 1944), to be polite is to observe each other's face. Linguistic indirectness manifested in small talk and supportive moves is a strategy adopted by all participants to constantly assess the situation so as to make appropriate face adjustments to others and self. The lengthy small talk preceding and following the main topic, e.g., request in a requestive event, was documented by Scollon and Wong-Scollon (1991), who rightly said that it served as "a kind of extended facework", gauging the mood and attitude of the participants, adjusting the distance and relationship between them and creating an amiable atmosphere to conduct transactions. The ensuing small talk, on the other hand, finetunes the face distance of both parties for a harmonious conclusion. Such interactive adjustment aims at a face-balance between the interlocutors in a communicative event. If facework is instrumental to politeness and harmony, face-balance is central in the facework.

Supportive moves are often NCID utterances, realized on the surface in a variety of speech acts seemingly unrelated to the proposed action (Weizman, 1989, 1993), for example, compliment, statement of problems, etc. in a requestive event (Du, this volume; Kirkpatrick, 1991). High in deniability potential, they provide both parties with opportunities to openly and respectably deny his/her true intentions in case they prove too face damaging. Supportive moves also serve as a means of negotiation, steering the course of the interaction in the direction of one's intended goal, and in the course of that, act as face-saving strategies to supply the chance for both parties to perform a polite act, e.g., offering and thanking, while deferring the occurrence of an inherently impolite one, e.g., requesting and refusing. Such a strategy is related so closely to the Chinese value of politeness that a request without some kind of preface is considered direct, and often, impolite.

The discourse function of "small talk" in a speech event has not received sufficient attention. Specifically, we have little knowledge about the favored, or "safe", topics for small talk, the dynamics between types of small talk or supportive moves and types of situation, and the effect of social variables in the choice of small talk types, etc. Although anecdotes are abundant, systematic studies of discourse structure in Chinese have only dealt with invitation events (Gu, 1990; Mao, 1994) and written requests (Kirkpatrick, 1991).

In order to capture the dynamics of verbal interaction and culture-specific discourse behavior, we need to move beyond specific SAs to incorporate a wider range of phenomena such as discourse structure and management. Any communication involving negotiations, ritualistic or substantive, needs to take into consideration such factors as information sequencing (Scollon & Wong-Scollon, 1991; Kirkpatrick, 1991), length and types of supportive moves (Faerch & Kasper, 1989), face implications of speech events (Cottrill, 1990; Gu, 1990), the function and nature of NCID (Weizman, 1989, 1993), and the meaning of indirectness and its manifestation in different contexts (Scollon & Wong-Scollon, 1991; Kirkpatrick, 1991). The analysis of the following two roleplays will address these issues and illustrate the Chinese way of indirect speech behavior more specifically.

ROLEPLAYS

THE TWO ROLEPLAYS ON REQUESTIVE TOPICS were conducted between two female native speakers of Chinese. Both subjects were graduate students at the University of Hawai'i. One used to be the instructor of the other, but at the time of the roleplay, they were no longer in a teacher-student relationship. In both real life and roleplay situations, the subjects were good friends but not quite close. Relationships of this kind are most likely to invite indirect language use (Wolfson, 1989). Both roleplays deal with request situations. In Roleplay #1, one student asks the other to help with the upcoming exam; in Roleplay #2, one student asks the other to save a seat for her at a seminar.

On the role cards, the following conditions were specified: occupation (students), relationship (fellow students), events (exam, seminar), request intention (for the requester), event related problems (for the requestee). No outcome was postulated. The roleplays were carried out without the presence of the researcher. They were audio-recorded and later transcribed and translated (see Appendix for the original Chinese roleplay transcripts). In the retrospective interviews held two months later, the two subjects and nine native speakers of Chinese listened and commented upon the roleplays and answered a set of questions in Chinese. Furthermore, the naturalness of the roleplays was rated by ten native speakers of Chinese. On a scale of five, five being completely natural and authentic, the average rating was 4.5, with a range between 4 and 5. Because the transcript (below) is based on the audio-recording, non-verbal backchannelling behavior, which is predominant in Chinese interaction (Tao & Thomson, 1991), could not be captured.

The analysis will focus on the following three areas: (1) the realization of Chinese indirectness; (2) indirectness as a strategy in interactive facework; and

(3) the dynamics between indirectness, request goals, and politeness. The analysis will also draw on the retrospective interviews.

ROLEPLAY #1:
STUDYING FOR THE EXAM (TRANSLATED VERSION)

Speaker	Speech Activity	Utterance	SA
A:	* I've been rather busy recently studying.	1	stating circumstance
	* But some people always come to ask me questions.	2	complaining
	* It wouldn't be nice if I didn't answer their questions, since we are all classmates,	3	complaining
	* but it takes too much time to answer all their questions.	4	complaining
	* It is especially difficult to deal with those stupid people. They never understand your explanations.	5	complaining
	* What's more, they resent your attitude and you can't even show any impatience, you know. My gosh.	6	complaining
B:	* Speaking of the exam, I feel really bored and extremely (unclear).	7	complaining
	* Look, I don't even have a clue as to how to review.	8	stating problem
	* Sometimes, you know, it seems not so easy to ask for help from the teacher or the students.	9	stating problem
	* Hey, do you think they will like it if I go and ask them some questions? Or is it...	10	seeking advice
A:	* If you really must ask, you'd better not ask those exam-related questions.	11	giving advice

	* Even if they decide to answer your questions, you know, they feel more intimidated to answer exam-related ones.	12	giving advice
	* They don't even dare to show any unusual facial expressions for fear that you would say 'yes, I got it'. The other day when I was talking to this person, his facial expression was very strange and I knew immediately that this item would be on the exam.	13	telling supporting anecdote
B:	* Usually you know the teacher will give some review topics and things like that.	14	stating fact
	* Unfortunately, I didn't come to class last week.	15	stating problem
	* Of course, you know, I can study by myself,	16	stating solution
	* but I really hope, you know, to receive some help, you know, from the teacher or fellow students. What do you think?	17	stating hope
	* As you said just now, there's always a crowd bothering you before every exam,	18	offering sympathy
	* **so now I feel like, you know, asking but am afraid that people will resent me.**	19	**Request 1**
	* I feel very uncomfortable, you know.	20	stating problem
A:	* That depends.	21	stating principle
	* I don't mind if they are good friends.	22	stating principle
	* Otherwise, I hate to help,	23	stating principle

	* especially those who come to you only when they need you, you know.	24	stating principle
	* Also you must be very careful when you give help.	25	stating potential problem
	* If you give the wrong information by accident, you know, for example, people will say, look, you told me such-and-such.	26	stating potential problem
	* Of course they are not blaming you	27	stating potential problem
	* but what they say will make you uncomfortable.	28	stating potential problem
	* Therefore, I usually take it easy with those who are not my friends.	29	stating principle
	* But I must appear to be serious. I must [pretend it is real.	30	stating problem
	* That is very hard.	31	stating problem
B:	[Really. * I am extremely anxious now that the exam is only two weeks away. I don't know where to start and what to review.	32	eliciting sympathy
	* **Do you think you can help me if you know? Just tell me what the teacher said the other day and give me a rough idea, like some direction.**	33	Request 2
A:	* No problem.	34	complying
	* I'll xerox a copy of the review sheet for you and that will take care of everything, right?	35	offering
B:	* That's wonderful.	36	thanking

A:	* This won't take too much time.	37	minimizing cost
	* Probably the two of us can study together.	38	suggesting
	* I can learn something from you, too.	39	complimenting
	* All you missed was one day. Then...	40	
B:	* That's wonderful.	41	thanking
A:	* But we mustn't let everybody know it.	42	warning
	* Don't attract a big crowd... Look, let's set up a time.	43	warning
B:	* OK. When do you have time?...	44	negotiating appointment

(See Appendix for conclusion)

In this request event, B asks A for help with the upcoming examination. B's on-record request is realized in two steps. The first one "I feel like asking but..." (19) comes about at the end of the 4th turn. The second one "Do you think you can help me if you know?" (33) is realized after two more turns. On the utterance level, B's first request is a *Hedged Performative*, with ambiguous specification of the agent, which could be the teacher, fellow-students, or A. Her second request consists of two utterances: a CID with the conventionalized form "能 *néng*" (can) followed by a conditional clause as syntactic downgrader, and an imperative.

The pre-request supportive moves used by both interlocutors consist of several SAs. A's opening remarks (1–6) clearly have the force of a complaint. This is interpreted as an expression of reluctance by B, who commented in the retrospective interview that unless it was an emergency situation as she perceived the present roleplay situation to be, she would not go any further at this point in her request. As A does not relate her reluctance with any expression of refusal, B ignores it and precedes with her request through a statement of problems to elicit sympathy (8–9) and to seek advice (10, 17). A takes B literally. Instead of offering help, she gives advice (11–12), as B has asked (10, 17). Having explicitly expressed her problems and wishes (17) without encountering definite refusal, B tries, in an propositionally ambiguous yet illocutionary clear way, the request (19), which is met with a statement of principle (21). It is not until more worries are expressed (32) and more principles are stated that B makes the on-record request (33) and A complies (34).

In this discourse context, seeking advice, stating problems, expressing worries and wishes are all supportive moves leading to the request. Complaining, giving advice, and stating principle do not serve their primary illocutionary functions either, instead, they are intended to make B take action accordingly, i.e., withdraw the request.

The elaborate employment of supportive moves or "roundabout" talk in this case is determined by the nature of the request act, the relationship between the interlocutors and the obvious goal conflict. Throughout the discourse, each A and B know perfectly well what the other wants (interview data). Yet each tries to get the other to accept what she does not want, i.e., A does not want to be asked for help and B does not want to be refused. This kind of goal conflict is especially face-threatening and requires proper face-redressive work. That B does not put forward the request at the outset is motivated by face concerns for both A and herself, for to request directly in a non-routine situation is likely to be perceived as being inconsiderate, harmful to one's *liàn*. To be rejected in one's request is something rather face (面子 *miànzi*) losing. The primary concern in situations like this lies in first, not having to make the request explicitly, second, in having the interlocutor make an offer, and last, in making a successful request. In the roleplay above, the goal conflict has not produced verbal conflict, for the indirectness strategies chosen by A and B have helped to maintain harmony and to protect the 面子 *miànzi* of both participants. B's on-record request comes at a point where both have tested each other's territory sufficiently and felt that some kind of understanding and a "contract" have been reached in terms of the degree of A's commitment and B's expectations of and gratitude to A. It is only then that A complies readily by saying "No problem" (34), a polite act which not only gives 面子 *miànzi* to B but enhances that of A in every way.

ROLEPLAY #2:
SAVING SEATS (TRANSLATED VERSION)

Similar strategies of request are also employed in the second roleplay, in which A asks B to save a seat for her at a seminar.

Speaker	Speech Activity	Utterance	SA
A:	* Are you going to the seminar this evening?	1	pre-request inquiry
B:	* Well, I don't know yet.	2	evasive response
	* Look, I'm kind of upset whenever I think about it.	3	complaining
	* I have no idea why I am so unlucky that some people always ask me to save seats for them at every seminar.	4	complaining
	* It's not a big deal if it's only once or twice but it happens every time.	5	complaining
	* I feel it's unfair.	6	complaining
	* Well, I don't know what to do now.	7	complaining
A:	* Yeah, if you're to save seats for others, you need to go early, right?	8	offering sympathy
	* Meanwhile, they can take care of their own business, take it easy, and still have a good seat.	9	complaining
	* Of course, it would be better if people could take turns.	10	suggesting
	* On the other hand, some people are terrible —	11	complaining

	* they always ask you to save seats for them, butwhen you have some emergency and ask them to save a seat for you, they are reluctant, right?	12	complaining
	* Speaking of which, I have got something to do for tonight and **I would like to ask you to help save a seat for me.** Do you think it's OK?	13	Request
B:	* You're OK.	14	complying
	* I'm not busy and I am going tonight.	15	explaining
	* I'll do that for you today and next time you must save a seat for me, [because I always…	16	enforcing obligation
A:	* [I know.	17	acknowledging
	* People always think that I am a "bum".	18	self-criticism
	* Well, to tell you the truth, I am one of those who always asks others to save seats.	19	self-criticism
	* Today, through talking to you, I've realized my [problems.	20	self-criticism
B:	* [I didn't mean you.	21	denying
	* I just feel that I have to always do that for others.	22	explaining
	* As a matter of fact, it's not a big deal, I am going anyway and saving a seat is just something in passing.	23	explaining
	* But I don't always feel comfortable about it.	24	complaining

	* I kind of wish that people would say something nice to you like they appreciate it and things like that.	25	stating hope
A:	* Actually it's my fault.	26	self-criticism
	* I ask people to save a seat for me so that I can save some time for myself.	27	self-criticism
	* As a matter of fact I can't save that much time, ten minutes, twenty minutes at most, and I become the culprit as a result.	28	self-criticism
	* Next time, I'll be careful.	29	promising
	* In the past, I was not very considerate of other people, always being a bum with people and you know me...	30	self-criticism
	* Next time, I'll save a seat for you.	31	promising
B:	* No problem.	32	accepting
A:	* I promise to save a seat for you next time.	33	promising
B:	* No problem, buddy.	34	accepting

A's question (1) is sensed by B as an indirect request, for "saving seats" is written as a potential problem in the role card. B's complaint (3–7) as a reply to A's question is taken for an expression of reluctance (interview data). Since compliance from B is unlikely at this point, A is faced with two options — giving up or proceeding. A has chosen the latter but instead of eliciting sympathy by stating her plight as in the previous situation, she takes sides with B on the issue regardless of her real intention. Her on-record request, "I just would like to ask you to save a seat. Do you think it's OK?" (13) is a *Hedged Performative* with politeness marker (a verb "please") and consultative downtoner "Do you think it's OK?" (plus friendly laughter). The on-record request is realized after A has offered B a certain amount of emotional support through identifying with B's feelings (8-9, 11-12). It is met with ready compliance (14), which, according to B at the follow-up interview, has never been a problem despite her initial complaint about the matter. However, both the interlocutor and other native speakers of Chinese disagree, saying that B's complaint is not a totally innocent one, given the fact that she has sensed A's intention from the beginning. She later denies it precisely because she could lose 面子 miànzi gained in the interaction despite her compliance. However, that she could deny her intention is due to the deniability potential of her NCID utterances.

On the surface, A's request is rather abrupt and her strategy is face-damaging to herself, for she is the target of her own criticism. Yet, her "self-bashing" speech accommodates to B's emotional state at the moment. It "strokes" B's 面子 miànzi and "pokes" her own through depicting herself as a reasonable person who understands B's concerns. Yet her own request, which degrades her and virtually categorizes her with "those people", is realized almost in the middle of her reiterated support of B's objection to "those people". A request embedded within a self-degrading context creates an imbalance of 面子 miànzi which the requestee is obliged to rehabilitate through compliance. Self-denigration being a "ritual" or "normative" politeness gesture in Chinese culture (Gu, 1990), when a person denigrates him/herself, the other is obliged to elevate him/her. By the same token, when one elevates the other, e.g., through a compliment, the other must denigrate him/herself. Part of the goal is to reach balance. In the context of A's offer of sympathy, understanding and support, her request appears to be something different from those B is complaining about. Hers does not appear to take things for granted, nor does it seem to be callous.

The interaction does not stop at B's compliance. What follows is pure facework on both parts. This is necessary because A has forced her way through B's reluctance and dissatisfaction about her intended act and there might be some residue of that dissatisfaction left despite B's compliance. B's compliance, on the other hand, makes her previous grievance superfluous and potentially harmful to her positive 面子 miànzi. Something needs to be done in order to reach a harmonious ending. A launches into self-denigration speech by criticizing herself (18-20, 26-31), a polite act to further elevate B's face. Her self-criticism starts to act on B's conscience, who has to exclude A from her previous complaint "I didn't mean you" (21). This, together with her compliance, enhances A's face as well. Balance is achieved and symbolically manifested in the solidarity form "buddy" B uses to address A at the conclusion (35).

In these two samples of a request event, the indirect request is expressed through a series of pre-request supportive moves in which several SAs are employed to convey request intentions. The sequence of indirect request in Chinese, as manifested in these two roleplays, appears to be structured in the pattern:

Supportive moves (expressing worries and problems, seeking advice, offering sympathy, stating wishes, self-criticism)
Request
Supportive moves (self-criticism, promising, thanking)

CONCLUSION

INDIRECT SA THEORY and the cross-cultural study of SA realizations have focused mainly on individual utterances. This line of research makes it possible to define decontextualized illocutionary utterances and construct a directness-indirectness scale based on the relationship between locution and illocution. It also facilitates the comparison between the means and values of the realizations of linguistic indirectness across cultures. Politeness construed as a face-redressive strategy is expressed in the choice of different levels of (in)directness.

The Chinese language encodes the information of indirectness not so much in the grammatical features of the language as in the sequencing of information in ongoing discourse. Indirectness in this sense is a discourse phenomenon, characterized by distinctive structures:

Supportive move   (e.g., NCID SAs)
Main topic   (e.g., request)
Supportive moves   (e.g., NCID SAs)

Supportive moves are realized in a number of NCID SAs other than those which define the event. They play the role of specific illocutions which, for politeness reasons, cannot be realized explicitly at that point. The lengthy *Hints* serve to provide the interlocutors with chances to avoid performing an impolite act, to perform a polite act, and to perform an impolite act in a non-conflicting way. Politeness is best achieved when both parties constantly observe and balance each other's face throughout the discourse.

What is the significance of the above discussion for language teaching and learning? It is generally acknowledged that language learning is a cultural experience. In order to be able to function in a second language, both the linguistic and social behavior of the target culture should be observed and enacted properly. Sociopragmatic as well as pragmalinguistic ability should be developed in the course of learning (Thomas, 1983). In order to do that, knowledge about target cultural norms and patterns of linguistic behavior need to be imparted to the learner. With regard to Chinese indirect speech behavior, the following insights gained from the above study will be of pedagogical value.

1. Since Chinese indirectness exhibits a rather distinctive structure, it could be taught explicitly for both comprehension and production, oral and written. Sensitivity to the information embedded in the supportive moves should be developed during the language learning process.

2. Contrary to American perception, self-denigration in Chinese culture is by no means a symbol of weakness or a gesture of hypocrisy. It is a face-balancing interactional strategy which aims at installing good feelings in the addressee about him- or herself and eventually, about the speaker. One should not isolate the self-denigrating gesture of a Chinese from the speech event in which it occurs; conversely, one should learn and always be ready to denigrate oneself in interactions.

3. Linguistic strategies circumlocuting direct, flat negative responses should be taught and learned. The two roleplays present some resources which can be used in training. Receptively, listener's sensitivity to an indirect negative response must be cultivated to avoid being perceived as imposing and unreasonable.

4. Keeping Chinese face concerns in mind, learners should learn how to perform a particular SA in a non-confrontational way, if only in a ritual manner.

In the end, what indirectness in Chinese culture does is to maintain a harmonious relationship, however ostensible and superficial it may be. The accomplishment of transactional goals is only possible with sufficient good feelings all around ◆

ACKNOWLEDGEMENTS

I would like to express my deepest gratitude to my advisor over the last two and half years, Professor Kasper, whose keen interest, unfailing support, and critical thinking have benefitted me both as a student and as a researcher. Equally important in my academic life are those countless "subjects", in particular, Xin Chen, Yi Jin, Nengjia Wang, and Chuan Chen. Their ready cooperation has made the present paper possible. Finally, I would like to thank Karl Rensch for editing, and Lei Ye, Xixiang Jiang, and Beverly Hong for discussing various points "directly" or "indirectly" with me. The errors in the paper remain mine.

APPENDIX: ROLEPLAY TRANSCRIPTIONS AND DCT SITUATION 14

The roleplay transcription follows the standard format. There are three paragraphs within each turn: the first paragraph is transcribed in both Chinese characters and pinyin system, the second paragraph is a literal translation, and the third paragraph is an English version.

The Chinese version is a word-for-word transcription. The literal translation of the roleplay follows as much as possible the Chinese structure. The English version is comparable to the original Chinese version in meaning and force.

Transcription symbols:
[simultaneous speech production
[ ] interjection of one speaker within the turn of the other speaker.

ROLEPLAY #1: STUDYING FOR THE EXAM

A: 最近我啊學習特別忙。可是呢，老有一群人吧，老到我這兒來呢。有的時候呢，你說問問題呀，這兒那兒的，大家都要考試了。然后呢，不答吧，不合適，大伙都是同學。答了呢，太費功夫。尤其那些呢比較不開竅的人，這要不開竅的人呢，你跟他怎麼解釋他還不明白。他不明白他還賴你態度不好。你還不能急，你知道嘛，好傢伙。

Zuìjìn wǒ a xuéxí tèbié máng. Kěshì ne, lǎo yǒu yī qún rén ba, lǎo dào wǒ zhèr lái ne. Yǒude shíhòu ne, nǐ shuō wèn wèntí ya, zhèr nàr de, dàjiā dōu yào kǎoshì le. Ránhòu ne, bù dá ba, bù héshì, dàhuǒr dōu shì tóngxué. Dá le ne, tài fèi gōngfu. Yóuqí nèixiē ne bǐjiào bù kāiqiào de rén, zhè yào bù kāiqiào de rén ne, nǐ gēn tā zěnme jiěshì tā hái bù míngbai. Tā bù míngbai tā hái lài nǐ tàidù bù hǎo. Nǐ hái bù néng jí, nǐ zhīdào ma. Hǎo jiāhuo.

Recently I study rather busy. But, always a crowd of people, always come to my place. Sometimes, you say ask questions, this and that, everyone almost exam. Then, not answer, not proper, all are fellow students. Answer, too take time. Especially those relatively non-enlightened people. For non-enlightened people, you to him however explain he still not understand. He not understand, he blame you attitude not good. You can not get impatient, you know. My gosh.

I've been rather busy recently studying. But some people always come to ask me questions. It wouldn't be nice if I didn't answer their questions, since we are all classmates, but it takes too much time to answer all their questions. It's especially difficult to deal with those stupid people. They never understand your explanations. What's more, they resent your attitude and you can't even show any impatience, you know. My gosh.

B: 咳，就說考試，整個一個沒勁。我覺得是特別（不清楚）。而且吧，就說你說要復習吧，整個兒沒邊兒沒著落的甚麼的，可有時候吧，你就說你要是去問老師，或者去問同學吧，好象也是挺、挺不容易的。哎，你說要是要是嗯有些問題甚麼的去找老師或者找同學甚麼問問，你說他們能那個，能有意見嗎？就是說還是…

Hai. Jiùshuō kǎoshì, zhěnggè yī ge méijìn. Wǒ juéde shì tèbié (unclear). Érqiě ba, jiù shuō nǐ shuō yào fùxí ba, zhěnggèr méi biānr méi zhāolùo de shénmede. Kě yǒu shíhòu ba, nǐ jiù shuō nǐ yàoshi qù wèn lǎoshī, huòzhě qù wèn tóngxué ba, hǎoxiàng yě shì tǐng, tǐng bù róngyì de. Ai, nǐ shuō yàoshi yàoshi e yǒuxiē wèntí shénmede qù zhǎo lǎoshī huòzhě zhǎo tóngxué shénme wènwen, nǐ shuō tāmen néng nàge, néng yǒu yìjiàn ma? Jiùshi shuō háishì…

Well, talk about exam, totally boring. I feel very (unclear). In addition, say you say review, totally no limit no ideas, something like that. But sometimes, you say you go ask teacher or go ask students, not so easy. Hey, you say if if have some questions, etc., go find teachers or find students ask ask, you say they will will have resentment? Say or...

Speaking of the exam, I feel really bored and extremely (unclear). Look, I don't even have a clue as to how to review. Sometimes, you know, it isn't so easy to ask for help from the teacher or the students. Hey, do you think they'd like it if I went and asked them some questions? Or is it...

A: 你去問，你要問問題呢，你不能離著那個考試特近的。就是說你快考試你去問，你說咳，考甚麼范圍啊？另外呢，人家也不一定就是說答，你知道嘛，你越接近的范圍呢，他越不敢多說話。他怕好，一會兒，他不敢面部有任何表情。到時候你說哎唷，我猜著了，那天我跟他說的時候吧，他這就他臉上就不對勁兒。那時候我就知道難保有這道題。

Nǐ qù wèn, nǐ yào wèn wèntí ne, nǐ bù néng wèn lí zhe nèige kǎoshì tè jìn de. Jiùshi shuō nǐ kuài kǎoshì nǐ qù wèn, nǐ shuō hai, kǎo shénme fànwéi a. Lìngwài ne, rénjia yě bù yīdìng jiùshi shuō dá, nǐ zhīdao ma, nǐ yuè jiējìn de fànwéi ne, tā yuè bù gǎn duō shuōhuà. Tā pà hǎo, yīhuǐr, tā bù gǎn miànbu yǒu rènhé biǎoqíng. Dào shíhou nǐ shuō eiyou, wǒ cāi zhao le. Nèitiān wǒ gēn tā shuō de shíhou ba, tā zhèjiù tā liǎnshang jiù bù duìjìnr. Nèi shíhou wǒ jiù zhīdao zhǔnbǎo yǒu zhèi dào tí.

You go ask, you want ask questions, you cannot ask from that exam very close. That is to say you will examine soon you go ask, you say hey examine what limit? Besides, others may not say answer, you know. You more close to the exam area, he less dares more talk. He afraid OK, a little while, he not dare face has any expression. Then you say yes I guess it. That day I talk to him, he this then his face looked unusual. Then I knew sure there be this item.

If you really must ask, you'd better not ask those exam-related questions. Even if they decide to answer your questions, you know, they'll feel more intimidated to answer exam-related ones. They don't even dare to show any unusual facial expressions for fear that you would say 'yes, I got it'. The other day when I was talking to this person, his facial expression was very strange and I knew immediately that this item would be on the exam.

B: 那通常你看老師總給復習范圍甚麼的。我上星期吧，剛好沒來，然后我又，自個兒復習吧，當然就是說也沒事兒，可是就特別希望就是說找老師或者同學甚麼的就是說給點撥點撥那樣的，看可以不可以甚麼那種？不過可是就象你剛剛說的，就你吧，比方說，每次要考試之前恨不得一大幫人來老纏著你甚麼的，<u>你看我現在就是說又想問吧，可是又怕同學說</u>。特別的別扭那種的。

Nà tōngcháng nǐ kàn lǎoshī zǒng gěi fùxí fànwéi shémede. Wǒ shàng xīngqī ba, gānghǎo méi lái. Ránhòu wǒ yòu, zìgěr fùxí ba, dāngrán jiùshi shuō yě méi shìr. Kěshi jiù tèbié xīwàng jiùshi shuō zhǎo lǎoshī huòzhě tóngxué shénmede jiùshi shuō gěi diǎnbo diǎnbo nèiyàngde. Kàn kěyǐ bù kěyǐ shénme nèizhǒng? Bùguò kěshì jiù xiàng nǐ gānggāng shuō de, jiù nǐ ba, bǐfang shuō měicì yào kǎoshì zhīqián hènbùde yīdabāng rén lái lǎo chán zhe nǐ shénmede. <u>Nǐ kàn wǒ xiànzai jiùshi shuō yòu xiǎng wèn ba, kěshi yòu pà tóngxué shuō</u>. Tèbié de biàniu nèizhǒng de.

He usually you see teacher always gives review limit, etc. I last week, just didn't come. Then I again, myself review, of course say no problem. But especially hope say find teacher or students etc. say direct direct. See OK or not OK, something like that. But as you just now said, you, for example, every time exam before, always a big crowd come always bother you, something like that. <u>You see I now say want ask but afraid students talk.</u> Very uncomfortable etc.

Usually, you know, the teacher will give some review topics and things like that. Unfortunately, I didn't come to class last week. Of course, you know, I can study by myself, but I really hope, you know, to receive some help, you know, from the teacher or fellow students. What do you think? As you said just now, there's always a crowd bothering you before every exam, <u>so now I feel like, you know, asking, but I'm afraid that people will resent me.</u> I feel very uncomfortable, you know.

A: 嗯，那反正得看。假如是好朋友，我也就不在乎。要不是那好朋友，特別是用人臉朝前，不用人臉朝后的主兒，我就不愛管，你知道嗎。然后呢，你呢幫助人的時候，你還得特別小心。你一不小心，告錯了，你知道嗎，比如說，這東西呀你也拿不准是甚麼東西，結果呢，你弄錯了，然后呢，到時候，人家還說你看，就你告兒我的吧。當然他不會怪你哈。但是，他說了這麼兩句話讓你心裡怪別扭的。嗯，所以呢，一般來講呢，我不是朋友的話，我就應付。但是我應付呢,我還得我還不能顯出來。我得 [裝得特象似的。所以也怪難的。

Nn, nà fǎnzheng děi kàn. Jiǎrú shì hǎo péngyou, wǒ yějiu bù zàihu. Yào bùshì nèi hǎo péngyou, tèbié shì yòngrén liǎn cháo qián, bù yòngrén liǎn cháo hòu de zhǔr, wǒ jiù bù ài guǎn, nǐ zhīdao ma. Ránhòu ne, nǐ nà bāngzhù rén de shíhou, nǐ háiděi tèbié xiǎoxin. Nǐ yī bù xiǎoxin, gào cuò le, nǐ zhīdao ma, bǐrú shuō, zhè dōngxi ya nǐ yě ná bù zhǔn shì shénme dōngxi, jiéguǒ ne, nǐ nòng cuò le, ránhòu ne, dào shíhou rénjia hái shuō nǐ kàn, jiù nǐ gàor wǒ de ba. Dāngrán tā bù huì guài nǐ ha. Dànshi tā shuō le zhème liǎng jù huà ràng nǐ xīnli guài bièniu de. Nn, suǒyǐ ne, yībān lái jiǎng ne, wǒ bù shì péngyou de huà, wǒ jiù yìngfu. Dànshi wǒ yìngfu ne, wǒ háiděi wǒ hái bù néng xiǎn chūlai. Wǒ děi   [zhuāng de tè xiàng shìde. Suǒyǐ yě guài nán de.

That will see. If be good friends, I don't mind. If not be good friends, especially use people face front, not use people face behind person, I don't like to help, you know. In addition, you help people when, you must be very careful. You once not careful, give wrong, you know, for example, this thing you not sure what thing, then you got wrong, then people will say you look, it's you told me so. Of course he will not blame you, but he said these two sentences make you heart rather uncomfortable. So, generally speaking, if not friends I do the minimum. But I do the minimum, I must I cannot appear so. I must
 [pretend very real. So also rather difficult.

That depends. I don't mind if they are good friends. Otherwise, I hate to help, especially those who come to you only when they need you, you know. Also you must be very careful when you give help. If you give the wrong information by accident, you know, for example, tell people something you are not sure of, people will say, look, you told me such-and-such. Of course they are not blaming you but what they say will make you uncomfortable. Therefore, I usually take it easy with those who are not my friends. But I must appear to be serious. I must [pretend it is real. That is a very hard job.

B: [是嘛。因為我現在特著急。看再有倆星期了,我整個還一個沒頭緒,都不知道該復習甚麼。你看你能不能幫我那個。A你要是知道的話,你就跟我說說老師那天說甚麼來著。就給我大概其地就讓我心裡起碼有點兒數兒。點撥點撥甚麼的。

[Shì ma. Yīnwèi wǒ xiànzai tè zhāojí. Kàn zài yǒu liǎ xīngqī le, wǒ zhěngge hái yīge méi tóuxù, dōu bù zhīdào gāi fùxí shénme. <u>Nǐ kàn nǐ néng bù néng bāng wǒ nèige, nǐ yàoshi zhīdao de huà</u>, nǐ jiù gēn wǒ shuōshuo lǎoshī nèi tiān shuō shénme láizhe. Jiù gěi wǒ dàgàiqí de jiù ràng wǒ xīnli qǐmǎ yǒu diǎnr shùr. diǎnbo diǎnbo shénmede.

[Really. Because I now very worried. Look has only two weeks away, I totally no idea, don't know review what. <u>You see you can not can help me if you know</u>, you just to me talk talk teacher that day said what. Just let me in general let me heart at least have some idea, direct etc.

[Really. I am extremely anxious now that the exam is only two weeks away. I don't know where to start and what to review. <u>Do you think you can help me if you know?</u> Just tell me what the teacher said the other day and give me a rough idea, like some direction.

A: 那沒問題啊。我給你複印一份老師給的那東西不就得了嗎，是吧。

Nà méi wèntí a. Wǒ géi nǐ fùyìn yī fèn lǎoshī gěi de nèi dōngxi bù jiù déle ma, shì ba.

That no problem. I for you photocopy teacher give review sheet, all settled, right.

That's no problem. I'll make a photocopy of the review sheet for you and that will take care of everything, right?

B: 那太棒了。

Nà tài bàng le.

That too wonderful.

That's wonderful.

A: 這也佔不了多少時間。嗯，另外呢，也沒准兒呢，咱倆兒要不咱倆一塊兒複習。我還可以向你學點甚麼東西呢。你不就那天沒去嗎。然后…

Zhè yě zhàn bù liǎo duōshǎo shíjiān. Nn, lìngwài ne, yě méizhǔnr ne, zánliǎngr yàobu zánliǎng yīkuàir fùxí. Wǒ hái kěyǐ xiàng nǐ xué diǎnr shénme dōngxi ne. Nǐ bù jiù nèi tiān méi qù ma. Ránhòu…

This won't take much time. Besides, perhaps, we two or we two together review. I also can from you learn something. You only that day didn't come. Then…

This won't take too much time. Perhaps the two of us can study together. I can learn something from you, too. All you missed was one day. Then…

B: 那太棒了。

Nà tài bàng le.

That too wonderful

That's wonderful.

A: 但是呢，咱把范圍縮小。咱別招一大幫子。現在呢，一成立互助組人就要多，人一多了呢，[B:就亂了] 就亂了。東一嘴西一嘴，另外呢，還不夠折騰的呢。[B: 行。] 瞧咱們倆訂個功夫，訂個時間。

Dànshi ne, zán bǎ fànwéi suōxiǎo. Zán bié zhāo yī dà bāngzi. Xiànzai ne, yī chénglì hùzhùzǔ rén jiù yào duō. Rén yī duō le ne, [B: jiù luàn le] jiù luàn le. Dōng yī zuǐ xī yī zuǐ. Lìngwài ne, hái bùgòu zhēteng de ne. [B: Xíng] Qiáo zánmengliǎ dìng ge gōngfu, dìng ge shíjiān.

But, we limit scale. We don't find a big crowd. Nowadays once set up study groups, people will be many. Once a lot of people, [B: get messy] get messy. East a mouth west a mouth. Besides, not worth troubling [B: OK]. Look, let's set a time, set a time.

But we must not let everybody know it. Don't attract a big crowd. Nowadays, everybody wants to join a study group. Whenever there are too many people, [B: there will be a mess] there will surely be a mess. A word here and a word there and it's really a mess. Look, let's set a time.

B: 對，你看你甚麼時候有時間？反正我這一個星期，下一個星期還差不多還都挺鬆的。晚上也成。

Duì, nǐ kàn nǐ shénme shíhou yǒu shíjiān? Fǎnzheng wǒ zhèi yī ge xīngqī, xià yī ge xīngqī hái chàbuduō hái dōu tǐng sōng de. Wǎnshang yě chéng.

Right. You see you when have time? Anyway I this week, next week almost all rather leisure. Evening also OK.

OK. When do you have time? I'm not very busy either this week or next week. Evening is also good for me.

A: 嗯，我想想啊。要不咱們這樣，咱們呀，白天啊，自個兒學習。等到晚上的時候咱們碰碰頭。然后呢，咱們一塊兒說說。因為呢，白天你學了半天呢，到晚上你再學新的東西也進不去了。咱晚上呢，復習一下呢，反而好。[B: 行。] 這樣可以吧。

En, wǒ xiǎngxiang a. Yàobu zánmen zhèyang, zánmen ya, báitiān a, zìger xuéxí. Děngdao wǎnshang de shíhou zánmen pèngpeng tóu. Ránhòu ne, zánmen yīkuàr shuōshuo. Yīnwèi ne, báitiān nǐ xué le bàntiān ne, dào wǎnshang nǐ zài xué xīn de dōngxi yě jìn bù qù le. Zán wǎnshang ne, fùxí yīxia ne, fǎn'ér hǎo. [B: Xíng]. Zhèyàng kěyǐ ba.

En, I think think. Let's this way. We, daytime, self study. Wait till evening we meet. Then we together talk talk. Because daytime you study half day, in evening you again learn new things will not learn. *We evening, review a bit, is better.* [B: OK]. *This OK?*

Well, let me see. Let's do it this way. Let's study on our own during the day, and we'll meet in the evening. After studying so much in the daytime, it is not easy to learn new things in the evening anymore. So would be much better to review then. [B: OK]. Is this all right with you?

B: 行，那怎麼著？咱們就這麼著。

Xíng, nà zěnmezhao? Zánmen jiù zhème zhāo.

OK, then how is it? We like this.

OK then. Let's do it that way.

A: 咱們就這麼樣吧。然后呢，咱們就碰頭。縮小范圍啊。別那個別告別人啊。咱倆兒蔫不出溜的就行了。

Zánmen jiù zhème yàng ba. Ránhòu ne, zánmen jiù pèngtóu. Suōxiǎo fànwéi a. Bié nèige bié gào biéren a. Zánliǎngr niānrbuchūliu de jiù xíng le.

We like this. Then we meet. Limit it. Don't, er, don't tell other people. We two quietly do it.

OK, let's do it that way. We'll meet then. Limit the number of people. Don't tell other people. Keep it between the two of us.

ROLEPLAY #2: SAVING SEATS

A: 今兒晚你去聽講座嗎？

Jīnrwǎn nǐ qù tīng jiǎngzuo ma?

This evening you go listen the seminar?

Are you going to the seminar this evening?

B: 咳，我還不知道呢。你說真是的，我想想有時候就特生氣。每次吧，你說聽講座吧，我也不知怎麼那麼倒霉哈，每次老有人找我給他佔位子。你說要，要說一次兩次的行，那天天天天去給人家佔位子，心裡想想特虧。咳，真是的，我也不知道該怎麼辦。

Hai, wǒ hái bù zhīdào ne. Nǐ shuō zhēnshide, wǒ xiǎngxiang yǒu shíhou jiù tè shēngqì. Měicì ba, nǐ shuō tīng jiǎngzuò ba, wǒ yě bù zhī zěnme nàme dǎoméi ha, měicì lǎo yǒurén zhǎo wǒ gěi tā zhàn wèizi. Nǐ shuō yào, yàoshuō yīcì liǎngcì de xíng. Nà tiāntiān tiāntiān qù gěi rénjia zhàn wèizi, xīnli xiǎngxiang tè kuī. Hai, zhēnshìde. Wǒ yě bù zhīdào gāi zěnme bàn.

Ah, I still don't know. You say really, I think think sometimes very upset. Every time, you say listen to seminar, I don't know why so unlucky, every time always people find me for him/her keep seats. You say if, if say once twice OK. But everyday everyday go for others keep seats, heart think think very unfair. Ah, really, I don't know should how to do.

Well, I don't know yet. You know, I get upset whenever I think about it. I have no idea why I am so unlucky, some people always ask me to save seats for them at every seminar. It's not a big deal if it's only once or twice but it happens every time, every time. I feel it's unfair. Well, I don't know what to do now.

A: 嗯…對。其實就是。要給人佔位子（不清楚）也是，你想你得早去，對吧？然后吶，別人可以幹自己的事兒。松松快快的，然后呢，到那以後呢還有個好位子。當然了，如果能輪流就好了。不過呢，有的人也挺討厭，他老讓人佔位子。等到你真有事兒了要求人佔位子的時候吧，人就不樂意了。你知道嗎？這麼說著吧，今兒晚上我就有點兒事兒，<u>我就想請你幫著佔個位子</u>。你看行不行？

En... Duì. Qíshí jiùshi. Yào gěi rén zhàn wèizi (unclear), yěshì. Nǐ xiǎng nǐ děi zǎo qù, duì ba? Ránhòu na, biéren kěyǐ gàn zìjǐ de shìr, sōngsongkuàikuai de. Ránhòu ne, dào nà yǐhòu ne hái yǒu ge hǎo wèizi. Dāngrán le, rúguǒ néng lúnliú jiù hǎo le. Bùguò ne, yǒude rén yě tǐng tǎoyàn, tā lǎo ràng rén zhàn wèizi. Děngdào nǐ zhēn yǒu shìr le yāoqiú rén zhàn wèizi de shíhou ba, rén jiù bù lèyi le, nǐ zhīdao ma? Zhème shuō zhe ba, jīnr wǎnshang wǒ jiù yǒu diǎnr shìr. <u>Wǒ jiù xiǎng qǐng nǐ bāng zhe zhàn ge wèizi.</u> Nǐ kàn xíngbùxíng?

Well... Yes. Actually yes. For others keep seats (unclear), yes. You think you must early go, right? Then, others can do their own things, leisurely. Then, get there still have a good seat. Of course, if can take turns would be better. But some people very annoying, he always ask others keep seats. Wait till you really have matter, ask people keep a seat time, people not willing, you know. This talking, tonight I have a little thing, <u>I think ask you help keep a seat</u>, you see OK or not?

Yeah, if you're to save seats for others, you need to go early, right? Meanwhile, they can take care of their own business, take it easy, and still have a good seat. Of course, it would be better if people could take turns. On the other hand, some people are terrible: they always ask you to save seats for them, but when you are in an emergency and ask them to save a seat for you, they are reluctant, right? Speaking of which, I have got something to do for tonight and <u>I would like to ask you to help save a seat for me</u>. Would that be all right?

B: 要你還差不多。我覺行。沒事兒。因爲今天晚上我去，不過，今兒我給你佔了，下次你得給我佔噢。
   [因爲我老是…

Yào nǐ hái chàbuduō. Wǒ jué xíng. Méi shìr. Yīnwèi jīntiān wǎnshang wǒ qù. Bùguò, jīnr wǒ gěi nǐ zhàn le, xiàcì nǐ děi gěi wǒ zhàn ao.
   [*Yīnwèi wǒ lǎoshi...*

You are OK. I think OK. Have no matter. Because tonight I go. But today I for you keep, next time you must for me keep.
   [Because I always...

You're OK. I'm not busy and I'm going tonight. I'll do that for you today and next time you must save a seat for me,
[because I always...

A: 我知道。我這人也挺賴的，說句實話，我就是屬于那種老讓人佔位子的主兒。但是呢，我那個今兒你告兒我了，我也意識到自己的 [缺點錯誤。

Wǒ zhīdào. Wǒ zhè rén yě tǐng lài de, shuō jù shíhuà, wǒ jiùshi shǔyú nèizhǒng lǎo ràng rén zhàn wèizi de zhǔr. Dànshi ne, wǒ nèige jīnr nǐ gàor wǒ le, wǒ yě yìshi dào zìjǐ de [*quēdiǎn cuòwu.*

I know. I this person very "bum", say truth, I belong to those always ask others keep seats persons. But, I today you told me, I also realized my own [problems and shortcomings.

I know. People always think that I am a "bum". Well, to tell you the truth, I am one of those who always asks others to save seats. Today, though, you've told me, and I've realized my [problems.

B: 不不是說你。我就是說呀我老覺得老天天給人佔位子吧，咳，其實反正總得去哈。就是說順便佔了就佔了。就是說吧，老心裡不是特舒服。希望到時候，咳，別人起碼能跟你說一聲兒甚麼的，就是說嗨，人家領情了那種的還差不多。

Bù bùshi shuō nǐ. Wǒ jiùshi shuō ya wǒ lǎo juéde lǎo tiāntiān gěi rén zhàn wèizi ba, hai, qíshí fǎnzheng zǒngděi qù ha. Jiùshi shuō suíbiàn zhàn le jiù zhàn le. Jiùshi shuō ba, lǎo xīnli bù shì tè shūfu. Xīwàng dào shíhou, hai, biéren qǐmǎ néng gēn nǐ shuō yī shēngr shénmede, jiùshi shuō hài, rénjia lǐngqíng le nèizhǒngde hái chàbuduō.

Not say you. I say I always feel always everyday for others keep seats, well, actually anyway will go. That is to say in passing keep a seat, seat kept. That is to say, always heart not very comfortable. Hope people then, hay, others at *least can to you say something, etc. that is to say, hay, others appreciate it, etc. more like it.*

I didn't mean you. I just feel that I have to always do that for others. Well, as a matter of fact, it's not a big deal, I am going anyway and saving a seat is just something in passing. But I don't always feel comfortable about it. I kind of wish that people could say something nice to you like they appreciate it and things like that.

A: 其實我也是，你說我要是讓別人佔位子呢，我自己跟那兒省這點兒時間我也省不了多少。十分二十分撐死了。還落一不是，你瞧瞧。下次呢，我也得真的注意，以前我也從來沒就是說沒特別想別人。不太跟人家。老跟人犯賴。我這人比較賴。老跟人家犯賴。"給佔個位子呀，"嘻皮笑臉的。人也沒辦法說哈。下次我給你佔。

Qíshí wǒ yě shì. Nǐshuō wǒ yàoshi ràng biéren zhàn wèizi ne, wǒ zìjǐ gēn nàr shěng zhe diǎnr shíjiān wǒ yě shěng bù liǎo duōshǎo. Shífēn èrshífēn chēng sǐ le. Hái lào yī bùshì, nǐ qiáoqiao. Xiàcì ne, wǒ yě děi zhēnde zhùyi. Yǐqián wǒ yě cónglái méi jiùshi shuō méi tèbié xiǎng biéren. Bù tài gēn rénjia, lǎo gēn rén fàn lài. Wǒ zhè rén bǐjiao lài. Lǎo gēn rénjia fàn lài. "Gěi zhàn ge wèizi ya", xīpí-xiàoliǎn de. Rén yě méi bànfǎ shuō ha. Xiàci wǒ gěi nǐ zhàn.

Actually I am. You say I if ask others keep a seat, I myself there save this bit time I save not much. Ten minutes twenty minutes at most. Yet get blamed, you see. Next time, I must really pay attention. Before I never that is to say never particularly think about others. Not with people, always with others be "bum". I this person rather bum. "Keep a seat", smiling skin smiling face. Others no way say anything. Next time I for you keep.

Actually it's my fault. I ask people to save a seat for me so that I can save some time for myself. As a matter of fact I can't save that much time, 10 minutes twenty minutes at most, and I become the culprit as a result. Next time, I'll be careful. In the past, I was not very considerate of other people, always being a bum with people and, you know me, I'm a bum, kind of smiling and joking around when I say "Please save a seat for me?" People simply cannot refuse. Next time, I'll save a seat for you.

B: 沒問題。

    Méi wèntí.

    No problem.

    No problem.

A: 我肯定給你佔。

    Wǒ kěndìng gěi nǐ zhàn.

    I sure for you keep.

    I promise to save a seat for you next time.

B: 咱們哥們兒沒的說。

    Zánmen gēmenr méi de shuō.

    We brother no thing to say

    No problem, buddy.

DCT SITUATION 14: THE LECTURER

胡云教授給研究生趙軍打電話。希望趙軍能同意提前一周作有關惠特曼的課堂報告，因爲那會對課時安排更合適。如果您是胡云教授，您會怎樣對趙軍講，使他同意您的要求？

Hú Yún jiàoshòu gěi yánjiūshēng Zhào Jūn dǎ diànhuà. Xīwàng Zhào Jūn néng tóngyì tíqián yīzhōu zuò yǒuguān Whitman de kètáng bàogào, yīnwèi nà huì duì kèshí ānpái gèng héshì. Rúguǒ nín shì Hú Yún jiàoshòu, nín huì zěnyàng duì Zhào Jūn jiǎng, shǐ tā tóngyì nín de yāoqiú?

Hu Yun Professor call graduate student Zhao Jun. Hope Zhao Jun can agree a week earlier do about Whitman class presentation, because that will fit better schedule. If you were Hu Yun Professor, you will how say to Zhao Jun, make him agree to your request?

Professor Hu Yun calls a graduate student, Zhao Jun, to ask him to do his class presentation on Whitman a week early since it would fit the schedule better. If you were Professor Hu Yun, what would you say to get Zhao Jun to agree to your request?

Response:

趙軍嗎？我是胡云。我想和你商量一件事。學校最近要求我們擠出一周時間來給學生作社會調查。因此我的教學安排不得不有所變動。這樣就牽涉到你的惠特曼課堂報告。你是否也能抓緊時間，提前一周完成這個報告？這樣才能和變動的時間表一致。如果時間太緊的話，你那份讀書報告，可以推遲兩周再交。怎麽樣？你看行嗎？

Zhào Jūn ma? Wǒ shì Hú Yún. Wǒ xiǎng hé nǐ shāngliang yī jiàn shì. Xuéxiào zuìjìn yāoqiú wǒmen jǐ chū yīzhōu shíjiān lái gěi xuéshēng zuò shèhuì diàochá. Yīncǐ wǒde jiàoxué ānpái bùdébù yǒusuǒ biàndòng. Zhèyàng jiù qiānshè dao nǐ zuò de Whitman kètáng bàogào. Nǐ shìfǒu yě néng zhuā jǐn shíjiān, tíqián yīzhōu wánchéng zhège bàogào? Zhèyang cáinéng hé biàndong de shíjiān biǎo yīzhì. Rúguǒ shíjiān tài jǐn de huà, nǐ nàfen dúshū bàogào, kěyǐ tuīchí liǎngzhōu zài jiāo. Zěnmeyàng? Nǐ kàn xíng ma?

Is it Zhao Jun? I am Hu Yun. I would with you talk about something. School recently require us give one week to students to do social investigation. So my teaching *schedule has to somewhat change. This relates to your class report on Whitman. You can or not hurry up, finish the report in advance. This way can fit the changed schedule. If time too short, your reading report can two weeks later turn in. How about it? You think OK?*

Is this Zhao Jun? This is Hu Yun. I'd like to talk with you about something. The school has recently required us to give the students one week for studies on society. So my teaching schedule has to be changed, which in turn, will affect your oral report on Whitman in class. Could you hurry up a bit and do the report one week earlier? This way, it will fit the changed schedule. If time is too short, you may turn in your book report two weeks late. How about that? Do you think it's OK with you?

Xing Chen, Lei Ye, and Yanyin Zhang

REFUSING IN CHINESE

THE CONCEPT OF REFUSAL IN CHINESE

THE SPEECH ACT OF REFUSING is a responding act in which the speaker denies to engage in an action proposed by the interlocutor. For example, a professor suggests to a student a topic for her presentation, but she does not think the topic is appropriate for her. A possible exchange might be:

Professor: 下次上課你重點談談這個題目吧。
Xiàci shàngkè nǐ zhòngdiǎn tántan zhège tímù ba.
How about giving a presentation focusing on this topic for the next class?

Student: 對這個題目我沒有充分把握。能否換一個?
Duì zhège tímù wǒ méiyǒu chōngfèn bǎwo. Néngfǒu huàn yī ge?
I don't feel that I am very familiar with this topic. Can I change to another topic?

Chinese words for 'refusal' are 拒絕 *jùjué* or 回絕 *huíjué*. Literally, 拒絕 *jùjué* means 'to refuse; not to accept'. However, 拒絕 *jùjué* contains the slightly negative association of refusing directly though not necessarily rudely. 回絕 *huíjué* is more neutral and specific to 'refuse in reply'. In Chinese, there are a number of idioms expressing refusing politely (謝絕 *xièjué* or 婉言謝絕 *wǎnyán xièjué*) and refusing rudely or flatly (一口回絕 *yīkǒu huíjué* or 斷然拒絕 *duànrán jùjué*). Literally, 謝絕 *xièjué* means 'to refuse an offer with gratitude', and 婉言謝絕 *wǎnyán xièjué* means 'to refuse with gentle/mild

Chen, X., Ye, L., & Zhang, Y. (1995). Refusing in Chinese. In G. Kasper (Ed.), *Pragmatics of Chinese as native and target language* (Technical Report #5, pp. 119–163). Honolulu, Hawai'i: University of Hawai'i, Second Language Teaching & Curriculum Center.

words'; whereas 一口回絕 *yīkǒu huíjué* means 'to refuse flatly' and 斷然拒絕 *duànrán jùjué* means 'to refuse absolutely without hesitation'. These expressions reflect a preferred pattern of Chinese cultural conventions.

Chinese and American acts of refusing are regulated by different face-concerns. While American interaction is based on positive or negative face deriving from individuals' "face wants" (Brown and Levison, 1987), Chinese refusal is rooted in maintaining 面子 *miànzi* and 臉 *liǎn*, which are oriented toward a person's public image (Mao, 1994), realized through reciprocal avoidance of face-to-face confrontation. In refusing situations, Chinese perceive it as imperative to 留面子 *liú miànzi* 'preserve face' for the refusee, and to 留后路 *liú hòulù* 'leave oneself a way out' for the refuser. Honor is felt in such situations, with the assumption being that the refuser would not be the recipient of the initiating act (a request, suggestion, invitation, or offer) if she were not honored by the refusee. In this kind of situation, the refuser should show her recognition of the honor being given. Consequently, she should preserve the 面子 *miànzi* of the refusee by maintaining a position which makes her refusal effective but not rude. By doing so, she can also preserve her own face. In the above example, the student refuses the professor's suggestion by explaining why she does not want to give the presentation. In addition, she offers a way for her response to be perceived other than a total rejection. Thus she acknowledges the honor given her by the professor and also shows willingness to give a presentation of another topic which she is familiar with.

A refusal is perceived as having a potential negative impact on future interaction. However, since 留面子 *liú miànzi*, a fundamental principle for social interaction, is based on reciprocity, a speaker's own 面子 *miànzi* cannot be preserved unless the other person's 面子 *miànzi* is maintained as well. Because of these concerns, the refuser would be reluctant to refuse directly or immediately because she does not want to hurt the refusee's 面子 *miànzi* in return of having been given 面子 *miànzi* by the refusee. Nor does she want to be at the receiving end of a blunt refusal when her turn comes to request, suggest, offer, etc.

Refusals like the one illustrated above express the speaker's intention not to comply with the interlocutor's proposed action plan. The speaker says "no" (albeit politely) and means "no". This type of negative response will be referred to as "substantive refusal". However, in Chinese interaction, speakers may say "no" to initiations such as offers and invitations when in fact they are willing to accept. This type of denial will be called "ritual refusal". Each refusal type will be examined in turn.

PART 1: SUBSTANTIVE REFUSAL

IN ORDER TO EXAMINE SUBSTANTIVE REFUSAL in Chinese, a study was carried out, probing into the strategies Chinese employ to carry out refusals and the distribution of these strategies in response to different situations and in different interlocutor relationships.

METHOD

The study involved fifty male and fifty female native speakers of Mandarin Chinese who had resided in the U.S. for an average of 2.4 years at the time of the study[1]. All but four subjects had received higher education. Their mean age was 32.3 years.

Data were collected by means of a 16-item Production Questionnaire. Following Beebe, Takahashi, and Uliss-Weltz (1990), items were designed to elicit refusals in response to four types of initiating acts: requests, suggestions, invitations, and offers. Each item specified the speaker's (S) social status relative to the interlocutor (H) (S higher than H, S lower than H, S equal to H) and the social distance between the interlocutor and speaker (very close, close, distant, very distant). The questionnaire design is outlined in Table 1.

---

[1] A parallel study involving thirty subjects in Mainland China was carried out by Chen (1992). Comparison of the responses given by the two groups of Chinese subjects shows high similarities in their refusal patterns. The refusal behavior of the Chinese subjects living in the U.S. thus did not yet evince acculturation to American pragmatic norms. Because of the larger sample size, it was decided to base the present study on the Chinese native speakers living in the U.S.

Table 1: Design of refusal questionnaire

Item	Refuser status relative to interlocutor	Social distance	Initiating act
1	Equal	Close	Request
2	Higher	Distant	Request
3	Higher	Very close	Request
4	Lower	Close	Suggestion
5	Higher	Very distant	Suggestion
6	Lower	Distant	Suggestion
7	Lower	Distant	Suggestion
8	Equal	Close	Request
9	Lower	Distant	Request
10	Equal	Close	Request
11	Equal	Very distant	Request
12	Lower	Very close	Invitation
13	Higher	Distant	Invitation
14	Equal	Very close	Request
15	Lower	Distant	Offer
16	Higher	Distant	Offer

The content of the questionnaire items was as follows:

Borrowing Money   A person wants to borrow $500 from his/her neighbor.
Study Abroad   A teacher requests leave from the department chair to study abroad.
Recorder   A sister wants to borrow a tape recorder from her elder brother.

Color	An older person suggests that her younger neighbor buy some clothes with a purple color.
Tie	A salesman recommends an expensive tie to a customer.
Changes	An editor suggests a writer make some changes for his/her paper.
Topic	A professor suggests that a student present a topic that is not suitable for him/her.
Study Help	A student requests his/her classmate to help him/her with his/her missed lesson.
Extra Hours	A director wants his/her office worker to work extra hours.
Seat	A person wants his/her friend to save a seat for him/her.
Ticket	An old man wants a young man to buy a ticket for him.
Party	A person invites her nephew/niece to a dinner party.
Dinner	An older office worker invites his supervisor to dinner.
Job Transfer	A staff member requests his best friend's approval of a job transfer for another staff member.
Promotion	A department chair offers a promotion to a lecturer.
Handicraft	An elderly janitor offers to pay for a broken handicraft.

Thus, a questionnaire item looked like this:

Situation 1: *Borrowing Money*:

> Because of some urgent need, you have just withdrawn ¥500 from the bank. Your neighbor Young Zhang approaches you.

Zhang: Xxx, I want to borrow ¥500 from you to buy a gold necklace for my girlfriend.

You: _____

Subjects were asked to fill in what they thought was appropriate in each context. In order not to bias their responses, subjects were not specifically asked to produce refusals.

ANALYSIS

For the data analysis, the coding categories proposed by Beebe et al. (1990) were adapted to Chinese. We followed these authors in distinguishing between refusal strategies, i.e., semantic formulæ which in the given contexts carry the force of a refusal, and adjuncts to refusals, which modify the refusal but do not in themselves carry refusing force such as a) *Agreement:* 行，我去 *xíng, wǒ qù.* 'Okay, I'll go'; b) *Positive opinion:* 這條的確不錯 *zhèi tiáo díquè bùcuò* 'This one is really good'; c) *Empathy:* 我可以理解你的心情 *wǒ kěyǐ lǐjiě nǐ de xīnqíng* 'I can understand how you feel'; and d) *Gratitude/appreciation:* 謝謝你的建議 *xièxie nǐ de jiànyì* 'Thanks for your suggestion'.

Our present analysis focuses on refusal strategies. The following categories were adopted to classify Chinese refusal strategies.

Classification of refusal strategies

Direct Refusal: Direct denial of compliance without reservation

> <u>No</u>: Direct use of a denying lexical item
>
> 不行。
> *Bù xíng.*[2]
> No.   (*Recorder*)
>
> <u>Negative Willingness/Ability</u>: Utterances showing unwillingness or inability
>
> 我不想買。
> *Wǒ bù xiǎng mǎi.*
> I don't want to buy it.   (*Color*)

---

[2] Examples are given in the order of 1) Chinese characters; 2) pinyin; and 3) functionally equivalent translation.

Insistence: Insistence on the refuser's original plan of action

>我還是想出國。
>
>Wǒ háishì xiǎng chūguó.
>
>I still want to go abroad. (*Promotion*)

Regret: Utterances expressing regret

>對不起。
>
>Duìbuqǐ.
>
>I am sorry. (*Borrowing Money*)

Reason: Giving reasons for non-compliance

Excuse: Use of excuses

>我不打算去聽這個講座。
>
>Wǒ bù dǎsuan qù tīng zhège jiǎngzuò.
>
>I am not going to attend the lecture. (*Seat*)

Third Party: Putting blame on a third party

>我丈夫不喜歡這種顏色。
>
>Wǒ zhàngfu bù xǐhuan zhèzhǒng yánse.
>
>My husband doesn't like the color. (*Color*)

Alternative: Suggesting an alternative course of action

I can do X instead of Y

>我想換個題目。
>
>Wǒ xiǎng huàn ge tímu.
>
>I would like to change the topic. (*Topic*)

You can do X instead of Y

>你可以問問別人。
>
>Nǐ kěyǐ wènwen biéren.
>
>You could ask someone else. (*Seat*)

Let us/him/her/them do X instead of Y

> 讓我太太代表我吧。
> *Ràng wǒ tàitai dàibiǎo wǒ ba.*
> Let my wife be my representative. (*Party*)

Querying alternative option

> 我能不能試定一個題目？
> *Wǒ néngbùnéng shìdìng yī ge tímu?*
> Could I try to set a topic? (*Topic*)

Principle: Stating principle that would conflict with compliance

> 我從來不愛穿紫色的衣服。
> *Wǒ cónglái bù ài chuān zǐse de yīfu.*
> I have never liked purple clothes. (*Color*)

Folk Wisdom: Use of folk wisdom, usually in the form of clichés

> 舊的不去，新的不來。
> *Jiùde bù qù, xīnde bù lái.*
> If the old is not gone, the new will not come. (*Handicraft*)

Dissuade Interlocutor: Attempt to persuade the refusee to give up her action plan

> Threat or statement of negative consequences
>
> 我要是替您買了票，說不定明天我的對象就吹了。
> *Wǒ yàoshi tì nín mǎi le piào, shuōbudìng míngtiān wǒde duìxiàng jiù chuī le.*
> If I bought a ticket for you, my partner would probably break up with me tomorrow. (*Ticket*)

Guilt Trip: Pointing out things the refusee failed to do in the past

上次我借你的录音帶，你爲甚麼不借我？
Shàngci wǒ jiè nǐ de lùyīndài, nǐ wèishénme bù jiè wǒ?
Last time I tried to borrow your tape, why didn't you lend it to me?
(Recorder)

Criticism: Criticize the request/requester

你這樣做不是給我添麻煩嗎？
Nǐ zhèyàng zuò bùshì gěi wǒ tiān máfan ma?
Aren't you giving me trouble by acting this way? (Dinner)

Acceptance that functions as a refusal: Focusing on what one can accept

Non-specific or indefinite reply

好看是好看。3
Hǎo kàn shì hǎo kàn.
I agree it looks nice. (Color)

Lack of enthusiasm

如果需要修改的話，我可以再看一下。
Rúguǒ xūyào xiūgǎi de huà, wǒ kěyǐ zài kàn yīxià.
If editing is needed, I can read it again. (Changes)

Avoidance — Verbal: Avoiding direct response to proposed course of action

Topic switch

那件藍色的看起來不錯，樣式也差不多，我想我可以看看。
Nà jiàn lánsède kànqǐlai bùcuò, yàngshi yě chàbuduō, wǒ xiǎng wǒ kěyǐ kànkan.
That blue one looks nice and the style is not bad, either. I think I might have a look at it. (Color)

---

3 See the discussion in "Chinese concessive tautologies" in Wierzbicka, A. (1991). *Cross-cultural pragmatics*. Berlin: Mouton de Gruyter. pp. 423–426.

Joke

你看,我剛想找你給我佔位子呢。
Nǐ kàn, wǒ gāng xiǎng zhǎo nǐ gěi wǒ zhàn wèizi ne.
You see, I was about to ask you to save a seat for me.   (*Seat*)

Repetition of part of a request, etc.

修改?
Xiūgǎi?
Edit?   (*Changes*)

Postponement

等等再說吧。
Děngděng zài shuō ba.
Let's talk about it later.   (*Promotion*)

Hedging

我儘力而爲,但不保證。
Wǒ jìnlì-érwéi, dàn bù bǎozhèng.
I'll try my best, but I don't guarantee anything.   (*Seat*)

Results

As shown in Table 2 below, *Reason* is the most frequently used refusal strategy in Chinese (32.6%). This strategy is supplied in a variety of situations, as shown in the following examples:

(1) 我是很想去,但是我星期一剛好有一個重要的考試,可能沒辦法參加。
Wǒ shì hěn xiǎng qù, dànshi wǒ xīngqīyī gāng hǎo yǒu yíge zhòngyào de kǎoshì, kěnéng méi bànfǎ cānjiā.
I'd very much like to go, but I've got an important exam on Monday, so I probably won't be able to.   (*Party*)

Table 2: Overall Distribution of Refusal Strategies in %

Strategy	Frequency
Reason	32.6
Alternative	14.0
Direct Refusal	12.9
Regret	10.9
Dissuade Interlocutor	10.0
Avoidance (Verbal)	7.5
Acceptance that Functions as Refusal	3.6
Principle	1.1
Folk Wisdom	0.3
Others	7.1

(2) 星期天我和同學已經約好要去看電影。
Xīngqītiān wǒ hé tóngxué yǐjing yuēhǎo yào qù kàn diànyǐng.
My classmates and I have already planned to go to a movie on Sunday. (*Party*)

(3) 系裡現在很需要你。
Xìli xiànzài hěn xūyào nǐ.
Our department needs you very much right now. (*Study Abroad*)

(4) 我買不起；太貴了。
Wǒ mǎi bùqǐ, tài guì le.
I can't afford it; it's too expensive. (*Tie*)

(5) 我妻子打電話讓我早點回去。
Wǒ qīzǐ dǎ diànhuà ràng wǒ zǎo diǎn huíqu.
My wife called and asked me to go home early. (*Dinner*)

Note that the reasons for refusal given in these examples refer to prior commitments or obligations beyond the speaker's control, rather than stating speaker's deliberate preference for non-compliance. Such reasons appear to be the best justification for refusal without running the risk of losing or hurting 面子 *miànzi* on either side.

The second most frequently used strategy in Chinese refusal is *Alternative* (14%). *Alternative* provides a way to avoid a direct confrontation. Moreover, it illustrates the operation of preserving H's 面子 *miànzi* by showing S's concern for H's needs. Although S cannot do what H asks him/her to do, *Alternative* can possibly meet H's need or at least show S's sincerity and concern which might otherwise be concealed by S's refusal. This function of *Alternative* is apparent in the following examples:

(6) 你能否考慮明年？
Nǐ néngfǒu kǎolǜ míngnián?
Can you consider next year? (*Study Abroad*)

(7) 你看看能否去借隔壁毛毛的錄音機用一下？
Nǐ kànkan néngfǒu qù jiè gébì Máomao de lùyīnjī yòng yīxià?
Can you go and check if you can borrow a tape recorder from our neighbor Maomao? (*Record*)

(8) 讓別人替我一下吧。下次我替他。
Ràng biéren tì wǒ yīxià ba. Xiàcì wǒ tì tā.
Why don't you ask someone else to do it for me. I'll do it for him next time. (*Extra hours*)

(9) 以後我們一家人聚會的時候，我再來。
Yǐhòu wǒmen yījiārén jùhuì de shíhòu, wǒ zài lái.
I'll come later on when our family gets together. (*Party*)

(10) 哥給你出錢，拿到街上去修一下好了。
Gē gěi nǐ chū qián, ná dào jiē shangqu xiū yīxià hǎo le.
Have it fixed at the shop on the street. I'll pay for you. (*Handicraft*)

(11) 先問別的同學借一下。
    Xiān wèn biéde tóngxué jiè yīxià.
    Ask another student to lend it to you.   (*Recorder*)

(12) 是否讓我考完試以後。
    Shìfǒu ràng wǒ kǎo wàn shì yǐhòu.
    Can you let me do it after my exam?   (*Study Help*)

The high frequency of offering *Alternatives* in refusals shows the influence of the notion of "respectfulness" and "modesty" in Chinese politeness conceptions, on which this strategy is based (Gu, 1990). *Alternative* is thus used to soften the threatening power of refusals.

The next most frequent strategy is *Direct Refusal* (12.9%), as illustrated in the following examples:

(13) 不行。
    Bù xíng.
    No.   (*Recorder*)

(14) 現在不行。
    Xiànzài bùxíng.
    Not now.   (*Recorder*)

(15) 算了。
    Suàn le.
    Forget it.   (*Handicraft*)

(16) 這不可以。
    Zhè bù kěyǐ.
    This can't be done.   (*Ticket*)

(17) 不行。
    Bùxíng.
    No way.   (*Job Transfer*)

Direct Refusal is the most explicit, and thus a very effective refusal strategy. However, it is appropriate only in certain situations (which will be discussed in the next section).

Regret ranked fourth in frequency order (10.9%). As the formula 對不起 *duìbuqǐ* 'I am sorry' used in refusing situations projects a refusal, it carries a strong force of non-compliance. Here are some examples:

(18) 對不起，我自己就要買兩張票，沒辦法再幫您多買一張。
Duìbuqǐ, wǒ zìjǐ jiù yào mǎi liǎng zhāng piào, méi bànfǎ zài bāng nǐ duō mǎi yī zhāng.
Sorry, I myself need to buy two tickets. I have no way to buy an extra one for you. (*Ticket*)

(19) 對不起，我有事。
Duìbuqǐ, wǒ yǒu shì.
Sorry, I have other business. (*Extra hours*)

(20) 對不起，現在單位沒有名額。
Duìbuqǐ, xiànzài dānwèi méiyǒu míng'é.
Sorry, there is no vacancy for hiring at the moment. (*Job Transfer*)

(21) 對不起，你後邊慢慢排著吧。
Duìbuqǐ, nǐ hòubian mànman pái zhe ba.
Sorry, please wait patiently at the end of the line. (*Ticket*)

Moreover, the use of this strategy is often attached to other strategies; it then typically occupies the final position in a refusal sequence.

(22) 我已經排了兩個小時了，實在對不起。
Wǒ yǐjing pái le liǎng ge xiǎoshí le, shízài duìbuqǐ.
I have been standing in line for two hours. [I am] really sorry. (*Ticket*)

(23) 每人只能限買兩張票。你再想別的辦法吧。實在對不起了。
Měi rén zhǐnéng xiàn mǎi liǎng zhāng piào. Nǐ zài xiǎng bié de bànfǎ ba. Shízài duìbuqǐ le.
Each person can only buy two tickets. Maybe you can find another way [to get your ticket]. I am really sorry. (Ticket)

Notice that the expression of regret in Chinese 對不起 *duìbuqǐ* is not as applicable to different contexts as its English equivalents such as "I'm sorry" and "excuse me". Just as with its English counterparts, the use of the formula 對不起 *duìbuqǐ* does not necessarily indicate the speaker really feels sorry. Rather, it means that she cannot control the situation. If she feels sincere regret, the refuser will show it by making a statement of alternative. In other words, Chinese see offering alternatives as an action of regretting. In child socialization, for instance, parents admonish children to offer alternatives when the child expresses regret for (not) having done something. 對不起 *duìbuqǐ*, on the other hand, is rather used to signal "no more negotiation" in the event, and thus carries a strong refusing force. This may explain why Chinese prefer *Alternative* to *Regret*.

In *Dissuading the Interlocutor*, S both expresses consideration of H's 面子 *miànzi* and reminds H of considering S's own 面子 *miànzi*. Thus, this strategy shifts the focus of the refusing act from the refuser to the refusee. It is preferred in situations where refusals may hurt H's 面子 *miànzi*. Here are some examples of the use of this strategy:

(24) 請不必介意。
Qǐng bùbì jièyì.
Please don't be upset. (Handicraft)

(25) 如果我要了他，工作完不成找誰呀？
Rúgǒu wǒ yào le tā, gōngzuò wán bù chéng zhǎo shuí ya?
If I hire him, who do I look to if the work is not done? (Job Transfer)

(26) 這裡也可以攻讀博士學位，爲甚麼要去美國？
Zhèli yě kěyǐ gōngdú bóshì xuéwèi, wèishenme yào qù Měiguó?
You can get a Ph.D. degree here too; why do you want to go to the U.S.? (Study Abroad)

Although *Avoidance (Verbal)* may be thought to be "indirect", it can still be perceived as being impolite. As any act occurring immediately after an initiating act is taken as a meaningful responding act, avoiding direct positive response indicates refusal, and a refusal that evades the issue proposed in the initiating act can be perceived as impolite. This may be one of the reasons why *Avoidance (Verbal)* is less frequently used. Following are some examples.

(27) 我到別的店裡再去看看。
Wǒ dào biéde diànli zài qu kànkan.
I am going to have a look in other shops. (*Color*)

(28) 我先看看別的再說。也許有更合適的。
Wǒ xiān kànkan biéde zài shuō, yěxǔ yǒu gèng héshì de.
I'll take a look at some others first; there may be something more suitable. (*Color*)

(29) 讓我考慮考慮。
Ràng wǒ kǎolù kǎolù.
Let me think about it. (*Study Abroad*)

(30) 讓我看看其它的款式再決定。
Ràng wǒ kànkan qítā de kuǎnshì zài juédìng.
Let me see some other styles before deciding. (*Tie*)

One feature of using *Avoidance* is the preference for *Postponement* over other substrategies, as shown in the following:

(31) 等等再說。
Děngdeng zài shuō.
[We'll] talk about it later. (*Dinner*)

Acceptance that Functions as Refusal is rarely used in the data. Examples are as follows:

(32) 好看是好看。
Hǎokàn shì hǎokàn.
I agree it looks nice. (*Color*)

(33) 如果需要修改的話，我可以再看一下。
Rúgǒu xūyào xiūgǎi de huà, wǒ kěyǐ zài kàn yíxià.
If editing is needed, I can read it again. (*Changes*)

Finally, in contrast to the stereotype that in Chinese communication generalizing pronouncements are used a lot, stating *Principle* and *Folk Wisdom* were provided very infrequently. Perhaps the stereotype derives from the rare occurrence of such generalizing statements in American English. That is, their absence in American English can make the occurrence of these strategies in Chinese salient despite their low frequency. Also, this result suggests that in the teaching of Chinese, stating *Principle* and *Wisdom* should be taught for receptive purposes, but not necessarily for students' productive use, and that this strategy certainly should not be overemphasized.

Contextual distribution of refusal strategies

Because a refusal is the second part of an adjacency pair, the choice of refusal strategy depends on the type of initiating act. Furthermore, the social role relationship between the interlocutor and the speaker has an impact on strategy choice. In the following, the impact of the type of initiating act and social status on the choice of refusal strategy will be discussed.

Type of initiating act

Table 3 below displays the distribution of refusal strategies according to type of initiating act, i.e., whether the first pair part represents a request, suggestion, invitation, or offer.

In response to requests, suggestions, and invitations, *Reason* is the most preferred refusal strategy. This strategy reaches its highest frequency of occurrence in response to suggestions, followed by invitations; compare (34) through (37).

(34) 沒有錢借給你買項鍊。
Méiyǒu qián jiè gěi nǐ mǎi xiàngliàn.
I don't have money to lend you to buy a necklace.
(Request: *Borrowing Money*)

(35) 這條領帶配我的衣服不諧調。
Zhè tiáo lǐngdài pèi wǒ de yīfu bù xiétiáo.
This tie doesn't go with my wardrobe. (Suggestion: *Tie*)

Table 3: Distribution of refusal strategies in response to type of initiating act in %

Strategy	Request	Rank	Suggestion	Rank	Invitation	Rank	Offer	Rank
Reason	29.6	1	44.3	1	36.6	1	15.2	3
Alternative	15.3	2	21.1	2	5.2	6	3.4	4
Direct Refusal	10.8	4	8.0	4	16.8	2	27.7	2
Regret	15.0	3	3.4	5	12.6	3	2.3	5
Dissuade Interlocutor	10.3	5	2.4	6	2.1	7	30.5	1
Avoidance (Verbal)	6.5	6	13.8	3	6.3	5	2.3	5
Acceptance that Functions as Refusal	1.9	7	3.4	5	9.9	4	3.4	4
Others	10.6		3.6		10.5		15.2	

(36) 今天我外甥生日，我非去不可。
Jīntiān wǒ wàisheng shēngrì, wǒ fēi qù bùkě.
Today is my nephew's birthday; I must go to his party.
(Invitation: *Dinner*)

(37) 今天晚上我早和一個同學約好了去聽音樂會。
Jīntiān wǎnshang wǒ zǎo hé yíge tóngxué yuē hǎo le qù tīng yīnyuèhuì.
I already have an appointment to go to a concert with a classmate.
(Invitation: *Party*)

However, *Reason* is not subjects' first choice in response to offers. A possible reason is that refusing an offer actually minimizes H's costs, and thus bears less risk of hurting H's 面子 *miànzi* than the other three types of refusals.

Therefore, it is less necessary to use reasons or excuses to soften the usually face-threatening nature of refusal. Moreover, an offering situation in Chinese entails an offering of 面子 *miànzi*. Because obtaining 面子 *miànzi* is a much desired goal in social interaction, it would sound strange for one to offer a reason to reject it.

Alternative is the second most preferred strategy for refusing both requests and suggestions (see examples (40) and (39)) but is not used frequently for invitations and offers.

(38) 可不可以等到有個合適的人頂你才走?
Kě bù kěyǐ déngdao yǒu ge héshì de rén dǐng nǐ cái zǒu?
Can you wait until we find a qualified person to take your place?
(Request: *Study Abroad*)

(39) 讓我再試試別的顏色。
Ràng wǒ zài shìshi biéde yánse.
Let me try other colors. (Suggestion: *Color*)

This pattern of preference reflects the pragmatic constraints inherent in the initiating acts. Requests and suggestions entail a greater demand for compliance than invitations and offers do. Using *Alternative* can help soften the strong force of non-compliance in refusal as it leaves a door open to future compliance. On the other hand, compliance to invitations or offers entails acceptance of H's cost for the benefit of S; thus, refusing either of these two acts without offering alternatives can emphasize S's consideration of H. For this reason, *Alternative* is not selected frequently in order to refuse invitations and offers.

Instead, *Direct Refusal* is favored for refusing invitations and offers as the second most preferred strategy but only the fourth for refusing requests and suggestions. (40) through (42) illustrate the use of *Direct Refusal* for declining invitations and offers:

(40) 別請我了。
Bié qǐng wǒ le.
Don't invite me. (Invitation: *Dinner*)

(41) 算了。
   Suàn le.
   Forget it.   (Offer: *Handicraft*)

(42) 不要賠了。
   Bùyào péi le.
   Don't pay me for it.   (Offer: *Handicraft*)

Again, the nature of the initiating act plays an important role in strategy selection. In the case of invitations, if the first strategy selection (*Reason*) is absent for some reason, *Direct Refusal* could be chosen out of efficiency because a response to an invitation should be explicit enough to reduce H's cost entailed in the consequence of an invitation.

The same reason may account for the most frequent use of *Direct Refusal* to offers. Since offering involves H's cost benefiting S, a direct refusal in response will show S's concern about reducing H's cost. This can been observed from the direct refusal utterances of which the focus is in H's perspective, not S's, as in examples (41) and (42). The use of *Direct Refusal* also reflects the concept of Chinese politeness, where one's 面子 *miànzi* is obtained in reciprocity. According to the Chinese perception, an acceptance of an offer does not only increase H's cost, but also puts S in a higher position than H. Therefore, to reject an offer openly is to show that S is considering H's 面子 *miànzi* to be as important as S's, thus enhancing S's own 面子 *miànzi*. This suggests that *Direct Refusal* is needed for the sake of politeness, especially in response to offers, in which the directness of the refusal denies any suspicion of hesitation to refuse.

Regret is chosen more often for refusing requests and invitations (see examples (44) and (45)) than for suggestions and offers.

(43) 對不起，我五百塊錢是另有用途的。
   Dùibuqǐ, wǒ wǔ bǎi kuài qián shì lìng yǒu yòngtú de.
   Sorry, I have to spend my ¥500 on something else.
                                    (Request: *Borrow money*)

(44) 對不起，我不能來。
   Duìbuqǐ, wǒ bù néng lái.
   Sorry, I can't come.   (Invitation: *Party*)

The frequent use of *Regret* for refusing requests and invitations reflects the need of an explicit answer for these two types of initiating acts. As discussed in the overall distribution of the refusing strategies, *Regret* carries a strong force of non-compliance in Chinese refusal; therefore, it is not much selected in refusing suggestions. Moreover, the use of *Regret* to an offer carries a strong force of rejection, leaving little 面子 *miànzi* for H; thus it is not often chosen in these situations, either.

Dissuade Interlocutor is the most preferred strategy for refusing offers, yet not much used for the other acts. Denying the need for an offer is perceived as appropriate as it indicates that S does recognize the 面子 *miànzi* being given but cannot accept it only because it is not much needed, as in *Handicraft* and *Promotion*:

(45) 不用了。
      Bùyòng le.
      No need.   (*Handicraft*)

(46) 不需要了。
      Bù xūyào le.
      No need.   (*Promotion*)

(47) 我看不必了。
      Wǒ kàn bùbì le.
      I don't think it's necessary.   (*Handicraft*)

Theoretically, there is a similar concern of 面子 *miànzi* in refusing an offer or an invitation; thus the selections and preferences should not be very different. However, the results show a different preference order in the response strategies towards these two situations. Responses to the offering situations in this study (*Promotion* and *Handicraft*) reflect the respondents' sensitivity of the immediate given situations interacting with the general trend of selection of refusal strategies. Note that these two set of responses have concerns specifically related to the given situations. In *Promotion*, the choice between studying abroad and getting a promotion is an important factor for the selection. Although getting a promotion does not necessarily conflict with studying abroad, the offer of a promotion from a supervisor in responding to a request for studying overseas is virtually a refusal in the first place. Therefore, *Dissuade Interlocutor* fits such a situation because it avoids a direct refusal to an offer of promotion (which can be legitimate but often is not) as well as maintains one's preference to study overseas (which is used as the reason for the lack of need to get a promotion).

The selection of *Dissuade Interlocutor* for *Handicraft* also reflects the situation-specificity of strategy choice in refusals. This situation concerns an offer of money from a person of lower social status. In Chinese culture, it is regarded as inconsiderate and even cruel to accept money offered by a person whose social status is low and who has financial difficulty. To show sympathy for a poor cleaner reveals the influence of the notion of "helping the poor". Denying the need for an offer in such a situation also indicates that S considers maintaining 面子 *miànzi* more important than the money.

Avoidance (Verbal) is more often chosen for refusing suggestions than the other three acts, as shown in the following examples:

(48) 那件藍色的看起來不錯,樣式也差不多,我想我可以看看。

Nà jiàn lánsè de kàn qilai bùcuò, yàngshì yě chà bùduō, wǒ xiǎng wǒ kěyǐ kànkan.

That blue one looks nice and the style is not bad, either. I think I will have a look at it. (*Color*)

S's major concern with refusing suggestions is how to express her non-compliance and still preserve H's 面子 *miànzi*. The selection of *Avoidance (Verbal)* shows that when *Reason* is absent, respondents would rather choose to avoid explicit non-compliance with a given suggestion.

Acceptance that Functions as Refusal is mostly used for refusing invitations, as shown in the following:

(49) 行,不過我要是臨時有事就去不成了。

Xíng, bùguò wǒ yàoshi línshí yǒu shì jiù qù bu chéng le.

Okay, but I may not be able to go if something else comes up.
(*Invitation: Party*)

(50) 我會設法來的,但不要等我。

Wǒ huì shèfǎ lái de, dàn bùyào děng wǒ.

I'll try my best to come, but don't wait for me. (*Invitation: Party*)

The illocutionary force of refusing in examples (49) and (50) is conveyed by the second half of the response starting with 但 *dàn*, 'but'. Moreover, 不要等我 *bùyào děng wǒ* 'don't wait for me' in example (50) does not mean that the speaker is simply going to be late. Rather, she is trying to get herself out of the obligation. That is, saying 我會設法來的 wǒ huì shèfǎ lái de 'I'll try my best to come' does not mean she has accepted the invitation, but does not mean she has rejected the invitation, either. It is this interplay between the propositions and the illocutionary force that allows the speaker to maintain a position that shows both her wish to accept the invitation and a potential inability to fulfill the obligation of accepting the invitation.

In this particular case, the dinner party may be an important factor affecting the selection of strategies. Since S's single absence from a party may not have great impact on H's cost, *Acceptance that Functions as Refusal* allows S to focus on the acceptance of H's 面子 miànzi rather than her eventual non-compliance with H's invitation.

Interestingly, using *Acceptance that Functions as Refusal* in response to invitations can be seen as complementary to ritual refusal (which will be discussed in a later section), where the Chinese pragmatic force of politeness is expressed through paradoxical realizations of linguistic formulas.

The preference patterns of refusal strategies reflect the internal factors of the initiating acts. Moreover, the specific refusal contexts play an important role in strategy selection. The respondents' sensitivity to the situations demonstrates the interactive nature of speech events.

Social status

In addition to stimulus types, the refuser's social status relative to the interlocutor is another factor affecting the choice of refusal strategies. Table 4 below indicates how refuser's status influences strategy choice.

In Chinese society, social hierarchy plays an important role in refusal strategy choices. To act appropriately means to act according to one's social position or social status. Though enormous changes have taken place in Chinese society since the founding of the People's Republic, cultural tradition remains dominant in guiding individuals' behavior, speech behavior included. This is clearly evident from the refusal data.

While *Reason* is the preferred strategy in all status relationships, its use increases as S's social status decreases. By providing the interlocutor with a justification for non-compliance, S appeals to H's understanding why the course of action proposed by H is not followed. *Reason* thus appears to be the most effective refusal strategy regardless of status relationship; however in refusing a higher status person's initiation, justifying the refusal seems more strongly required. Many of the offered reasons are excuses, as illustrated in the examples (51) and (52).

Table 4: Distribution of strategies in relation to refuser's social status in %

Strategy	Refuser's Status					
	Higher Rank		Equal Rank		Lower Rank	
Reason	26.0	1	31.7	1	38.6	1
Alternative	13.4	4	11.9	3	16.7	2
Direct Refusal	14.5	3	10.7	4	13.8	3
Regret	6.1	6	19.1	2	6.6	5
Dissuade Interlocutor	18.0	2	9.8	5	3.5	6
Avoidance (Verbal)	6.7	5	6.1	6	9.7	4
Others	15.3		10.7		11.1	

(51) 不過我媽不喜歡紫色的。
　　 Bùguò wǒ mā bù xǐhuan zǐse de.
　　 But my mom doesn't like purple. (Color)

(52) 我晚上已經和同學約好去看電影。
　　 Wǒ wǎnshang yǐjing hé tóngxué yuē hǎo qù kàn diànyǐng.
　　 I have already agreed to go with my classmates to see a movie. (Party)

Excuses are particularly frequent in the case of lower status refusers, whereas higher status refusers, because of their more powerful role, offer excuses less often to lower status interlocutors.

The choice of *Alternative* relative to other strategies is clearly dependent on status relationship. When their status changes from higher to equal and equal to lower, respondents opt more for *Alternative* than other strategies accordingly. As in the case of *Reason*, the power associated with superior social status creates less of a need to suggest alternative options to the interlocutor, while lower status refusers will feel a need to soften the impolite impact of refusals and therefore offer alternative courses of action.

Direct Refusal is used the least frequently when the interlocutors are of equal status. One explanation is that because of its uncompromising and potentially confrontational tone, frequent use of *Direct Refusal* may pose a serious threat to relationships between same status participants such as friends, fellow students, and co-workers. When S is of lower or equal status, *Insistence* is preferred over the other two substrategies (i.e., *No* and *Negative Willingness/ Ability*), as illustrated in (53) through (55).

(53) 我還是想先去讀博士學位。
Wǒ háishì xiǎng xiān qù dú bóshì xuéwèi.
I still wish to study first for a Ph.D. degree.   (*Promotion*)

(54) 我想還是買那件灰色的吧。
Wǒ xiǎng háishì mǎi nà jian huīsè de ba.
I think I would still like to buy that gray one.   (*Color*)

(55) 我還是想保留那一部份。
Wǒ háishì xiǎng bǎoliú nà yī bùfen.
I still wish to keep that section.   (*Change*)

Just as *Direct Refusal* is least often chosen among status equals, *Regret* is expressed most frequently in status equal relationships, cf. (56) and (57).

(56) 眞對不起，雖然我剛從銀行取回五百圓錢，但我現在有急用。
Zhēn duìbuqǐ, suīrán wǒ gāng cóng yínháng qǔ huí wǔ bǎi yuán qián, dàn wǒ xiànzài yǒu jí yòng.

I am really sorry. Although I have just withdrawn five hundred *yuan* from the bank, I need it now for an emergency.

(*Borrow money*)

(57) 對不起，我實在沒有時間。
Duìbuqǐ, wǒ zhízài méiyǒu shíjiān.
Sorry, I really don't have time.   (*Study Help*)

This usage of *Regret* indicates that further negotiation is not possible, but unlike *Direct Refusal*, it expresses non-compliance through a conventionally approved politeness routine. While *Direct Refusal* is less often chosen because of its detrimental effect on the interlocutors' relationship, *Regret* can effectively express S's intention of non-compliance without damaging H's 面子 *miànzi*.

A dramatic linear status effect is seen in the use of *Dissuade Interlocutor*. When S is in the status higher position, *Dissuade* ranks second after *Reason*, whereas in low to high relationships, it is clearly not preferred as a refusal option, showing the lowest frequency of all refusal strategies. Among status equals, *Dissuade Interlocutor* ranks second lowest on the scale of refusal options. The function of dissuasion is to lessen the threatening impact of refusal since, instead of rejecting H's proposition, it opens a chance for H to reconsider and withdraw her proposed plan of action, as shown in (58):

(58) 但我怎麼向其他領導同志交待呢？
      Dàn wǒ zěnme xiàng qítā lǐngdǎo tóngzhì jiāodài ne?
      But how can I explain this to other supervisors?   (Job Transfer)

While this strategy contains an element of letting H off the hook so as to save her 面子 *miànzi*, it appears to take the authority of a status superior to license the use of *Dissuade Interlocutor* because implicit in the strategy is some judgment of the action proposed by H. This may explain why *Dissuade Interlocutor* is used more frequently in high to low interactions than in the other two status relationships.

Although much less pronounced, the usage pattern of *Avoidance (Verbal)* is reverse to that of *Dissuade*: Lower status speakers avoid refusal more frequently, whereas equal and high status speakers avoid less often. While it is obvious that status superiors should have less of a need to avoid refusing an interlocutor's proposition, it may seem surprising that *Avoidance* is the least frequently chosen option among status equals. Possibly, avoiding H's proposal may be seen as less cooperative compared to response alternatives which display more direct uptake of the initiating act, and thus seem to be inconsistent with the mode of interaction between status equals.

As is apparent from Figure 1, status relationships affect the choice of refusal strategies in complex ways. Two strategies, *Reason* and *Dissuade Interlocutor*, follow a complementary linear pattern. Selection of strategies is thus consistent with Brown and Levinson's (1987) politeness theory, according to which strategic options vary directly with social power. Yet in four out of the six refusal strategies, the impact of status on strategy choice is non-linear: equal status relationships either increase (as in *Regret*) or decrease (as in *Alternative*,

Figure 1: Summary of choice of refusal strategies in the three status relationships

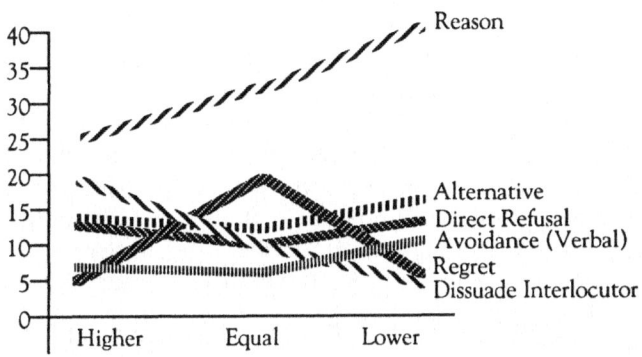

Direct Refusal, and *Avoidance*) the choice of a particular refusal strategy relative to the unequal status constellations. Most of the strategic options seem therefore more readily explained in terms of Wolfson's (1989) Bulge Theory, which postulates greater politeness investment in status equal as opposed to status unequal relationships. Upon closer inspection, however, two of the nonlinear distribution patterns — those of *Alternative* and *Avoidance* — align the strategy preferences of the higher status speakers more with those seen in the status equal encounters than in the low to high relationships. The status inferior position seems to motivate more strongly the display of respect and concern for H's 面子 *miànzi* which underlies *Alternative*, and the entire circumvention of behavior which might possibly be taken as disrespectful through the use of *Avoidance*. Strategy choice is thus affected by status in complex ways, and even though theories such as Brown and Levinson's and Wolfson's can account for some of the strategy choices, the culture-specific principles of Chinese interaction must be taken into consideration in order to explain the impact of status on options of refusal strategies.

Sequencing of refusal strategies

As has been obvious from the examples presented above, refusal strategies typically occur in combination. Therefore, it is important to ask what the most frequent combinations are, and how multiple refusal strategies are sequenced. The most preferred sequence for refusing in Chinese is *Reason–Alternative*. These two refusal strategies highlight two different but related aspects in S's attempt to attend to both S's and H's 面子 *miànzi* in the act of refusing. *Reason* focuses on S's negative response to H's initiating act, attempting to alleviate the disruptive impact of the refusal by explaining to H why compliance is not possible or desirable. *Alternative*, by contrast, focuses on H's needs and goals, presenting to H an alternative course of action than the one proposed by H yet one which H might consider an agreeable second option. In proposing an alternative, S thus presents herself as willing to cooperate and support H's goals. One might thus say that while *Reason* is speaker-related, emphasizing justification of S's non-compliance, *Alternative* is hearer-related, focusing on the satisfaction of H's goals, albeit in a modified manner compared to H's original proposition. As for the sequential occurrence of the two strategies, it stands to reason that an explanation why H's initiation is not complied with should precede the offer of an alternative course of action.

The following examples illustrate the *Reason–Alternative* sequence:

(59) 這錢我有急用，能不能過幾天我想法湊些錢借給你。

Zhè qián wǒ yǒu jí yòng, néng bù néng guò jǐ tiān wǒ xiǎngfǎ còu xiē qián jiè gěi nǐ.

I need this money for an emergency. Can I try to collect some money to lend to you a few days from now?   (*Borrow money*)

(60) 我有一個很重要的約會，能不能另找人加班。

Wǒ yǒu yíge hěn zhòngyào de yuēhuì, néng bù néng lìng zhǎo rén jiābān.

I've got an important appointment. Can you find someone else to work overtime?   (*Extra hour*)

(61) 我星期天有很重要的事要辦，實在抽身不得。趕明兒我專程去看小表弟好不好？

Wǒ xīngqītiān yǒu hěn zhòngyào de shì yào bàn, shízài chōushēn bùdé. Gǎnmínger wǒ zhuānchéng qù kàn xiǎo biǎodì hǎo bù hǎo?

I have something very important on Sunday that I just can't get away from. How about if I pay a special visit to my little cousin another day?   (*Party*)

(62) 我晚上有重要事情要處理,下次有空再說吧。
Wǒ wǎnshang yǒu zhòngyào shìqing yào chǔlǐ, xiàcì yǒu kòng zài shuō ba.
I have important business to attend to. I'll go the next time I have time.　　　　　　　　　　　　　　　　　　(Dinner)

(63) 這條太貴。我還是另選一條吧。
Zhè tiáo tài guì. Wǒ háishì lìng xuǎn yī tiáo ba.
This one is too expensive. Let me choose another one.　　(Tie)

(64) 我現在沒有時間。我們訂一個別的時間吧。
Wǒ xiànzài méiyǒu shíjiān. Wǒmen dìng yíge biéde shíjiān ba.
I don't have time now. Let's make it another time.　　(Study Help)

(65) 系裡非常需要你。下次有機會,一定優先批準你。
Xìli fēicháng xūyào nǐ. Xiàcì yǒu jīhuì, yīdìng yōuxiān pīzhǔn nǐ.
You are very much needed in the department. The next time the opportunity arises, you'll certainly have priority for approval.
(Study Abroad)

(66) 那題目我實在陌生,談不深。下次熟悉了再談談,好不好?
Nà tímù wǒ shízài mòshēng, tán bù shēn. Xiàcì shúxi le zài tántan, hǎo bù hǎo?
I feel really unfamiliar with that topic, so I am not able to present it in depth. How about if I present it next time when I know it better?　　　　　　　　　　　　　　　　　　　　(Topic)

The analysis of Substantive refusal in Chinese has demonstrated that offering a *Reason* for non-compliance is the preferred strategic choice. As studies by Beebe and Cummings (in press) and Chen (1992) demonstrate, this finding is consistent with preferences for refusal strategies by native speakers of American English. A culturally distinctive feature is found in the frequent option for *Alternative* the Chinese respondents. However, choice of specific refusal strategies is mediated by the type of initiating act and social factors. While their strategy selection is generally status-sensitive, Chinese respondents display concern for their own and the interlocutors 面子 *miànzi* in the act of refusing, and this concern is reflected in strategy choices which differentially attend to 面子 *miànzi* in different status relationships.

The common theme in the otherwise diverse refusal contexts in the preceding study was the speaker's assumed intention to substantively refuse the hearer's proposition. Surely this overall purpose determines to a large extent the kinds of strategies chosen. However, as noted initially, there are occasions where speakers in fact wish to accept the hearer's proposal yet perform an act of refusal for the sake of politeness. Part Two of this paper will examine the functions and forms of the act of pretended non-compliance, or refusal.

PART 2: RITUAL REFUSAL

WHILE SUBSTANTIVE REFUSAL IS A FACE-THREATENING ACT according to both Chinese and Western concepts of politeness, ritual refusal is closely tied to Chinese cultural values and thus may be a rich source of cross-cultural miscommunication.

Ritual refusal takes place in response to an initiating *commissive-directive act* (Hancher, 1979), such as an offer or an invitation. These acts are commissives in that the speaker commits herself to a future course of action which is beneficial to the hearer. At the same time, they are directives in that they influence a future course of action on the hearer's part. Their success hinges on the hearer's being able and willing to engage in the proposed action, and on the speaker's honoring the commitment she made. During the course of obtaining these two conditions, both interlocutors' 面子 *miànzi* interacts and ritual refusal, fundamentally similar to substantive refusal, is played out against the concern for and attending to self as well as other's 面子 *miànzi*.

In Chinese culture, an invitation to dinner often functions as a leave-taking act and an expression of good will/wish on the part of the inviter. One can often hear a host say 留下來吃飯吧 *liúxiàlai chīfàn ba* 'please stay for dinner/lunch', at which point the visitor declines and takes leave. It is equally frequent to hear the same utterance of 'invitation' during leave-taking initiated by the visitor. The invitation made then is often, if not always, a ritual one. It is either a strategy to have the visitor leave the house, as in the former case, or a conventionalized way of saying good-bye. By using an invitation in leave-taking, the host not only gives 面子 *miànzi* to the visitor by showing she is a welcome guest, but also enhances her own 面子 *miànzi* by offering hospitality. An invitation to dinner or a meal is considered a polite act, indicating positive feelings on the part of the inviter to the invitee. Its use extends to many social occasions when it is felt necessary to express one's good feelings, appreciation, and gratitude. In this case, a *sincerity condition* (Searle, 1969) does not obtain because the invitation is either a pure social gesture or an indirect speech act of saying good-bye. Extending a dinner invitation assumes a ritual character which the invitee must observe correctly.

Similarly, ritual refusal is a polite act to indicate the speaker's consideration of the hearer. It is performed as a response to a substantive offer or invitation. Because by issuing an offer or invitation, the speaker proposes to exert herself on behalf of the hearer, it is improper for the hearer to immediately accept the offered good or action. The denial of acceptance in form sustains the hospitality offered by the hearer as well as indicating the speaker's appreciation so that both parties' 面子 *miànzi* is preserved. Ritual refusal came into existence as a response to the substantive invitation and eventually became a culturally standard way to react to any given invitation and offer.

Defined in this way, ritual refusal has two functions. First, it gauges the real intentions of the inviter/offerer to determine the sincerity of the act. If the result of the estimation indicates the invitation to be a ritual one, a decline is the only appropriate response and more often than not, initial ritual refusal will quickly give way to substantive refusal, indicated by the speech act realizations employed. For by definition, ritual refusal indicates eventual acceptance. On the other hand, if the assessment shows that the inviter is sincere and serious, ritual refusal will lead to acceptance. In either case, both interlocutors must actively participate in the interaction and give respective linguistic signals. And in either case, ritual refusal develops over a series of exchanges which are highly structured and conventionalized. The following discussion will focus on the sociopragmatic and pragmalinguistic differences between ritual and substantive refusals, and the differences between ritual and substantive invitation. The propositional content of refusal strategies, their sequence, and interlocutor's face concerns will also be examined.

REALIZATION OF RITUAL AND SUBSTANTIVE REFUSAL

As noted in the section on substantive refusal, if an invitee wishes to decline an invitation, it is imperative for the invitee to give reasons, excuses, etc. in order to mitigate threat to both parties' 面子 *miànzi*. However, the perspective in which these reasons are supplied are different in ritual refusal and substantive refusal. In ritual refusal, the invitee constantly gives reasons derived from consideration of costs to the inviter. She declines the invitation, as she would say, for fear of causing too much trouble to the inviter. For example, in responding to an initial invitation to dinner, the speaker would say (examples from Gu (1990)):

> 不來了，太麻煩
> bù lái le, tài máfan
> [I'm] not coming, it's too much trouble [for you].

and

> 那也得燒哇
> nà yě děi shāo(wa)
> [you] still need to cook.

to inviter's downgrading the effort involved in the cooking. The following examples from Mao (1994) are in response to an invitation extended to the invitee's family:

> 別客氣了。你只有兩個星期的假期，一定有很多事情要做
> bié kèqi le. Nǐ zhǐyǒu liǎngge xīngqī de jiàqī, yīdìng yǒu hěn duō shìqing yào zuò
> Don't be polite. Your stay here is only for two weeks, and I am sure you have a lot to do with your family.

and to an initial invitation and to an inviter's denial of other engagements:

> 這次就別麻煩了，這樣太花時間了
> zhècì jiù bié máfan le, zhèyàng tài huā shíjiān le
> Please don't bother this time; it takes (you) too much time.

The invitee's replies are inevitably oriented toward her concern of the cost such an event will involve for A. Linguistically, ritual refusal is realized by a set of formulas designed to offset a set of persuasive formulas by the inviter, for example, 太麻煩 tài máfan 'too much trouble', 那也得燒 nà yěděi shāo '[you] still need to cook', 你們也挺忙的 nǐ (men) yě tǐng máng de 'you are also rather busy', etc. Eventual acceptance is also phrased in cost minimizing formulas, e.g. 就隨便一點 jiù suíbiàn yīdiǎn 'make it simple/casual' or humbling 真不好意思 zhēn bù hǎo yìsi '[I'm] rather embarrassed', etc.

As stated above, in substantive refusal, the invitee stresses her inability, not unwillingness (never!), to accept the invitation by relating it to her own most unfortuitous circumstances. Her justifications serve partly as a gesture to assume responsibility for not fulfilling a social obligation. Substantive refusal of invitations is realized by means of formulaic expressions; it relates to specific circumstances, and is almost exclusively self-oriented.

RITUAL AND SUBSTANTIVE INVITATION

How to refuse appropriately depends how one estimates the nature of the invitation. As mentioned above, a ritual invitation is frequently issued at the end of the visit at the host's house, at meal time (e.g., 12:00 noon, 6:00 p.m.), and during leave-taking. These situational contexts, however, are not absolute indicators of the nature of an invitation. The decisive factor is linguistic. The ritual inviter usually extends the invitation using suggestory formulæ 在這兒吃飯吧 *zài zhèr chīfàn (ba)* 'How about staying here for dinner?' instead of impositives 明天來吃晚飯啊 *míngtiān lái chī wǎnfàn (a)* 'Tomorrow come eat dinner' (cf. Gu, p. 252), 這個星期六你和你先生到我們家來吃飯啊 *zhè ge xīngqī liù nǐ hé nǐ xiānsheng dào wǒmen jiā lái chīfàn a* 'This Saturday, you and your husband come to my place to have dinner' (cf. Mao, p. 40). Secondly, a ritual invitation gets increasingly weaker while a substantive invitation becomes increasingly stronger. The ritual inviter will not insist through the use of various strategies to downgrade the cost sustained by her and will be likely to suggest a future invitation very soon 那下次（吧）*nà xià cì (ba)* 'Then next time', also a ritual one, in most cases. On the other hand, a substantive invitation will see the inviter deny the cost and trouble and will often "denigrate" her (10 course) dinner/meal to an insignificant or casual get-together. Therefore, to decline a ritual invitation, light (vs. heavy and serious) self-oriented excuses are used, e.g., 不了，我還有事 *bùle, wǒ hái yǒu shì* 'Not today, I have something going on', 'My wife/husband/mother, etc. is waiting for me for dinner', etc. It is also appropriate to take up the host's future invitation, e.g., 好吧，下次一定來 *hǎoba, xiàcì yīdìng lái* 'OK, next time [I] promise to come'.

SEQUENCE OF INVITATION/REFUSAL

An invitation/offer situation in Chinese culture is highly structured and conventionalized (Gu, 1990; Mao, 1994). The most apparent structural aspect is the sequence and number of turns before the conclusion. Both parties expect a particular sequential pattern and engage in the speech event following an almost scripted version of verbal exchange.

The following three sets of examples from Gu (1990) and Mao (1994) illustrate these conventionalized sequences:

Example set 1: (Gu, 1990)

A: [1] 明天來吃晚飯（啊）
Míngtiān lái chī wǎnfàn (ar).
tomorrow come eat dinner

B: [2] 不來（了）。太麻煩。
Bù lái (le). Tài máfan.
not come too much trouble

A: [3] 麻煩甚麼（呀）
Máfan shénme (ya).
trouble nothing

[4] 菜都是現成（的）
Cài dōu shi xiànchéng (de).
dishes all are ready-made

B: [5] 那也得燒（哇）
Nà yěděi shāo (wa).
that still cook

A: [6] 你不來我們也得吃飯。
Nǐ bù lái wǒmen yěděi chīfàn.
you not come we also must have meal

[7] 一定來（啊），不來我可生氣（了）。
Yīdìng lái(ar), bù lái wǒ kě shēngqì (le).
must come not come I shall feel offended

B: [8] 好（吧），就隨便一點。
Hǎo (ba), jiù suíbiàn yīdiǎn.
all right, just potluck

Example set 2: (Mao, 1994)

Y: [1] 嘿，小李，這個星期六你和你先生到我們家來吃飯啊。我正好回來，我們大家碰碰頭。

Hèi, Hsiǎo L, zhège xīngqīliù nǐ hé nǐ xiānsheng dào wǒmen jiā lái chīfàn a. Wǒ zhènghǎo húilái, wǒmen dàjiā pèngpèng tóu.

Hey, Hsiao L, this Saturday you with your husband come to our house eat rice. I just come back, we meet each other.

Hey, Hsiao L, how about you and your husband coming to have dinner with us this coming Saturday. Now that I am back home, it will be fun to see you guys.

L: [2] 別客氣了。你只有兩個星期的假期，一定有很多事情做。

Bié kèqi le. Nǐ zhǐyǒu liǎngge xīngqī de jiàqī, yīdìng yǒu hěnduō shìqing zuò.

No polite. You only have two weeks vacation, certainly have many things need do.

Don't be polite. Your stay here is only for a couple of weeks, and I am sure you have a lot to do with your family.

Y: [3] 除了休息以外，我沒甚麼事情要做。你們來嘛，又沒其他人。

Chú le xiūxi yǐwài, wǒ méi shénme shìqing yào zuò. Nǐmen lái ma, yòuméi qítā rén.

Except rest in addition, I have no any things need do you come, really no other people.

Except resting, I really have nothing else to do. Why don't you come — there aren't any other people.

L: [4] 這次就別麻煩了，這樣太花時間了。

Zhècì jiù bié máfàn le, zhèyàng tài huā shíjiān le.

This time no need bother, this way too much take time.

Please don't bother this time; it takes too much time.

Y: [5] 一點不花時間,吃頓便飯嘛。
Yīdiǎn bù huā shíjiān, chī dùn biànfàn ma.
Not at all take time, eat a casual dinner.
Not at all. It is only a potluck.

L: [6] 我們還是來談談好了,不要吃飯了。
Wǒmen háishi lái tántán hǎo le, búyào chīfàn le.
We still come chat chat good, no need eat dinner.
Why don't we come and chat, but no dinner really.

Y: [7] 來了怎麼可以不吃飯呢!
Lái le zěnme kěyǐ bù chīfàn ne!
Come how can not eat dinner!
If you come, how should have dinner with us!

G: [8] 好了,別再客氣了!這是很隨便的。我們
就想聚一聚,看看大家。你們一定要來的。
Hǎo le, bié zài kèqì le! Zhèshì hěn suíbiàn de. Wǒmen jiùxiǎng jù yī jù, kànkan dàjiā. Nǐmen yīdìng yào lái de.
All right, no longer again polite! This is very casual, and we just want get together, see you all You must come.
Stop being polite any more, please! It's a very casual dinner. We just want to get together and see you guys. You must come.

L: [9] 你們太客氣了,老是請我們吃飯。
Nǐmen tài kèqi le, lǎoshi qǐng wǒmen chīfàn.
You too polite, always invite us eat dinner.
You are being too polite; you always invite us to eat with you.

Y: [10] 別瞎說了。就這樣定了。
Bié xiāshuō le. Jiù zhèyàng dìng le.
No nonsense talk. Just this way settled.
That is not true at all. OK, it is agreed then.

L: [11] 好吧,那我們就來。要我們帶甚麼來嗎?
        Hǎo ba, nà wǒmen jiù lái. Yào wǒmen dài diǎn shéme lái ma?
        OK, we come. Want us bring something?
        OK, we will come. But do you want us to bring some food?

Y: [12] 不要帶,一點也不要帶。
        Bùyào dài, yīdiǎn yě bùyào dài.
        No need bring, one bit no need bring.
        No, nothing. Bring nothing.

L: [13] 好吧,我們這次就全都聽你的了。
        Hǎoba, wǒmen zhècì jiù quán dōu tīng nǐ de le.
        OK, we this time just all listen to you.
        OK, we will do whatever you say this time.

Y: [14] (She then asks L how to prepare one dish).

Example set 3: (Mao, 1994)

X: [15] 怎麼,還有這麼多面條留著。你們拿點去吧。
        Zěnme, háiyǒu zhème duō miàntiáo liú zhe. Nǐmen ná diǎn qù ba.
        What, still have these many noodles left. You take some.
        Look, there are still so many noodles left. Why don't you take some.

Mrs. W: [16] 不必了。你們留著自己吃吧。
        Bùbì le. Nǐmen liú zhe zìjǐ chī ba.
        No need. You leave yourselves to eat.
        It is not necessary. You can save them for yourselves.

X: [17] 這麼多我們也吃不掉！

Zhème duō wǒmen yě chī bù diào!

These many we also eat not them up!

There are so many left; we cannot finish them all!

Mrs. W: [18] 這不對啊，吃了還要拿。

Zhè bù duì a, chī le hái yào ná.

This not right, having eaten still need to take.

This is not right; we've already had a lot, and now we are going to take more.

X: [19] 別客氣了。既然好吃，就留一點嘛。
這種面條不馬上吃掉也就不好吃了。

Bié kèqi le. Jìrán hǎo chī, jiù liú yīdiǎn ma. Zhè zhǒng miàntiáo bù mǎshàng chī diào yě jiù bù hǎo chī le.

No polite. Since they good eating, then leave some. This kind noodles not at once eat up also then no good eating.

Don't be polite. Since they taste good, why not take some. This kind of noodles cannot stay too long, or they become tasteless.

Mrs. W: [20] 那我們就不客氣了。

Nà wǒmen jiù bù kèqi le (overlapping with 21).

Then we not polite.

Then, we will stop being polite.

Mr.W: [21] 好，那我們就拿一點吧。

Hǎo, nà wǒmen jiù ná yīdiǎn ba.

Good, then we only take some.

OK, we will only take some.

X: [22] 多拿一點，你們不拿我們也吃不掉。
        Duō ná yìdiǎn, nǐmen bù ná wǒmen yě chī bù diào.
        Take some more, you not take we also cannot eat up.
        Take more; if you do not take more, we cannot eat them all. (Mr. Wang begins to scoop the noodles into his bowl.)

Mrs. W: [23] 你真是太客氣了。
        Nǐ zhēnshì tài kèqi le.
        You really too polite.
        You are really being too polite.

X: [24] 多拿一點嘛。
        Duō ná yìdiǎn ma (addressing and gesturing to Mr. W).
        Take some more.
        Take more.

In all three dialogues, the invitee starts his/her response to the invitation with a refusal, focusing on the trouble and cost the inviter will have to bear. Expecting some kind of refusal in the first place, the inviter, through the strategies used by the invitee, is able to infer the nature of the refusal, i.e., ritual or substantive. The other-oriented strategies in these cases indicate to the inviter that the refusal is a ritual one. The inviter reinforces her invitation, as is expected. This invitation/offer-refusal sequence is played out three times in all the above dialogues before acceptance.

For ritual refusals, this invitation/offer-refusal sequence need not be performed more than three times in an invitation event. Over-doing it might send wrong signals, such as over-politeness to increase social distance, insincerity about the cost to the inviter, or substantive refusal.

LEARNERS AND THE RITUAL REFUSAL

As an invitee

Initial decline is expected. Upon hearing an invitation, one can try out a refusal by saying something like 太麻煩你了 *tài máfan nǐ le* 'too much trouble for you'. Since it is the semantic orientation of the refusal content which is crucial, the learner must not mention anything relating to her own circumstances in a ritual refusal. Being a cultural outsider in China, the learner is not expected to behave exactly like a Chinese, and therefore the informal folk rule of refusing three times may not apply to her. As reported by both learners and native speakers of Chinese, once or at most twice is more than enough. Learners' instant acceptance of an invitation or an offer will not be judged as rude (although it may be perceived as rather direct and sudden), provided the nature of the invitation is assessed accurately.

As an inviter

The most prevalent misstep Americans take as inviters/offerers, as reported by learners and Chinese, is that they take the first refusal by a Chinese interlocutor at face value and stop further inviting and offering right away. That often makes Chinese feel embarrassed (and leaves them hungry). It should be noted that explicit instructions such as "make yourself at home", "take whatever you like", etc. do not help in such situations because they are conventional scripts employed by hosts in American culture but not in a Chinese context. When acting as host/offerer vis-a-vis a Chinese person, one needs to repeat the inviting/offering act in addition to the instruction, and be especially sensitive to the semantic perspectives in the refusal.

SUMMARY

SUBSTANTIVE AND RITUAL REFUSALS ARE TWO TYPES OF REFUSAL with different functions. As non-native speakers tend to transfer their native sociopragmatic knowledge to the use of their target language, both substantive and ritual refusals may seem confusing, and give rise to misunderstanding. Therefore, it is most important to distinguish these two types of refusals in interpersonal interactions. Understanding the Chinese notion of politeness and the concept of 面子 *miànzi* can provide guidance in the observation and study of this speech act.

Moreover, learners should keep in mind that one strategy of a similar semantic form in both English and Chinese may function differently when placed in different pragmatic systems. Therefore, observing native speakers communicative practice and making use of their preferred strategies can help non-native speakers develop the sociopragmatic knowledge of the target language.

Further research is needed into both substantive and ritual refusal. Observation of refusal in a variety of authentic speech events may provide more accurate information, especially about the negotiation processes involved in the enactment of both refusal types. for the research. In addition, examination of sociolinguistic factors such as age and gender can offer further insight into the complex business of refusing in Chinese ◆

Jinwen Steinberg Du

PERFORMANCE OF FACE-THREATENING ACTS IN CHINESE: COMPLAINING, GIVING BAD NEWS, AND DISAGREEING

INTRODUCTION

IT IS GENERALLY CONSIDERED one of the most important aspects of second language learning to acquire pragmatic abilities in the second language. However, because of different cultural norms and orientations, language use differs across speech communities. One social or situational phenomenon will motivate two kinds of linguistic strategies in two different cultures, or one linguistic strategy will produce two or more social or situational responses. It is therefore important for second language learners to know which linguistic strategies can be used appropriately in order to accomplish a particular communicative goal in a specific social situation in the target culture. This is especially important when the intended communicative goal entails a 'face-threatening act' ("FTA", Brown & Levinson, 1987), i.e., an action which in some way demonstrates lack of social appreciation of the hearer or of something she did (thus posing a threat to the hearer's 'positive face'), or which goes against the hearer's wishes (thus posing a threat to the hearer's 'negative face' in the sense of Brown and Levinson).

This paper examines the realization in Chinese of three face-threatening acts — *Complaining, Giving Bad News,* and *Disagreeing*. First, a brief discussion will be offered of the definitions of the three face-threatening acts, the illocutionary verbs denoting these acts in Chinese, and the semantics of face in Chinese culture. Then, a data based study of the three speech acts will be reported. Finally, conclusions will be drawn with respect to learning Chinese as a foreign language.

Du, W. S. (1995). Performance of face-threatening acts in Chinese: Complaining, giving bad news, and disagreeing. In G. Kasper (Ed.), *Pragmatics of Chinese as native and target language* (Technical Report #5, pp. 165–205). Honolulu, Hawai'i: University of Hawai'i, Second Language Teaching & Curriculum Center.

DEFINITION OF THE THREE SPEECH ACTS

Complaining

According to Brown and Levinson (1987), the speech act of complaining implies that "S (the speaker) has a negative evaluation of some aspect of H's (the hearer's) positive face" (p. 66). From S's point of view, the following preconditions are needed in order for the speech act of complaining to take place:
1. H performs a socially unacceptable act (SUA) which is contrary to a social code of behavioral norms shared by S and H.
2. S perceives the SUA as having unfavorable consequences for him/herself, and/or for the general public.
3. The verbal expression of S relates *post facto* directly or indirectly to the SUA, thus having the illocutionary force of censure (Olshtain & Weinbach, 1993).

The Chinese terms describing the action of *Complaining* are 發牢騷 *fā láosao*, 有怨言 *yǒu yuànyán*, and 有意見 *yǒu yìjian*. The first two terms are synonymous, and can be glossed as 'voicing discontent or grievances'. Usually, they are performed informally, behind the back of the person involved. 有意見 *yǒu yìjian*, however, can be expressed both formally and informally with or without the presence of the person involved.

Giving Bad News

The giving of bad news about H is defined in the literature as an act demonstrating that "S doesn't care about (or is indifferent to) H's positive face" (Brown & Levinson, 1987, pp. 66–67). In the present study, *Giving Bad News* comes in two types: first, in the sense of giving embarrassing information and second, in the sense of warning. In the first type, the performative verbs in Chinese are 告訴 *gàosu*, and 提醒 *tíxǐng*. A general verb with little connotation, 告訴 *gàosu* describes the action of telling, regardless of the manner or the content. 提醒 *tíxǐng*, however, carries the meaning of reminding that something may or could be amiss.

Although both 告訴 *gàosù* and 提醒 *tíxǐng* can be used in the sense of warning, depending on the seriousness of the situation, the following two verbs, 警告 *jǐnggào* and 告誡 *gàojiè*, express such actions more appropriately. Both verbs carry the meaning of warning and admonishing. 告誡 *gàojiè*, however, also encodes the sense of giving advice.

Disagreeing

Together with challenges, *Disagreeing* or contradiction expresses a negative evaluation by S of some aspect of H's positive face. By disagreeing, contradicting and challenging, S indicates that she thinks H is wrong, misguided, or unreasonable about some issue, such wrongness being associated with disapproval (Brown & Levinson, 1987, p. 66). *Disagreeing* in Chinese is 异議 *yìyì*, 爭議 *zhēngyì*, and 爭論 *zhēnglùn*. 异議 *yìyì* denotes different opinions or ideas one has, whereas 爭議 *zhēngyì* and 爭論 *zhēnglùn* refer to controversial issues.

CHINESE FACE (臉 *liǎn*, 面子 *miànzi*; or 臉面 *liǎnmiàn*) AND FTAS

In Chinese culture, *Giving Bad News* about H is not categorically perceived as a FTA. It often shows genuine concern of S about H's welfare and is not considered as an act depriving H of face.

The deviation of the conceptual definition of FTAs in Chinese culture from current western literature is to be expected. Since Chinese face values differ from, say, English and American face values (Mao, 1994), FTAs in Chinese culture have to be defined according to Chinese face values. Western face wants, as expounded by Brown and Levinson (1987), revolve around an individual's private concerns of his or her personal identity and territory, whereas Chinese face (臉 *liǎn*, 面子 *miànzi*) (Gu, 1990; Mao, 1994) is socially oriented and reciprocal among interactants (Mao, 1994; Zhang, this volume). In any interactive event, each participant's face is exposed. The face dynamics in interaction in Chinese culture dictates that both S and H observe, comply with, and act upon the face needs of the self and the other and attempt to adjust to and eventually achieve face balance in the on-going discourse.

Complaining

Complaining is a FTA pure and simple. Being complained against, from H's point of view, is rather face-losing, for nothing is more face-damaging than the fact that a person's behavior is not approved or accepted by other social members. Since S is aware of the inherent face-threat that her complaint entails, she has two problems to solve. The first is how to get the message across to H with as little threat to H's 臉 *liǎn* as possible. Depriving H of too much 臉 *liǎn* creates imbalance and possible conflict. Second, in the course of damaging H's 臉 *liǎn*, as complaining obviously does, how to give H certain 面子 *miànzi* so as to reassure H that she is still being respected as a social member despite the topicalized misdemeanor. Since in the act of complaining a balance has to be struck between depriving H of 臉 *liǎn* and giving 面子 *miànzi*, Chinese people in general avoid face to face complaints unless absolutely necessary.

Giving Bad News

Face concerns in the speech act of *Giving Bad News* are different depending on the nature of the "bad news". In the present study, the situations eliciting this act involve two types of news. The first type is news as embarrassing information, e.g., a professor has a big tear in his shirt; second is news about an event which is detrimental to H's goals, e.g., a student was flunked by a professor but doesn't know it yet. When imparting the first type of news, S's action encodes two kinds of face-related information: S shows genuine concern for H's 臉 *liǎn* when the latter is unintentionally and unknowingly violating some marginal social conventions/expectations. By virtue of pointing out the problem, S is trying to save H's 臉 *liǎn* in the public eye. At the same time, S's action reflects the censure and disapproval on behalf of social conventions or his/her own standard. This amounts to criticism which is face-threatening. In such situations, whether or not S decides to perform the act hinges upon the outcome of the struggle between these two face considerations. The relationship between S and H plays an important role in such considerations. The closer the relationship, the more identified is S's face with H's and the more likely S will take it as his/her responsibility not to let H suffer any face loss. In imparting the second type of news, i.e., news that is detrimental to H, the idea of "embarrassment", as in the previous type of news, is normally absent. Chinese people do not consider such an act "face-threatening". Instead, it is generally regarded as a good deed for S to do since it is for the benefit of H. Unlike the previous "embarrassing news", probably no grudge will develop between S and H. Rather, H would feel grateful to S for making known to her what she must know eventually anyway.

Disagreeing

When *Disagreeing* takes place, interlocutors' face is directly confronted. In Chinese culture, open conflict is to be avoided and surface harmony to be maintained in any on-going interaction. *Disagreeing*, however, challenges this unwritten rule of social behavior and therefore puts the face of both interlocutors "on the spot". And yet, although the participants' face is challenged, it is not disregarded. In order to bring the *Disagreeing* situation to a compromising end, i.e., getting messages across and accepted, both sides must take care that the other person's opinion is not devalued too much, for being disagreed with is being denied the honor of one's opinion, which has everything to do with how one's face is viewed and valued. Therefore, in a *Disagreeing* situation, as in the case of many FTAs, to leave the interlocutor a certain amount of face, i.e., the option to exit respectably, is paramount to the success of the act as well as the preservation of surface harmony and amiable relationships.

METHOD

INSTRUMENT

THE INSTRUMENT FOR THIS STUDY was a 19-item production questionnaire (see Appendices A and B). Each item described a face-threatening situation after which the subject was asked to consider the situation and to write his or her response in the blank space provided. Some of the situations were selected from observed occurrences in mainland China, but similar or equivalent situations can be found in other cultures. In order to facilitate the informants' task and increase the validity of the data, ten of the situations were located in university settings, the remaining nine were daily life situations that can be seen everywhere. The reason for half of the items in the questionnaire having university settings is that all the respondents were either studying or working at a university, and university life was the most familiar to them. For the present study, the 12 items eliciting the three FTAs introduced above, that is, *Complaining*, *Giving Bad News*, and *Disagreeing*, will be analyzed.

The following is a list of the 12 situations and the key words by which they will be referred to in this paper.

Complaining situation

S2 *Noise* The daughter of your neighbor practices violin at home in the evening.

Bad news situations

S6 *Torn Shirt* You notice a big tear in the shirt your professor is wearing.

S7	*Poem*	Your classmate wants to publish a poem of his but you don't think it is good enough.
S8	*Spinach*	You see some spinach caught in the teeth of your classmate.
S10	*Breath*	Your classmate has garlic smell in his/her breath and you have a pack of chewing gum with you.
S12	*Ink Mark*	Your classmate has a black ink mark on his face.
S14	*Curtain*	A guest of your family always forgets to draw the curtain when changing clothes.
S17	*Dress*	Your roommate is wearing a dress which is very transparent.
S18	*Remark*	You overheard some negative remark your professor expressed about a good friend of yours.

Disagreeing situations

S13	*Blouse*	Your friend wants to buy a dress but you do not think it suits her.
S15	*Newspaper*	Your boss wants you to use his plan for the next issue of the newspaper, but you don't think the plan is very good.
S19	*Proposal*	You do not like some issues raised in a proposal submitted by another student.

Sample situation

S18	*Remark*	You go to see your professor and run into your good friend George, who is coming out of the office. When George is gone, you overhear your professor saying to other teachers in the office, "Unless this young man tries harder to catch up, I'm going to flunk him." Later that day, you run into George again. You would:

SUBJECTS

Thirty students (female and male) from Beijing Normal University responded to the questionnaire. Their ages ranged from 19 to 30 years.

RESULTS

COMPLAINING

THE SPEAKER'S OPTIONS IN RESPONDING TO THIS SITUATION are as follows: First of all, S has the possibility of completely opting out from performing the act, in other words, refraining from expressing censure altogether. Secondly, S has the possibility of expressing censure by choosing to carry out the act 'on-' or 'off-record' (Brown & Levinson, 1987). Off-record in the case of censure would be some hint relating to the inconvenience which results from the SUA. If S decides to complain on-record, she has a choice to realize the speech act with or without redress, i.e., S can choose whether or not to mitigate her speech act.

The *Complaining* situation (S2 *Noise*) in the questionnaire for this study involves a neighbor whose daughter takes violin lessons in the evenings and thereby makes a noise that prevents S from concentrating on her work.

The following are the strategies used by the respondents in this situation:

Complain

S informs H of his/her annoyance about the situation and advises H to take action to eliminate the source of trouble. On Olshtain and Weinbach's (1993) scale, this realization is still vague and indirect. By expressing general annoyance at the violation, S still tries to avoid open confrontation, which involves the more face-threatening acts of accusation, warning, and immediate threat.

當面找他們談這個問題。
Dāngmiàn zhǎo tāmen tán zhège wèntí.
(I would) talk to them face to face about the problem.

Complain in a Modest and Casual Manner

While complaining to H, S makes an effort to soften the complaining force by using mitigating devices such as softeners, hedging, or sounding casual in tone.

> 以一種輕鬆自在的方式向他們提出這個問題。
>
> *Yǐ yīzhǒng qīngsōng zìzài de fāngshì xiàng tāmen tíchū zhège wèntí.*
>
> (I would) talk to them about it in a very casual manner.

Suggest

While indicating that H should not give up practising, S suggests that H change the daughter's schedule or location of practice in order to avoid disturbing the neighbors.

> 白天練琴效果最好。
>
> *Báitiān liànqín xiàoguǒ zuìhǎo.*
>
> Daytime practice would yield best results.

Hope

S puts her suggestion as an expression of "hope" for improving the situation.

> 只是希望音量能怎麼著的減低點兒。
>
> *Zhǐshì xīwàng yīnliàng néng zěnmezhāo de jiǎndī diǎnr.*
>
> I'd hope that the sound volume could be somehow reduced.

> 希望她最好能在晚飯後練琴。
>
> *Xīwàng tā zuìhǎo néng zài wǎnfàn hòu liànqín.*
>
> I hope that maybe she could practice after dinner.

Negotiate

S puts forward suggestions of alternatives for H in a business-like manner.

> 找個机會和他們協商這個問題。
>
> *Zhǎo ge jīhuì hé tāmen xiéshāng zhège wèntí.*
>
> (I would) find a chance to negotiate with them.

Hint

S chooses to drop hints to the neighbor about the inconvenience they caused.

> 串門兒時，不經意地提到"近來失眠"。
>
> *Chuànménr shí, bù jīngyì de tídào "jìnlái shīmián".*
>
> When dropping by, casually mention "can't sleep lately".

The *Hope* and *Hint* strategies both fall under Olshtain and Weinbach's "below the level of reproach" strategy, which enables S to avoid explicit mention of the offensive event.

Praise + Suggestion

S brings up the topic of the violin practice in a positive way by praising the daughter's progress. After that, S makes "constructive" suggestions about the practice, such as the timing.

> 先夸"小姑娘真聰明，都會彈琴啦"。再和他們具體討論時間的問題。
>
> *Xiān kuā "xiǎo gūniang zhēn cōngming, dōu huì tánqín la". Zài hé tāmen jùtǐ tǎolùn shíjiān de wèntí.*
>
> First say "The little girl is so smart that she can play violin now!" Then discuss with them the time of her violin practice.

Retaliate

Instead of complaining directly, S chooses to make noises either to warn or to annoy the neighbors in return.

> （我會）在他們睡覺的時候放錄音機給他們聽。
>
> *(Wǒ huì) zài tāmen shuìjiào de shíhòu fàng lùyīnjī gěi tāmen tīng.*
>
> (I would) play my stereo real loud when they are sleeping.

Try to Cope

S would not complain but finds ways to bear with the noise.

> 糊窗戶，塞耳朵，或放很響的音樂。
>
> *Hú chuānghu, sāi ěrduo, huò fàng hěn xiǎng de yīnyuè.*
>
> Seal my windows, plug my ears, or listen to loud music.

找個安靜的地方。
Zhǎo ge ānjìng de dìfang.
Find a quiet place.

Remain Silent
Despite experienced discomfort, S would not say anything to the neighbor about the noise.

甚麼也不說。
Shénme yě bù shuō.
(would) not say anything.

我會很不高興的。
Wǒ huì hěn bù gāoxìng de.
(I would) be very unhappy.

Complain to Others
S chooses to vent all the annoyance behind the neighbor's back and criticize the neighbor to other people.

這種人真不自覺。也太過份了。左鄰右舍沒人能休息和工作。
Zhèizhǒng rén zhēn bù zìjué. Yě tài guòfèn le. Zuǒlín yòushè méirén néng xiūxi hé gōngzuò.
These folks are so inconsiderate! It's too much! Nobody around them can rest or work!

Wait and then Complain
S decides to wait and see if the situation will change for the better as the practice moves on. If the noise continues to bother S, S would then decide to complain to the neighbor.

Bear with It or Complain
S wants to consider other factors before deciding which action to take.

Table 1. Distribution of *Complaining* strategies (%)

Suggest	36
Try to Cope	20
Other	20
Hope	14
Complain	10

Table 1 shows the distribution of most frequently used *Complaining* strategies. The distribution of *Complaining* strategies indicates that on-record complaining is avoided. Rather, strategies proposing, in a constructive manner, how the source of irritation can be removed (*Suggest* and *Hope*) and strategies avoiding mention of the problem altogether by adjusting to the situation (*Try to Cope*) are favored ways of dealing with the disturbing event. These strategies attend to participants' face concerns and help maintain surface harmony, a crucial social factor governing Chinese daily life.

While the author who, as a member of the Chinese speech community, feels that the above data represent quite well the types of complaining strategies adopted by Chinese people in real life situations, the absence of one strategy, "non-verbal reminder", in the data does not seem representative of its frequent daily occurrence. In the author's experience, it appears to be the most frequently applied and most effective strategy in the kind of situation chosen for the study. An example from daily life in Beijing may serve as illustration. In the apartment buildings in Beijing, when such noise as amateur violin playing is constantly bothering the neighborhood, people will typically avoid making a face-to-face verbal complaint. Instead, the people who live close to the particularly noisy apartment would bang on the shared wall (if they live side by side to this neighbor), stamp their feet on the floor (if they live above), or poke the ceiling with a stick (if they live under), until the noise ceases. A more common method is to bang on the heating pipe. When the connected heating pipes are making a commotion in the whole building, the one apartment that is the cause of disturbing the neighbors is usually forced to give up. This strategy is both effective and, surprisingly, less face-threatening. In fact, many of the apartment buildings in Beijing thrive in greater harmony on this particular strategy. Because there is no finger pointing, "witch hunting", or direct confrontation, which would endanger both *liǎn* and *miànzi* the neighborhood continues to carry on their lives peacefully and amiably with each other as if nothing has happened — until the next commotion comes up.

GIVING BAD NEWS

Although Brown and Levinson (1987) defined the *Giving Bad News* about H as an act "that (shows) that S doesn't care about (or is indifferent to) H's positive face" (pp. 66–67), the data collected for this study suggest that the opposite is the case. Those who chose to inform H of something negative about her- or himself (relating to H's personal appearance or academic performance, for instance) generally showed genuine concern about H's welfare. The situations involving giving embarrassing information are S6 *Torn Shirt*, S7 *Poem*, S8 *Spinach*, S10 *Breath*, S12 *Ink Mark*, and S18 *Remark*. The following strategies were used in order to deliver bad news in these situations.

Inform Directly

S directly informs H of news which is either embarrassing or unfavorable to H.

王教授，您的襯衫開線了。
Wáng jiàoshòu, nín de chènshān kāixiàn le.
Prof. Wang, your shirt seam is open.　　　　　　　(S6 *Torn Shirt*)

是不錯，可要拿出去發表就難說了。
Shì bùcuò, kě yào ná chūqu fābiǎo jiù nǎnshuō le.
It's not bad, but whether it can be published is hard to say.
　　　　　　　　　　　　　　　　　　　　　　(S7 *Poem*)

你牙縫裡有菠菜。
Nǐ yáfèng lǐ yǒu bōcài.
You have spinach in your teeth.　　　　　　　　　(S8 *Spinach*)

Inform + Suggest

Besides informing H of bad news, S goes on to advise H on the actions H should take.

王教授，您的襯衫開線了。快找人縫縫吧。
Wáng jiàoshòu, nín de chènshān kāixiàn le. Kuài zhǎo rén féngfeng ba.
Prof. Wang, your shirt seam is open, better have it mended.
　　　　　　　　　　　　　　　　　　　　　　(S6 *Torn Shirt*)

你牙縫裡有東西,快去刷刷牙吧。
Nǐ yáfèng lǐ yǒu dōngxi, kuài qù shuāshua yá ba.
You have something in your teeth, better go brush your teeth.
(S8 Spinach)

Hint/Joking

S tries to inform H of the bad news through hinting or joking.

婉轉地提醒他檢查一下衣服是否穿整齊了。
Wǎnzhuǎn de tíxǐng tā jiǎnchá yīxià yīfu shìfǒu chuān zhěngqí le.
Ask him in a roundabout way to check if he is properly attired.
(S6 Torn Shirt)

提議這位同學再另寫一首。
Tíyì zhèwèi tóngxué zài lìng xiě yī shǒu.
Suggest to the classmate that he write another poem. (S7 Poem)

現在市場上的衣服質量太差。穿沒幾天就開線。
Xiànzài shìchǎng shàng de yīfu zhìliang tài chà. Chuān méi jǐ tiān jiù kāixiàn.
Nowadays the quality of clothes is so poor that they fall apart after only a few days... (S6 Torn Shirt)

您工作太忙。顧不上照顧自己。
Nín gōngzuò tài máng. Gù bù shàng zhàogu zìjǐ.
You've been too busy with your work to take care of yourself.
(S6 Torn Shirt)

如今想發表點兒東西可難著呢。
Rújīn xiǎng fābiǎo diǎnr dōngxi kě nán zhe ne.
It's really difficult to get anything published nowadays. (S7 Poem)

今兒看起來剛下戲臺。
Jīr kànqilai gāng xià xìtái.
Did you just step down from an opera stage? (S12 Ink Mark)

你是不是剛唱完花臉呀？
Nǐ shì bù shì gāng chàng wán huāliǎn ya?
Were you just singing the *Painted Role*? (S12 Ink Mark)

In these last two joking utterances, the allusion to Beijing Opera (e.g., 戲臺 *xìtái* 'opera stage', 花臉 *huāliǎn* '*Painted Role*') is made. The point of the allusion, as with many jokes, is associated with the conventional part of the event of analogy, in this case, with the extravagant facial make-up of the characters. In this way, the joke is understood to refer to the hearer's face, i.e., something is on his/her face.

Depends

S wants to consider such factors as personal relationships, age and status differences and the consequences of either informing or not informing H of the facts before deciding upon whether or not to give H the bad news.

如果我和這個教授很熟的話，我會告訴他。要不然的話，我會裝著沒看見。
Rúguǒ wǒ hé zhège jiàoshòu hěn shú de huà, wǒ huì gàosu tā. Yàoburán de huà, wǒ huì zhuāng zhe méi kànjiàn.
If I were very familiar with the professor, I'd tell him; otherwise, I'd pretend that I didn't see it. (S6 *Torn Shirt*)

如果教授是個女的就告訴她；否則甚麼也不說。
Rúguǒ jiàoshòu shì ge nǚ de jiù gàosu tā; fǒuzé shénme yě bù shuō.
If the professor were a woman, I'd tell her; otherwise, I wouldn't say anything. (S6 *Torn Shirt*)

如果這個同學是我的好朋友，我會坦率地告訴他我的想法。否則就甚麼也不說。

Rúguǒ zhège tóngxué shì wǒ de hǎo péngyou, wǒ huì tǎnshuài de gàosu tā wǒ de xiǎngfǎ. Fǒuzé jiù shénme yě bù shuō.

If the classmate were a good friend, I'd let him know my opinion; otherwise, I wouldn't say anything. (S7 Poem)

Say Nothing

S does not want to break the news in order not to risk embarrassment.

Pretend Not to See

This strategy pertains to situations involving H's appearance. S does not show any awareness about the fact that something is wrong with the way H looks.

Table 2. Distribution of *Giving Bad News* strategies (personal appearance) (%)

Hint/Joking	40
Tell + Suggest	25
Inform Directly	15
Say Nothing	12
Other	8

Table 2 represents the distribution of strategies in situations involving personal appearance. In responding to the *S6 Torn Shirt* situation, none of the respondents chose to give the information directly. Although 40% of the Chinese respondents did choose to inform the professor that his shirt was torn, they immediately added 快找人縫縫吧 *kuài zhǎo rén féngfeng ba* 'better have it mended' or 最好換一件 *zuìhǎo huàn yíjiàn* 'better change your shirt' which sound like suggesting or giving advice to the professor. 13% of the respondents decided to use a hint to the professor about the torn shirt by either asking what happened to the professor's shirt or asking the professor to "check his clothes".

Two situations (*S7 Poem* and *S18 Remark*) contain bad news concerning H's academic performance. Threatening someone's "academic face" is a very sensitive issue for the respondents who were themselves academics. As in Table 2, Table 3 shows that the majority of the responses elicited were also *Hint/Joking*. More people chose not to say anything than to confront H directly with the news.

Table 3: Distribution of *Giving Bad News* strategies
(academic performance) (%)

Hint/Joking	45
Tell + Suggest	22
Say Nothing	22
Inform Directly	8
Other	3

Why then is *Joking* such a highly preferred strategy in the act of *Giving Bad News*? In Chinese culture, surface harmony and smoothness in an interactive event is paramount to other considerations. Most of the times, the success of one's mission, be it *Complaining* or *Giving Bad News*, depends heavily on how one delivers the message. *Joking* often serves as a good means to deflect embarrassment and unpleasantness in situations which are inherently so, such as the present *Giving Bad News* situations. It is therefore not surprising that the respondents scored high on this strategy. Some of the jokes they made are in fact highly conventionalized, or even clichés, as the two *Joking* samples illustrated above. *Joking* provides H with a chance to laugh things off together with S; thus the sense of embarrassment is reduced or eliminated. Whether or not *Joking* is selected as a strategy depends on the interlocutor relationship. While it is used among status equals and from a status higher to a status lower person, it is not seen as an appropriate strategy to use from a status lower to a status higher interlocutor. Thus in the case of the professor's torn shirt, none of the respondents opted for this strategy.

Compared with the above two types of *Giving Bad News* situations, the news to be communicated in *S14 Curtain* and *S17 Dress* is the most sensitive to gender difference in responses. As Table 4 shows, the majority chose to tell H, a female participant, their opinion directly. Although some of the respondents expressed various degrees of indifference to these two situations with such remarks as "who cares" or "no big deal", most of them still tried to alert H about the potential embarrassment. The female respondents showed special concerns towards H. Some male respondents dismissed the situations for the reason that they never encountered such situations.

Table 4. Distribution of *Giving Bad News* strategies (physical exposure) (%)

Inform Directly	40
Hint/Joking	22
Other	20
Tell + Suggest	18

DISAGREEING

Disagreeing is another category of FTAs that expresses S's negative evaluation of some aspect of H's positive face. There are three *Disagreeing* situations in this study. In the *S13 Blouse* situation, the two parties, status-equals and of the same age, are at a garment store, and S does not think that H has made the right choice for a purchase. In the *S15 Newspaper* situation, a status lower and younger writer for a student newspaper has different opinions from her or his supervisor about the editing plan of their paper. Finally, in the *S19 Proposal* situation, a status higher student leader does not approve of a student's proposal concerning departmental affairs.

The following strategies were used by the respondents to disagree with their interlocutors:

Criticize

S not only directly expresses disagreement to H's choices, plans etc., but also criticize H's decisions.

> 顏色太鮮艷，式樣太摩登。要我可穿不出去。
>
> *Yánsè tài xiānyàn, shìyang tài módēng. Yào wǒ kě chuān bù chūqù*
>
> The color is too loud, the style is too modern. I wouldn't dare wear it anywhere. (S13 Blouse)

Offer Opinion

S directly expresses a different opinion, but gives H the benefit of choice.

告訴他我的看法，當然他自己拿主意。每個人品味不同。只要他喜歡就可以買。

Gàosu tā wǒ de kànfǎ, dānráng tā zìjǐ ná zhǔyì. Měige rén pǐnwèi bùtóng. Zhǐyào tā xǐhuan jiù kěyǐ mǎi.

Tell her my opinion, but add that everybody has different taste. If she really likes it, she can go ahead and buy it. (S13 Blouse)

亮出我的計劃，但說我可以做些改動。

Liàngchū wǒ de jìhuà, dàn shuō wǒ kěyǐ zuò xiē gǎidòng.

Tell him about my plan, but add that I can make changes. (S15 Newspaper)

告訴他我的想法。

Gàosu tā wǒ de xiǎngfǎ.

Tell him what I think. (S19 Proposal)

Praise + Disagree

Before expressing a different opinion, S praises the positive side of H's choice or plan.

先談他提到的好的地方，然后再指出他的弱點。

Xiān tán tā tídào de hǎo de dìfan, ránhòu zài zhǐchū tā de ruòdiǎn.

Talk about the good points he raised first and then point out the weaknesses of his proposal. (S19 Proposal)

指出他的計劃不現實，但希望他將來能提出更多的計劃。

Zhǐchū tā de jìhuà bù xiànshí, dàn xīwàng tā jiānglái néng tíchū gèngduō de jìhuà.

Point out that his proposal is impractical, but hope that he would bring up other proposals in the future. (S19 Proposal).

首先表揚他對系裡工作的熱情態度，並感謝他的計劃。然后指出他計劃中的不現實的地方。最后鼓勵他再接再勵。
Shǒuxiān biǎoyáng tā dui xìli gōngzuò de rèqíng tàidu, bìng gǎnxiè tā de jìhuà. Ránhòu zhǐchū tā jìhuà zhōng de bù xiànshí de dìfang. Zuìhòu gǔlì tā zàijiē-zàilì.

First praise his enthusiasm in departmental work, and thank him for submitting the proposal, then point out the impractical parts of his proposal. Finally, encourage him to keep up his enthusiasm in departmental affairs. *(S19 Proposal)*

Appreciation + Disagree

S expresses appreciation of H's intention before pointing out the impracticality of H's choice.

感謝他的積极熱情，但指出他提議中的不足之處。
Gǎnxiè tā de jījí rèqíng, dàn zhǐchū tā tíyì zhōng de bùzú zhīchù.

Thank him for his enthusiasm but point out the weakness of his proposal. *(S19 Proposal)*

Disagree + Encouragement

After disagreeing with H's choice or plan, S offers encouragement to H for future endeavors.

指出他的提案不切實可行，但歡迎他今后提出更多更好的建議。
Zhǐchū tā de tí'àn bù qièshí kěxíng, dàn huānyíng tā jīnhòu tíchū gèng duō gèng hǎo de jiànyì.

Point out that his proposal is impractical, but add that any proposals in the future would be welcome. *(S19 Proposal)*

Suggest

Instead of offering different opinions, S suggests alternatives to H's choices or plans for H to consider.

讓他修改。
Ràng tā xiūgǎi.

Ask him to revise his proposal. *(S19 Proposal)*

請他將其要點再與其他學生磋商一下。
Qǐng tā jiāng qí yàodiǎn zài yǔ qítā xuéshēng cuōshāng yīxià.
Ask him to talk to other students about the points he made.
(S19 Proposal)

Negotiate
S tries to strike a compromise with H about their differences in opinion.

找出兩個計劃的共同點。再設法擬一個新計劃。
Zhǎochū liǎng ge jìhuà de gòngtóngdiǎn. Zài shèfǎ nǐ yíge xīn jìhuà.
Try to find the common ground between the two plans and devise a third plan. (S15 Newspaper)

和這個學生商討一下。接受他的部份建議。
Hé zhège xuésheng shāngtǎo yīxià. Jiēshòu tā de bùfen jiànyì.
Negotiate with the student, accept part of his plan. (S19 Proposal)

Ask Questions
By asking questions, S tries to lead H to realize S's different opinion.

你真的喜歡這個嗎?
Nǐ zhēn de xǐhuan zhège ma?
You really like it? (S13 Blouse)

問他是怎麼想出那些條款的。
Wèn tā shì zěnme xiǎngchū nàxiē tiáokuǎn de.
Ask he how he came up with those points. (S19 Proposal)

Defer Response
Wait and look around before uttering any different opinions.

告訴他我會仔細地研究一下他的提案。
Gàosu tā wǒ huì zǐxì de yánjiū yīxià tā de tí'àn.
Tell him I would seriously consider his proposal.   (S19 Proposal)

Opt Out

S avoids disagreeing with H by remaining silent, making remarks, disregard H's suggestions, or complying with H's decisions.

要是喜歡就買吧。
Yàoshi xǐhuan jiù mǎi ba.
If you like it, go ahead and buy it.   (S13 Blouse)

這次用他的，下次用我的。
Zhècì yòng tā de. Xiàcì yòng wǒ de.
Use his plan this time, mine next time.   (S15 Newspaper)

用他的計劃。
Yòng tā de jìhuà.
Follow his plan.   (S15 Newspaper)

不提我的計劃。
Bù tí wǒ de jìhuà.
Not mention my plan.   (S15 Newspaper)

改變我的計劃。
Gǎibiàn wǒ de jìhuà.
Change my plan.   (S15 Newspaper)

In disagreeing with a friend's taste in the *S13 Blouse* situation (age and status equals), *Offer Opinion* and *Suggest* were the two most preferred strategies. It means that the majority of the respondents have left it to H to decide for herself. Only 6% of the respondents ventured to criticize H's choice. Another 10% of them chose to remain silent (see Table 5).

Table 5. Distribution of *Disagreeing* strategies (S13 Blouse) (%)

Offer Opinion	44
Suggest	30
Say Nothing	10
Other	10
Criticize	6

Table 6. Distribution of *Disagreeing* strategies (S15 Newspaper) (%)

Offer Opinion	50
Negotiate	44
Other	4
Say Nothing	2

In the *S15 Newspaper* situation (see Table 6), where a superior imposes a different plan on a younger colleague (status lower, younger person to status higher, older person), none of the respondents chose to criticize the superior's plan or even make suggestions. Half of them ventured to announce their different plans to their superior in an indirect way, by offering opinions. The other half (interestingly, all of them were male respondents) chose to negotiate or comply with their superior's plan.

Table 7. Distribution of *Disagreeing* strategies (S19 Proposal) (%)

Suggest	30
Offer Opinion	20
Plus Strategy	19
Negotiate	16
Other	15

In the *S19 Proposal* situation (see Table 7), where a student leader disagrees with an ordinary student's suggestion (status higher to lower), a frequently occurring strategy which did not appear in response to the other two *Disagreeing* situations is the so-called *Plus Strategy*. About 19% of Chinese respondents applied "praise", "appreciation", or "encouragement", or any combination of them in their *Disagreeing* utterances.

The above data indicate that the Chinese respondents are status and age conscious in disagreeing with other people. In the three situations under the study, more power in terms of age or status advantage affects the range of linguistic options in that a status higher person has more strategies to manipulate, whereas it does not seem a common practice for a status lower person to use a *Plus Strategy*, i.e., a combination of positive politeness strategies and *Disagreeing*, a negative politeness strategy.

When an American who speaks and writes perfect Chinese responded to both the English and Chinese version of the questionnaire, he gave two cross-culturally different responses to the *S13 Blouse* situation (disagreeing with a friend's taste in choosing clothes): In Chinese, he told H that he did not think the blouse she chose was any better looking than the one she was wearing and persuaded her to "go look around some more before coming back here" (现在看看，然后再回來買 xiànzài kànkan, ránhòu zài huílai mǎi); while in English, he "would not offer any unsolicited opinion because it is a matter of personal taste". In a retrospective interview with this informant, who had lived and worked as a journalist in Beijing for more than four years, explained that his response to the situation in Chinese was based on his experience and observation in China and that it reflected what he would do in the same situation in China. His observation is to the point. The data provided by the native speakers of Chinese in response to the *S13 Blouse* situation correspond to the American nonnative speaker's "Chinese" response. In general, Chinese people take much more liberty to comment on what Americans consider to be other people's personal matters, such as taste in clothes and hair style.

CONCLUSION

WITHIN THE SCOPE OF THE TWELVE SITUATIONS UNDER STUDY, a certain pattern of linguistic decision can be observed with respect to the three FTAs: *Complaining*, *Giving Bad News*, and *Disagreeing*. In the *Complaining* situation, the Chinese tend to use a *Suggest* strategy more often (if ever they indeed decide to confront the problem verbally). In the *Giving Bad News* situations, *Hint/Joking* are most preferred for conveying two out of three types of unwelcome information (personal appearance and academic performance, but not physical exposure). The *Disagreeing* situations elicited most frequently the strategies of *Offer Opinion* and *Suggest*. As was to be expected, strategy choice varied to some extent according to referential goal and interlocutor relationship. However, the general pattern emerging from this study is that FTAs in Chinese tend to be performed in a cooperative rather than confrontational manner. By emphasizing common ground and constructive problem solutions, attention is paid to both participants' 臉 *liǎn* and 面子 *miànzi*. Thus an effort is made to diffuse the potentially disruptive effect of FTAs. For the nonnative speaker of Chinese who may find it particularly difficult to carry out FTAs without causing offense the described pattern appears to be a safe approach to follow ◆

APPENDIX A

QUESTIONNAIRE
(Pinyin transcription did not appear in the original instrument)

年齡 _____ 姓別 _____ 出生地 _____
niánlíng   *xìngbié*   *chūshēngdì*

母語 _____
mǔyǔ

其他能講的語言 _____
qítā néng jiǎng de yǔyán

請您將自己置身于以下所列情形之中，寫出您在一般的情況下的眞實反應（即，您會說甚麽，會做甚麽，包括無聲反應）。倘若您的反應在某些情況下取決于對方的姓別、相對年齡等等，請您詳細解釋。

Qǐng nín jiāng zìjǐ zhìshēn yú yǐxià suǒliè qíngxíng zhīzhōng, xiě chū nín zài yībān de qíngkuàng xià de zhēnshí fǎnyìng (jí, nín huì shuō shénme, huì zuò shénme, bāokuò wúshēng fǎnyìng). Tǎngruò nín de fǎnyìng zài mǒuxiē qíngkuàng xià qǔjué yú duìfāng de xìngbié, xiāngduì niánlíng děngděng, qǐng nín xiángxì jiěshì.

1. 你的朋友來你家玩時，對你最心愛的工藝品讚口不絕，說它非常精緻漂亮。

    Nǐ de péngyou lái nǐ jiā wán shí, duì nǐ zuì xīn'ài de gōngyìpǐn zànkǒubùjué, shuō tā fēicháng jīngzhì piàoliang.

你會：

Nǐ huì:

2. 你和隔壁的鄰居相處一向不錯，可是近來每天晚上他們的女兒在家學拉提琴，吵得你甚麼事也幹不成。

    Nǐ hé gébì de língju xiāngchǔ yíxiàng bùcuò, kěshi jìnlái měitiān wǎnshang tāmen de nǚ'er zài jiā xué lā tíqín, chǎo de nǐ shénme shì yě gàn bù chéng.

你會：

Nǐ huì:

3. 你和你的朋友去逛百貨公司。你的朋友看到貨架上有一件他／她向往以久的商品，非常想買，可是沒有帶夠錢。他／她不斷地說"真是的！我一直想買這個，要是我帶夠錢就好了！"

    Nǐ hé nǐ de péngyou qù guàn bǎihuò gōngsī. Nǐ de péngyou kàn dao huòjià shang yǒu yíjiàn tā xiǎngwǎng de shāngpǐn, fēicháng xiǎng mǎi, kěshì méiyǒu dài gòu qián. Tā bùduàn de shuō: "zhēngshì de! Wǒ yìzhí xiǎng mǎi zhège, yàoshi wǒ dài gòu qián jiù hǎo le!"

你會：

Nǐ huì:

4. 你和一個朋友去看電影。你的朋友坐下後不斷問你"你的座位怎麼樣，你坐那兒看得清嗎？"

   Nǐ hé yíge péngyou qù kàn diànjǐng. Nǐ de péngyou zuòxia hòu bùduàn wèn nǐ: "nǐ de zuòwei zěnmeyàng, nǐ zuò nàr kàn de qīng ma?"

你會：

Nǐ huì:

5. 你的朋友想向你借一筆錢，並保證儘早還你。你又不想借給他／她錢，可又不好傷他／她的面子。

   Nǐ de péngyou xiǎng xiàng nǐ jiè yībǐ qián, bìng bǎozhèng jìnzǎo huán nǐ. Nǐ yòu bù xiǎng jiègěi tā qián, kě yòu bù hǎo shāng tā de miànzi.

你會：

Nǐ huì:

6. 你和你的教授準備一同去圖書館，還沒出他辦公室的門，你發現他穿的襯衫有一處開線的地方。

   Nǐ hé nǐ de jiàoshòu zhǔnbèi yītóng qù túshūguǎn, hái méi chū tā bàngōngshǐ de mén, nǐ fāxiàn tā chuān de chènshān yǒu yīchù kāixiàn de dìfang.

你會：

Nǐ huì:

7. 你的一個同班同學寫了一首詩，自鳴得意，準備拿去發表。你看了他的詩後，覺得此詩無望得以發表。

   Nǐ de yíge tóngbān tóngxué xiě le yīshǒu shī, zìmíngdéyì, zhǔnbèi ná qu fābiǎo. Nǐ kàn le tā de shī hòu, juéde cǐ shī wúwàng déyǐ fābiǎo.

你會：

Nǐ huì:

8. 吃過午飯，你和你的同班同學一起去上課。路上你看到他／她牙裡有一點韭菜渣。

    Chī guo wǔfàn, nǐ hé nǐ de tóngbān tóngxué yīqǐ qu shàngkè. Lù shang nǐ kàn dao tā yáli yǒu yīdiǎn jiǔcaizhār.

你會：

Nǐ huì:

9. 你的室友經常逃避值日，你對他／她很有意見，覺得有必要強調他／她的責任。

    Nǐ de shǐyǒu jīngcháng táobì zhírì, nǐ duì tā hěn yǒu yìjian, juéde yǒu bìyào qiángdiào tā de zérèn.

你會：

Nǐ huì:

10. 你和同班同學談話時發現他／她嘴裡大蒜氣味很濃。你身上剛巧帶了口香糖。

    Nǐ hé tóngbān tóngxué tánhuà shí fāxiàn tā zuǐli dàsuàn qìwei hěn nóng. Nǐ shēnshang gāngqiǎo dài le kǒuxiāngtáng.

你會：

Nǐ huì:

11. 在機場，你看見一位婦女吃力地抬著兩個大皮箱。你剛巧知道走廊拐彎的地方有行李車出租。

    Zài jīchǎng, nǐ kànjian yíwèi fùnǚ chīlì de tá zhe liǎngge dà píxiāng. Nǐ gāngqiǎo zhīdao zǒuláng guǎiwān de dìfang yǒu xínglichē chūzū.

你會：

Nǐ huì:

12. 在校園裡你碰見你的同班同學小林。小林的臉上有一塊墨跡。

    Zài xiàoyuán li nǐ pèngjian nǐ de tóngbān tóngxué Xiǎo Lín. Xiǎo Lín de liǎn shang yǒu yíkuài mòji.

你會：

Nǐ huì:

13. 在一服裝店裡，你的一個朋友看上了一件很時髦的紅色襯衫並決定買下一件。可你覺得這件襯衫不論從顏色和式樣上都不適合她。

    Zài yī fúzhuāngdiàn li, nǐ de yíge péngyou kàn shang le yíjiàn hěn shímáo de hóngsè chènshān bìng juédìng mǎi xia yíjiàn. Kě nǐ juéde zhè jiàn chènshān bùlùn cóng yánsè hé shìyang shang dōu bù shìhé tā.

你會：

Nǐ huì:

14. 你們家最近來了一位与你同歲的客人。在她住的日子裡，你發現她似乎在換衣服時總忘記拉上窗帘。你意識到住在對面房子裡的人們可以很清楚地看見這邊房子裡的一切。

    Nǐmen jiāli zuìjìn lái le yíwèi yǔ nǐ tóngsuì de kèren. Zài tā zhù de rìzi li, nǐ fāxiàn tā sìhu zài huàn yīfu shí zǒng wàngji lāshang chuānglián. Nǐ yìshi dao zhù zài duìmian fángzi li de rénmen kěyǐ hěn qīngchǔ de kànjian zhèbian fángzi li de yíqiè.

你會：

Nǐ huì:

15. 你是系板報組的編輯，對下期板報已有了很好的計劃。可是系輔導員把你叫到他的辦公室給你看一個他擬好的詳細的下期板報計劃。這個計劃和你的截然不同。

    Nǐ shì xì bǎnbào zǔ de biānji, duì xiàqī bǎnbào yǐ yǒu le hěn hǎo de jìhuà. Kěshi xì fúdǎoyuán bǎ nǐ jiào dao tā de bàngōngshǐ gěi nǐ kàn yíge tā nǐ hǎo de xiángxì de xiàqī bǎnbào jìhuà. Zhège jìhuà hé nǐ de jiérán bùtòng.

你會：

Nǐ huì:

16. 在教學樓的走廊上，你看見一位女教師的背上落了許多粉筆沫，她穿著一件暗綠色的連衣裙，粉筆灰非常顯眼。

    Zài jiàoxuélóu de zǒuláng shang, ní kànjian yíwèi nǚ lǎoshī de bèi shang luò le xǔduō fěnbǐmò, tā chuān zhe yíjiàn àn lǜsè de liányīqún, fěnbǐhuī fēicháng xiǎnyǎn.

你會：

Nǐ huì:

17. 你和室友準憊一同去參加一個舞會。你的室友打算穿她新買的連衣裙，但她似乎沒有注意到燈光下她的連衣裙很透明。

    Nǐ hé shǐyǒu zhǔnbèi yītóng qù cānjiā yíge wǔhuì. Nǐ de shǐyǒu dǎsuàn chuān tā xīn mǎi de liányīqún, dàn tā sìhū měiyǒu zhùyì dao dēngguāng xià tā de liányīqún hěn tòumíng.

你會：

Nǐ huì:

18. 在去會你的教授的時候你剛巧遇見你的好朋友小張從
    教授辦公室裡出來。小張走後，你聽見教授對辦公室的其他
    教師說"如果這個年輕人再不努力趕上其他
    的學生，我的課他別打算及格！"同一天晚些時候，
    你又碰見了小張。

    Zài qù huì nǐ de jiàoshòu de shíhou nǐ gāngqiǎo yùjian nǐ de hǎo péngyou Xiǎo Zhāng cóng jiàoshòu bàngōngshǐ li chūlai. Xiǎo Zhāng zǒu hòu, nǐ tīngjian jiàoshòu duì bàngōngshǐ de qítā jiàoshī shuō: "Rúguǒ zhège niánqīngrén zài bù nǔlì gǎnshang qítā de xuéshēng, wǒ de kè tā bié dǎsuàn jígé!" Tóng yì tiān wǎn xiē shíhòu, nǐ yòu pèngjiàn le Xiǎo Zhāng.

你會：

Nǐ huì:

19. 你是系學生會主席。系裡的一個學生向學生會提交了一份有關系裡
    事務的建議書。你看過這份建議書後，覺得裡面有些條文很
    不切合實際。

    Nǐ shì xì xuéshēnghuì zhǔxí. Xìli de yíge xuéshēng xiàng xuéshēnghuì tíjiāo le yīfèn yǒuguān xìli shìwu de jiànyishū. Nǐ kàn guo zhèfen jiànyishū hòu, juéde lǐbian yǒuxiē tiáowén hěn bù qièhé shíjì.

你會：

Nǐ huì:

APPENDIX B

ENGLISH TRANSLATION OF QUESTIONNAIRE

Information about you:

age _____ sex _____ birthplace _____
mother tongue _____
what other languages(s) do you speak? _____

Now please imagine yourself in the following situations, and write down exactly what kind of reaction you would *normally* have in such real life situations. (e.g., what you might say, or what you might do, including silence etc.) Should you find in certain situations your reaction would depend upon whether the person you are dealing with is a male or female, older or younger than you etc., please give specific explanations under the situation.

1. Your friend is visiting you at your home, and you find her lingering around your favorite handicraft — a miniature bamboo boat and repeatedly expressing her admiration: "It's so pretty, so real!"

    You would:

2. You and your next door neighbor usually get along well, but recently, their daughter is taking violin lessons at home in the evenings and you find yourself unable to do anything with the noise.

   You would:

3. You and your friend are in a department store. Suddenly something on the shelf catches his/her eyes and he/she exclaims: "My, I've been looking for this for a long time, I just have to buy one. I wish I had more money with me!"

   You would:

4. You go to a movie theater with a friend of yours, who keeps asking you after sitting down: "Are you comfortable sitting there?"

   You would:

5. Your friend asks you to lend him/her some money, and promises to return it to you as soon as possible. You don't want to either lend him/her the money or hurt him/her.

   You would:

6. You and your professor are heading for the library together, but just before leaving his office, you see a big tear in his shirt.

   You would:

7. Your classmate wrote a poem which he likes very much and is going to get it published. After reading the poem, you think that the poem really has no chance to be published.

   You would:

8. After lunch, you and your classmate are going to attend a class. You see that he/she has some spinach caught in his/her teeth.

   You would:

9. Your housemate always neglects his/her cleaning duty, it irritates you a lot and you feel that you have to point out to him/her that he/she should carry out his/her duty.

   You would:

10. You are talking with your classmate and find that his/her breath smells strongly of garlic. You happen to have a pack of chewing gum with you.

    You would:

11. At an airport, you see a woman struggling to carry two big suitcases, and you know there are baggage carts for rent right around the corner.

    You would:

12. You run into your classmate John on campus, and see that he has a black mark on his face.

    You would:

13. At a clothes store, your friend is very much taken by a fashionable red blouse and decides to buy it. However, you do not think the blouse is suitable for her either in terms of its style or color.

    You would:

14. A guest who is of the same age as you is staying with your family. You find that she seems to always forget to draw the curtain when she changes her clothes, and you know that the people living in the next house can see clearly through the window.

    You would:

15. You are the editor of a newspaper in your department. You already have a good plan for the next issue of the paper, but the department instructor asks you to come to his office and gives you a specific but different plan for the next issue of the newspaper.

    You would:

16. In the lobby outside your classroom, you see a woman teacher who has a lot of chalk dust on the back of her dark green dress.

    You would:

17. You and your roommate are going to a party. Your roommate is going to wear a new dress, but she does not seem to realize that in the light the dress is very transparent.

    You would:

18. You go to see your professor and run into your good friend George, who is coming out of the office. When George is gone, you overhear your professor saying to other teachers in the office, "Unless this young man tries harder to catch up, I'm going to flunk him." Later that day, you run into George again.

    You would:

19. You are the chairperson of the Student Committee in your department. One of the students submits a proposal concerning some of the departmental affairs. After reading the proposal, you think some issues that he/she raises are impractical.

    You would:

Lei Ye

COMPLIMENTING IN MANDARIN CHINESE

INTRODUCTION

PRAGMATICS HAS BECOME INCREASINGLY IMPORTANT to the study of linguistics. In the field of second language learning and teaching, pragmatic knowledge is regarded as a central component of communicative competence. Because interlanguage pragmatics research has clearly demonstrated that learners transfer their pragmatic knowledge from their first language to a second (Scarcella, 1983; Beebe, Takahashi, & Uliss-Weltz, 1990; Kasper, 1992; Takahashi & Beebe, 1993), it is crucial to determine the nature of their L1 pragmatic knowledge. This study, therefore, is designed to investigate one such aspect of L1 pragmatic competence: the speech event of complimenting in Mandarin Chinese.

LITERATURE REVIEW

A compliment is a polite speech act which explicitly or implicitly attributes credit to someone for something which is valued positively by the speaker and hearer (Holmes, 1986). How to give compliments and respond to them, therefore, constitutes a part of the communicative competence of every member of a speech community, which is taken for granted by the speakers. However, studies of compliments and compliment responses have shown that this small speech event is actually far more complicated and revealing than it appears, in terms of the relation between language, society, and culture (Pomerantz, 1978; Wolfson, 1981; Wolfson & Manes, 1981; Manes, 1983; Knapp, Happer, & Bell, 1984; Holmes, 1986; Holmes & Brown, 1987; Herbert, 1988, 1990, 1991; Herbert & Straight, 1989; Wolfson, 1989; Lee, 1990).

Ye, L. (1995). Complimenting in Mandarin Chinese. In G. Kasper (Ed.), *Pragmatics of Chinese as native and target language* (Technical Report #5, pp. 207–295). Honolulu, Hawai'i: University of Hawai'i, Second Language Teaching & Curriculum Center.

Studies of compliments have focused on the following areas: compliment formulas, topics, distribution and frequency, compliment rejoinders[1], function, and compliments as a sex-preferential strategy. Most of the studies have concentrated on complimenting in different varieties of English (Pomerantz, 1978; Wolfson, 1981; Wolfson & Manes, 1981; Knapp et al, 1984; Holmes, 1986; Pomerantz, 1987; Holmes & Brown, 1987; Herbert, 1988, 1990; Herbert & Straight, 1989; Wolfson, 1989; Lee, 1990); very few have examined compliments in other languages (Zuo, 1988; Lewandowska-Tomaszczyk, 1989; Herbert, 1991).

Compliment formulas

Systematic studies of the linguistic form of compliments reveal a regularity in compliments as formulas. Characteristics include uses of limited syntactic patterns and a small range of words with unspecifically positive meaning. Based on their studies of 686 American English compliments gathered through observation of everyday interactions, Wolfson and Manes (1981) concluded that "compliments in American English are formulaic in nature" (p. 115). Their analysis of the syntax of compliment utterances resulted in three most commonly occurring syntactic patterns, the first of which accounted for 50% of these three patterns in their corpus:

NP is/looks (really) ADJ
    Your dress is beautiful.
    Your hair looks nice.

I (really) like/love NP
    I really like your car.
    I love your hair.

PRO is (really) (a) ADJ NP
    That's really a nice dress.

---

[1] The term "rejoinder" is used here instead of "response", which is common in the literature. This is done to maintain a clear distinction between the complimentee's actual utterence in reply to a compliment ("rejoinder") and her performance ("response") either within the context of a compliment-giving situation, or more specifically, on the data collection instrument used in the present study.

Similarly, their investigation of the semantic formulas showed that the overwhelming majority of compliments contained a highly restricted set of adjectives and verbs. The most commonly used adjectives were those with unspecifically positive semantic load: "nice", "good", "beautiful", "pretty", and "great". In accordance with the use of adjectives, a very limited numbers of verbs expressing appreciation appeared in compliments, especially "like" and "love". Manes and Wolfson also examined the adverbs, intensifiers, and deictic elements, all of which demonstrated highly similar patterns. Moreover, Manes and Wolfson found that there were morphological constraints in addition to semantic constraints, which were seen in the base form of adjectives (rather than their comparative and superlative forms) and a strong constraint on the use of the tense of verbs. Furthermore, they pointed out that compliments typically reflect an interactional constraint concerning either the addressee or his/her objects being complimented. Manes and Wolfson concluded that "the speech act of complimenting is, in fact, characterized by the formulaic nature of its syntactic and semantic composition" (p. 123).

Following Manes and Wolfson's investigation, there were other studies which confirmed their finding of the formulas in other varieties of English. Holmes (1986) replicated their study with a corpus of 517 New Zealand English compliments and found a similar result; thus, she concluded that there were "remarkable regularities in compliment behavior which appear to extend across different English-speaking communities" (p. 491). Consistent with this finding, Lee's study (1990) of Hawai'i Creole English (HCE) showed that the most frequent positive semantic carriers in her data were adjectives — particularly "good" and "nice". Further, Lee's corpus showed that the verbs "like" and "love" were the only two verbs used in HCE compliments and the use of the verb "like" occurred almost 100% of the time in compliments with a verbal semantic load (p. 128).

Meanwhile, Lewandowska-Tomaszczyk (1989) and Herbert (1991) also found similar formulas in their Polish data. However, Herbert's study showed that adverbial compliments (i.e., adverbs used as positive semantic carriers) occurred with as high a frequency as 27% of his Polish corpus, in contrast to 2.7% of the English counterpart. Herbert considered this discrepancy to be a result of syntactic differences between English and Polish, because verbs of sensory perception, such as "like" and "taste", "regularly take adverbial modifiers in Polish and adjectival ones in English" (p. 388). The other difference that Herbert found in his study was a marked infrequency of first person compliments[2] in Polish.

It is interesting to note that in Zuo's study (1988) of Chinese compliments an even higher frequency of adverbial compliments was found, accounting for 43% of her data. Zuo noticed that Chinese adverbs often occurred with most of the positive adjectives and verbs, functioning as intensifiers. She also noted that Chinese compliments rarely employed the speaker's perspective "I" (p. 121).

The findings concerning compliment formulas indicate that compliments are readily recognizable items of discourse. This recognizability facilitates interaction; that is, the routinized formulas are facilitators for comprehension and production. They reduce the possibility of misunderstanding between the speaker and the hearer. This, in turn, may explain why similar formulas are found in different varieties of English and in some other languages.

Compliment topic

Here again, studies show that the vast majority of compliments fall into only a few general topics. Manes (1983) found that the most frequently occurring topics in American English were compliments on personal appearance and accomplishments. Moreover, she identified new acquisitions as a distinctive topic in American English compliments. Holmes' (1986) data on compliments in New Zealand also showed agreement with these general topics. However, Holmes pointed out that "more detailed analysis might reveal differences with the categories concerning which aspects of appearance or which particular possessions are considered appropriate for comment. Acceptable topics of compliments certainly vary cross-culturally" (p. 497). Lee's (1990) study demonstrated this point. Despite the fact that Hawai'i Creole English shared the two basic common topical categories with the U.S. and New Zealand data, Lee's study showed that food compliments were common in addition to other compliments on accomplishments or skills, which Lee took to reflect a cultural difference between Hawai'i Creole English speakers and speakers of other varieties of English. Lee's study also indicates that more cross-cultural data are

---

[2] First person compliments refer to the compliments which are given from the speaker's point of view, as in the example:
 I like your dress.

needed to investigate the relation between compliment topics and cultural values.

Herbert's study (1991) of Polish compliments revealed a cultural variation. Specifically, it showed that making compliments on possessions reached about 50% in his Polish sample. Herbert examined this phenomena from a sociological perspective and concluded that this relatively high frequency reflected the scarcity of commodities in Poland at the time of his field study. He further pointed out that compliments on this kind of acquisition were directed to the social ability rather than the personal judgment of the addressee, which interestingly led to a high frequency of acceptance as a response to compliments of this kind.

Compliment responses

One major study focus of the complimenting event is on compliment responses. Pomerantz (1978) noticed that a large proportion of compliment rejoinders deviated from the acceptance with appreciation token as the social norm model of responding to compliments. Therefore, she analyzed compliments in terms of constraint systems: the agreement/disagreement system, the acceptance/rejection system, and self-praise avoidance system. Pomerantz pointed out that the production of compliment rejoinders was sensitive to the operation of multiple constraint systems. Consequently, the actualization of compliment rejoinders could be classified into the following categories: 1) Acceptance which includes tokens of appreciation and agreement, 2) Rejection which entails disagreement, and 3) Self-praise avoidance mechanisms in which praise is downgraded (agreement and disagreement) and in which referent shifts (reassignment and return) occur (pp. 81–109).

Similarly, Holmes (1986) developed three categories of compliment rejoinders with a focus on the credit attribution component of compliments: Accept, Reject, and Deflect or Evade. She also analyzed complimenting behavior in terms of Brown and Levinson's (1987) Politeness Theory and considered compliments to be face-threatening acts, which accounted for the varieties of compliment responses. However, Holmes' study found that the most frequent response to a compliment was Accept (1989, p. 496). Lee's (1990) study, on the other hand, showed that denial was the most common response in Hawai'i Creole English. Lee pointed out that the denial response functioned as "a marker of cultural identity and a transfer" from Asian culture, in which the Modesty Maxim appeared to operate powerfully (p. 135).

Distribution and frequency

The distribution and frequency of compliments in a speech community have also attracted researchers' attention. Studies show that compliments tend to occur during openings and closings of speech events, often preceded by greetings and followed by farewells. Moreover, compliments may occur at transition points within a speech event, such as at the dinner table during a conversation (Holmes & Brown, 1987; Wolfson, 1989).

Although the distribution of compliments exhibits similarities among the speech communities studied, the frequency of complimenting varies in different cultures. As Herbert pointed out, "Utterances intended and perceived as compliments are frequent in (at least some) varieties of English, e.g. American" (Herbert, 1989, p. 7). This frequency singles out American cultural values even from all the other English-speaking communities, which leads us to look at the discussion of the specific cultural values embedded in compliments and the function of this speech event.

Function

Based on the observation and analysis of her U.S. data, Manes (1983) contended that the high frequency of compliments on appearance (especially to and from women) and on new acquisitions reflects the importance of personal appearance for women and the premium placed on newness in American society. Furthermore, Manes maintained that American English compliments function to establish and reinforce solidarity between the speaker and the addressee.

Herbert (1989) also approached the function of compliments by examining frequency. He pointed out that the relatively high frequency of compliments in American English was a reflection of the perception of native speakers of American English in complimenting situations — they feel culturally obliged to give positive comments and use their preferred politeness strategy when trying to handle a face-threatening act.

The function of compliments has particularly been examined in compliment responses. In light of Pomerantz's analysis, Herbert (1989) conducted a contrastive study on American and South African compliment responses. Unlike Pomerantz, Herbert classified his data into categories such as Agreements, Nonagreements, and Request Interpretations. Herbert's study showed that the difference in frequency distribution of occurrence was crucial for determining the function of compliments. Comparing the frequency distribution of his two data sets, Herbert found that Americans exhibited more compliment-offering but less compliment-accepting while South Africans exhibited less compliment-offering but more compliment-accepting (Herbert & Straight, 1989). From the analysis of the American data in contrast to their South African counterpart, Herbert noticed that American speakers often made use of compliments as a negotiation strategy, that is, they gave the hearer an opportunity to accept/negotiate an offer of solidarity. Consequently, Herbert proposed that solidarity-negotiating is the function of both parts of compliment events — compliments and compliment rejoinders (p. 25). He pointed out that "the isolated study of either compliment or compliment [rejoinder] conceals the negotiating function of the total speech event" (p. 26). The speaker's intention and the hearer's perception and interpretation can only be revealed in the process of interaction. Herbert concluded that the high frequency of compliments and the high rate of different compliment response types (other than Acceptance) in the U.S. data reflected American notions of equality and democratic idealism while the low frequency of compliments and the high rate of Acceptance were tied to elitism in South Africa.

Herbert and Straight (1989) continued to examine the same sets of data from a psycholinguistic view. According to Herbert and Straight, the American stance focused on comprehension, which is a listener-based pragmatic strategy. This strategy led to avoidance of self-praise, resulting in low compliment-accepting. On the other hand, the South African stance focused on production, which is a speaker-based strategy that highlighted agreement with others, resulting in high compliment-accepting. The difference of the focus and strategy was interpreted as indicative of a basic functional difference with regard to the interactional role of compliments. While American English compliments functioned to negotiate social solidarity, South African English compliments functioned to affirm such solidarity (p. 44).

These studies show, on the one hand, that the function of compliments can only be specified emically within a linguistic-cultural system. On the other hand, the distinctive features of each function become most apparent in contrast with other cultures, calling for an "etic" analysis. Although many contrastive studies reveal different cultural values and functions of compliments, the nature of this speech act is still veiled to a certain degree, due to the fact that most contrastive studies are done among similar cultures, especially among Western cultures. Therefore, a systematic study of compliments in different cultures may help reveal both universal and culturally specific features of compliments.

Compliments as a gender-preferential strategy

Complimenting has also been analyzed as a gender-preferential strategy. Holmes (1988) examined the compliment behavior of New Zealanders and found that women used compliments to each other in significantly different ways from men, in terms of frequency, syntactic form, topic, and responses. Specifically, women used compliments more often to other women than they did to men or than men did to each other. Moreover, women used a syntactic form which strengthened the positive force of the compliment more often than men did. Furthermore, compliments on appearance were the dominant topic for women, whereas men complimented on possessions. Finally, men's evasive compliment responses took the form of a marked avoidance strategy more often than women's compliment responses did (pp. 462–463). Based on these observations, Holmes concluded that compliments appeared to be functionally complex speech acts which served as "solidarity signals, cementing friendships, attenuating demands, smoothing ruffled feathers and bridging gaps created by possible offenses" (p. 464). Lee's (1990) research on Hawai'i Creole English found similar patterns. Moreover, Lee found that there were statistically significant differences between uni- and mixed-sex interactions in compliment rejoinder realization.

Herbert (1990) examined gender-based differences in American compliment behavior. He found that the gender of participants had significant impact on the variation of the structuring of compliment events and that the gender of the complimenter determined the type of response he/she received. Female speakers predominantly employed first person compliments regardless of the gender of addressee. In addition, their compliments would most likely not be accepted, whereas compliments from males would be, especially by female recipients. Based on the notion that acceptances were most common among status nonequals and among those whose status was not being negotiated, Herbert speculated that the increased frequency of acceptance responses to male compliments by female addressees might be "another manifestation of the linguistic consequences of status differences apparent in cross-sex interactions" (p. 217). Consistent with his contrastive study of American and South African compliments, Herbert pointed out that the different strategies of compliments and compliment responses between females and males reflect different conversational roles. Herbert thus claimed a "direct relation" between the function, the frequency, and the types as shown in the following:

Function:	offer praise	offer solidarity
Frequency:	infrequent	frequent
[Response]:	ACCEPTANCE	non-ACCEPTANCE
	(South Africans; males)	(Americans; females)

(from Herbert, 1990, p. 222)

Although Herbert notes that such a claim requires further testing, his claim does shed light on compliment events from a holistic perspective.

Research methods

In most studies, data were gathered by taking field notes of compliment events observed in natural encounters (Manes & Wolfson, 1981; Manes, 1983; Holmes, 1986; Herbert, 1989; Lewandowska-Tomaszczyk, 1989; Lee, 1990). However, some studies employed multiple data sources. Lewandowska-Tomaszczyk's data included elicitation tests, interviews, introspection, as well as written sources (Lewandowska-Tomaszczyk, 1989, p. 73), whereas Lee's data collection consisted of reported compliments and compliment rejoinders from native speakers, a complimenting elicitation method, natural observation, and a judgment questionnaire (Lee, 1990, p. 123–124). The sample size of all studies ranged from 321 to 1062 compliment events (Manes, 1983; Holmes, 1986; Herbert, 1989; Lee, 1990). Variables included gender, social relation, age, location, education, and occupation (Manes & Wolfson, 1981; Homes, 1986; Herbert, 1989; Lee, 1990). Categories including taxonomies of compliments were also described in different studies (Knapp, Hopper, & Bell, 1984; Holmes, 1986; Herbert, 1989; Lee, 1990).

From her study of New Zealand English compliments, Holmes (1986) found that small samples could be sufficient to investigate patterns of complimenting behavior in particular contexts or social groups. She also claimed that there was no significant difference between observations and elicitations in her study. Furthermore, she stated that more cross-cultural data were needed so that universal characteristics of complimenting behavior could be distinguished from the preferred cultural patterns of particular groups (p. 505).

Zuo's (1988) study investigated a field other than Western cultures, which widened the perspective of the research into compliments; however, her analysis was based on a scripted tape, which is more impressionistic than authentic.

SUMMARY

Studies on compliments and reponses to compliments demonstrate that a compliment is a structured speech act which reflects cultural values as well as similarities in human behavior. Cross-cultural data provide a source for us to examine the universal features and specific preferred cultural patterns. Studies show that the same forms of compliments may function differently in different linguistic-cultural systems. Thus, they may even fall into different categories. However, the number of cross-cultural data-based studies examining the varieties of participants' perception and production of compliments is still limited.

DESIGN OF THE STUDY

RESEARCH QUESTIONS

SINCE MOST STUDIES SO FAR HAVE FOCUSED ON VARIETIES of English and none has examined compliments on an empirical basis in an Asian context, a study of Chinese compliments may provide some useful information from another cultural perspective. The objectives of this study are to examine the overall characteristics of Chinese compliments with the following research questions:

1. What are the linguistic forms used in compliments?
2. How do interlocutors respond to compliments?
3. What are the characteristics of Chinese compliments and compliment rejoinders in relation to contextual factors?
4. Are there sex-preferential compliment and compliment response strategies?
5. What is the function of compliments in the Chinese cultural context?

METHOD

Data collection

As the analysis of this study is done outside the target speech community, that is, China, natural observation of compliment events is not possible. Therefore, a discourse completion task (DCT) is utilized in this study. DCT can collect, in a short time, large amounts of data that can be used to generalize about stereotypical Chinese complimenting behavior.

Table 1: Design of the variables

SITUATION	INDEPENDENT VARIABLES	
	COMPLIMENT	
	Gender of Complimentee	Compliment Topic
S1 Blouse	Female	Appearance
S2 Ping-Pong	Male	Performance
S3 Glasses	Male	Appearance
S4 Cook	Female	Performance
S5 Sneakers	Male	Appearance
S6 Dress	Female	Appearance
S7 Dance	Female	Performance
S8 Painting	Male	Performance
	RESPONSE	
SITUATION	Gender of Complimentor	Compliment Topic
S9 Clothes	Male	Appearance
S10 Swimming	Female	Performance
S11 Hair	Female	Appearance
S12 Shoes	Female	Appearance
S13 Essay	Female	Performance
S14 Cooking	Male	Performance
S15 Sweater	Male	Appearance
S16 Presentation	Male	Performance

The DCT consists of sixteen situations — eight situations for compliments (S1–S8) and eight for compliment responses (S9–S16). The three dependent variables are compliment structure, compliment focus, and compliment response strategy. The independent variables are gender and compliment topic (personal appearance and skill/performance). Gender-specific Chinese names are given to the fictional interlocutors in the DCT items in order to control for the gender variable. In addition, contextual factors are given in compliment responses. Variables such as interlocutors' social distance relationship, age, and education are controlled. The combination of all three sets of variables resulted in eight situations. The following table outlines the design of the variables:

In order to obtain more reliable data, each item is duplicated, producing sixteen situations in the final DCT format, as shown in the following:

Compliment

S1	*Blouse*	A student notices his/her female classmate wearing a new blouse in front of the library.
S2	*Ping-Pong*	A student finds his/her male friend is a good ping-pong player.
S3	*Glasses*	A student notices his/her male classmate wearing a new pair of glasses in the classroom.
S4	*Cook*	A student notices his/her female schoolmate is a good cook at a New Year's party.
S5	*Sneakers*	A student notices his/her male classmate wearing a new pair of sneakers for an outing.
S6	*Dress*	A student notices his/her female classmate wearing a new pretty dress at a party.
S7	*Dance*	A student finds his/her female classmate is a good dancer at a school dance ball.
S8	*Painting*	A person sees a painting in his/her male friend's home and is told that the painting is done by this friend.

Compliment response

S9	*Clothes*	A student is being complimented by his/her male classmate on his/her new clothes at school.

S10	*Swimming*	A person is being complimented on his/her swimming by a female friend
S11	*Hair*	A person is being complimented on his/her hairstyle by his/her female neighbor.
S12	*Shoes*	A student is being complimented on his/her new shoes at school by his/her female classmate.
S13	*Essay*	A student is being complimented on his/her essay writing by his/her female classmate.
S14	*Cooking*	A friend is being complimented on his/her cooking skills by a male friend.
S15	*Sweater*	A friend is being complimented on a new sweater by a male friend.
S16	*Presentation*	A student is being complimented on a presentation by a male classmate.

In addition, options for zero realization were also given in the DCT format by providing a choice of "You do not say anything" or "You do not respond" (see Appendix A for the original Chinese language instrument; Appendix B contains an English translation).

Subjects

Subjects were ninety-six native speakers of Chinese in the People's Republic of China. Forty-two were male and fifty-four were female. The respondents were university students, teachers, engineers, and civil officers. Their ages ranged from eighteen to thirty-eight years old. All of them were native speakers of Chinese with an education above the tertiary level. Although 90.6% of them had studied one foreign language for five to ten years, none of them had been to a foreign country.

Analysis

Units of analysis were the *compliment formula*, the *compliment focus*, the *compliment response strategy*, and *sex-preferential strategies*. Taxonomies from previous studies (Knapp, Hopper, & Bell, 1984; Holmes, 1986; Herbert, 1989; Lee, 1990) were adapted and percentages were calculated for the major semantic formula and compliment and compliment response strategies. All of the data were independently coded by two researchers and the interrater reliability was 97.2%. Chi-square analysis was used to determine significance in difference from chance distribution between gender and strategy and also between gender and topic. The critical value for these statistical analyses was set at $p < .05$.

Based on the observed data and two pilot studies, the analysis includes the following categories: compliment formula, compliment focus, and compliment response strategy.

Compliment formula

Compliment formulas can be analyzed by positive semantic carriers and compliment focus.

Positive semantic carriers

Positive semantic carriers can be grouped into *Adj/Stative Verbs*, *Adverbs*, *Nouns*, and *Verbs*. Here, both adjective and stative verb are classified into the same group due to Chinese language structure, in which words containing similar meaning to the English adjective can function both as adjectives and stative verbs, as in the following:

<u>as an adjective:</u>

穿漂亮衣服啦。

Chuān piàoliàng yīfu la.

[You] have pretty clothes on.

<u>as a stative verb:</u>

你的衣服真漂亮。

Nǐ de yīfú zhēn <u>piàoliàng</u>.

Your clothes [are] very pretty.

The category *Adverb* refers to the positive semantic carrier that functions as an adverb. In the Chinese language structure, a word does not show changes in form when it functions differently. However, it is still identifiable by examining its relation to other words. For example, the word 不錯 *bùcuò* 'not bad' can be an adjective or an adverb depending on its distributions, as in the following:

as an adjective:

這件衣服樣子很不錯。

Zhè jiàn yīfu yàngzi hěn bùcuò.

The style of this clothing is very good.

as an adverb:

你的球打得真不錯。

Nǐ de qiú dǎ de zhēn bùcuò.

Your ball playing is done very well. (You play ball very well).

Compliment focus

Compliment focus refers to the major focus of the compliment utterance. It can be categorized into *Object/Action* and *Agent*. *Object/Action* refers to those utterances which focus either on objects or actions of the complimentee, as shown in the following example:

你這雙鞋真不錯。

Nǐ zhè shuāng xié zhēn bùcuò.

This pair of shoes of yours is really good.

On the other hand, *Agent* refers to the complimentee him/herself, as in the following:

你真能幹。

Nǐ zhēn néng gàn.

You're really capable.

Compliment response strategies

Compliment response strategy is divided into three categories: *Acceptance, Acceptance with Amendment,* and *Non-acceptance.* Under these three there are subcategories as in the following:

Acceptance

> Appreciation token: utterances that recognize the status of a previous utterance as a compliment by showing gratitude.
>
> 謝謝。
> *Xièxie.*
> Thanks.
>
> Agreement: utterances to agree with the complimenter.
>
> 我也挺喜歡的。
> *Wǒ yě tǐng xǐhuān de.*
> I like it, too.
>
> Pleasure: utterances to show the complimentee is pleased.
>
> 我聽了眞高興。
> *Wǒ tīng le zhēn gāoxìng.*
> I am very happy to hear that.
>
> Smile: recognizing the compliment by smiling. (A number of subjects noted on their surveys that they would simply smile in response to a given compliment.)

Acceptance with Amendment

> Return: utterances to reciprocate the act of complimenting by offering praise to speaker.
>
> 你也不錯。
> *Nǐ yě bùcuò.*
> You are not bad, either.
>
> Downgrade: utterances to scale down the praise of a compliment.
>
> 馬馬虎虎。
> *Mǎmǎ hūhū.*
> Just so-so.

Magnification: utterances to increase the complimentary force of a previous utterance.

> 你不看看這是誰寫的？
>
> *Nǐ bù kànkàn zhè shì shuí xiě de?*
>
> Don't you see who wrote that? [i.e., Of course my writing is good!]

Confirmation: utterances to confirm and reassure the previous utterance.

> 是嗎？你眞覺得不錯？
>
> *Shì ma? Nǐ zhēn juéde bùcuò?*
>
> Is it? Do you really think it's not bad?

Comment: utterance to impersonalize the complimentary force by giving impersonal details.

> 朋友送的。
>
> *Péngyou sòng de.*
>
> It's given by a friend.

Transfer: utterances which switch the focus of the compliments.

> 你喜歡吃就多吃點兒。
>
> *Nǐ xǐhuan chī jiù duō chī diǎnr.*
>
> Have more since you like it.

Non-acceptance

Denial: utterances to deny the content of the compliment.

> 不行，不行。
>
> *Bù xíng, bù xíng.*
>
> No, No.

Delay: utterances which delay the delivery of the compliments.

吃了再說。

Chī le zài shuō.

Comment on it after you've tasted it.

Qualification: utterances to deny the quality complimented.

差遠了。

Chà yuǎn le.

It's far from it.

Idiom: utterances which are composed of idiomatic expressions to show the complimentee feels embarrassed or abashed.

不好意思。

Bù hǎo yìsi.

[I am] embarrassed.

Diverge: utterances to deny the complimentary force by directing it to other acts.

別逗了。

Bié dòu le.

No kidding/Don't make fun of me.

Avoidance: utterances that avoid responding to the complimenting content.

你太客氣了。

Nǐ tài kèqi le.

You are being too polite.

RESULTS

THIS SECTION IS CONCERNED WITH THE STATISTICAL RESULTS of the DCT data collection. The results are divided into compliments (responses to situations S1–S8), and compliment rejoinders (responses to situations S9–S16). Under each division, overall distributions, contextual factors (including topic and situation), and gender-specific distributions are examined.

COMPLIMENTS

In the following analyses, results from situations S1–S8 are grouped into compliment response types and compliment formulas.

Compliment response types

The data yielded four types of compliment responses: *No Response*, *Non-Compliment*, *Implicit Compliment*, and *Explicit Compliment*. These four types of compliment responses can be observed and analyzed by their overall distributions, contextual factors, and gender-specific distributions.

Overall distributions

There were 763 responses collected from the compliment situations in the data (situations S1–S8). The distribution of the responses is displayed in Table 2.

Over half of the responses are explicit verbal compliments (55.5%), while the rest are of other kinds (43.5%). In Table 2, *No Response* refers to the zero realization where the respondents chose "You would not say anything". As shown in Table 2, this option reaches a relatively high percentage (23.9% overall and 54.8% of all responses that are not *Explicit Compliment*) for the given complimenting situations. This suggests that in some situations, offering a compliment is not felt to be culturally obligatory,[3] either due to the perceived nature of the situations or to the constraints of the contexts.

Table 2: Percentage of overall distribution of compliment rejoinder types

No Response	23.9
Non-Compliment	13.6
Implicit Compliment	6.0
Explicit Compliment	56.6

Related but different from *No Response* is *Non-compliment*, where the respondents did give verbal rejoinders to the given situations but those rejoinders can hardly be categorized as compliments:

(1) 甚麼時候配的？
Shénme shíhou pèi de?
When did you have them made? (S3 *Glasses*)

(2) 這鞋多少錢？
Zhè xié duōshǎo qián?
How much are these sneakers? (S5 *Sneakers*)

These compliment rejoinders show that some situations are open to more than one interpretation. Interactionally, they serve to start a conversation topic which requires the interlocutor at the next turn to provide specific information requested in the previous utterance. Note that the requested information may be considered as personal by non-native speakers of Chinese, as in (2). These rejoinders thus suggest that there are culture-specific conditions governing the selection of topics for talk and that in cross-cultural encounters with Chinese interlocutors, participants need to be aware of the appropriate conditions for topic selection.

---

[3] "Culturally obligatory" refers to the cultural factors that motivate the choice of this particular speech event. The absence of the compliment is felt by the members of a culture when it is culturally obligatory.

Implicit Compliment refers to those compliments which are not explicitly directed to the complimentee's appearance or performance. The following are examples of some implicit compliments:

(3) 我跟你學學。
 Wǒ gēn nǐ xuéxue.
 Let me learn from you. (S4 Cook)

(4) 好好教我跳跳吧。
 Hǎohao jiāo wǒ tiàotiao ba.
 Please teach me how to properly. (S7 Dance)

(5) 在家是不是常幹呀？
 Zài jiā shìbushì cháng gàn ya?
 Do you do this a lot at home? (S4 Cook)

(6) 甚麼時候學的？
 Shénme shíhòu xué de?
 When did you learn it? (S7 Dance)

These compliments are typically conveyed in the form of requesting or questioning. However, they are not true requests or information inquiries. This can be seen from the rejoinders that follow these kinds of utterances.[4] For instance, a relevant second pair-part to (4) would be 我哪兒會呀 *wǒ nǎr huì ya* 'I don't know how to dance' or 我跳得不行 *wǒ tiào de bùxíng* 'I can't dance well', not 來，跟我跳 *lái, gēn wǒ tiào* 'come here and dance with me'. Also, a relevant response to (6) would not inform about a specific time in response to "when". This indicates that these utterances are interpreted as compliments because their second pair-parts of adjacency pairs operate on different response priorities from requests (Bilmes 1988). If the above examples were true requests, the first priority of a response should be compliance or giving specific

---

[4] It is true that one can play with the ambiguity in the previous utterance so as to negotiate meaning; however, responses which deliberately treat the previous utterances as requests would be more idiosyncratic than conventional to the given situations of *Dance* and *Cook*.

information; however, the typical response from native speakers[5] is a downgrade or a ritual denial, which is a priority of Chinese compliment responses.

The technical term *"Implicit Compliment"* is not that implicit emically. While the form of the utterances is implicit and allows the hearer to make other possible interpretations of meaning, this kind of utterance is perceived by native speakers as loaded explicitly with compliment force. Consequently, an implicit compliment needs an interpretation at the level of form in which the positive semantic carrier is missing.

Explicit Compliment, by contrast, refers to a direct positive comment in which the form contains at least one positive semantic carrier:

(7) 你的新襯衫很漂亮！
     Nǐ de xīn chènshān hěn piàoliang!
     Your new blouse is very pretty!   (S1 Blouse)

(8) 你的球藝真棒！
     Nǐ de qiúyì zhēn bàng!
     Your playing skill is excellent!   (S2 Ping-Pong)

As shown in Table 2, only a little more than half of the compliment responses fall into this category. This relatively low frequency indicates that the speech event of complimenting in Chinese may not occur very often.

Compliment Response Type by Compliment Topic

Compliment response types are further examined by the two compliment topics (i.e., appearance and performance), as shown in Table 3.

No Response occurs more than twice as often in situations with *Appearance* (35.2%) than in those with *Performance* (12.6%). This suggests that the high frequency of *No Response* may be the result of conscious avoidance since explicit descriptions of new appearance and wording "you notice..." are given in DCT (see Appendices A and B). In other words, the respondents chose to "opt out" (decline to respond) because they perceived the situations as inappropriate for offering compliments even though they noticed the changes

---

[5] This comment has to be based on the author's native speaker communicative competence because the DCT cannot provide such information.

in appearance. This indicates that complimenting on appearance is less preferred than complimenting on performance.

Table 3: Percentage of distribution of compliment rejoinder types by compliment topic

	APPEARANCE	PERFORMANCE
No Response	35.2	12.6
Non-Compliment	20.7	6.5
Implicit Compliment	1.0	11.0
Explicit Compliment	43.0	69.9

Furthermore, *Implicit Compliment* on appearance occurs less frequently (1.0%) than on performance (11.0%). Consistent with the high frequency of avoidance and lower frequency of *Explicit Compliment* on appearance, *Non-Compliment* on appearance (20.7%) is much higher than on performance (6.5%); the following examples illustrate *Non-Compliment* :

(9) 換了副新眼鏡？
Huàn le fu xīn yǎnjìng?
Are you wearing a new pair of glasses?   (S3 Glasses)

(10) 你的新球鞋是甚麼牌子？好不好穿？
Nǐ de xīn qiúxié shì shénme páizi? Hǎo bù hǎo chuān?
What's the brand of your new sneakers? Are they comfortable?
(S12 Shoes)

This suggests that a change in appearance may not be deemed as worthy of complimenting as an achievement in performance; new possessions or pretty clothes may not necessarily lead to positive comments in the observed Chinese speech community, whereas an achievement is more likely to be complimented. This further indicates that complimenting on performance is more likely to be felt as socially acceptable — thus safer — than making compliments on appearance.

In total, the combination of both *No Response* and *Non-Compliment* on appearance yields a frequency reaching as high as 55.9% contrasted with a much lower frequency of 19.1% on performance. This pattern reveals a preference of topic for complimenting in Chinese.

Compliment response type by gender

Results show that both males and females gave the same order of rank in their preference of compliment response types (see Table 4). However, female respondents (62.3%) gave more explicit compliments than male respondents (48.9%), while males gave more implicit compliments (8.8%) or non-compliments (17.2%). Statistical analysis shows that there is a significant difference between genders using these four compliment response types, $\chi 2$ (3, N = 763) = 19.0, $p < .05$.

Table 4: Percentage of distribution of compliment rejoinder types by gender of complimenter

	MALE	RANK	FEMALE	RANK
No Response	25.1	2	22.9	2
Non-compliment	17.2	3	10.9	3
Implicit Compliment	8.8	4	3.9	4
Explicit Compliment	48.9	1	62.3	1

The gender-specific distributions can be further examined in the interaction between the gender of complimenter and complimentee (see Table 5). The results show that each gender group of respondents treat the other group differently from their own group. When the complimentee was male, male respondents offer explicit compliments almost as often as female respondents did. However, more females (24.5%) chose to opt out than males (16.4%), while more males (25.5%) gave *Non-Compliment* than females (17.6%).

When the complimentee was female, females (69.9%) gave more explicit compliments than males (45.8%). However, males (11.4%) made more implicit compliment remarks than females (4.6%) and more males (33.7%) chose to opt out or give non-compliments than females (21.3%).

Table 5: Percentage of distribution of compliment rejoinder types by interaction between gender of complimenter and complimentee

	M–m	F–m	M–f	F–f
No Response	16.4	24.5	33.7	21.3
Non-Compliment	25.5	17.6	9.0	4.2
Implicit Compliment	6.1	3.2	11.4	4.6
Explicit Compliment	52.1	54.6	45.8	69.9

M, F = complimenter; m, f = complimentee

This difference shows that cross-gender complimenting is more restricted than is complimenting between interlocutors of the same gender. Both males and females give compliments less frequently when the complimentee is of the opposite gender. Although generally females offer compliments more often than males do (see Table 4), they compliment males less often than they do each other. Males, on the other hand, compliment less than females; when they do compliment, they compliment other males more often than females. Also, they give females the least explicit — but the most implicit — compliments among these four types of interaction. Even when they do not treat the given situations as complimenting events, they keep interacting with other males by giving non-compliments, but they opt out with females.

Compliment response type by topic and gender

Gender-specific distribution is also found to be significantly different when compliments are made by different genders for different topics, i.e., appearance, χ^2 (3, N = 381) = 11.5, $p < .05$; and performance χ^2 (3, N = 381) = 11.4, $p < .05$. (See Table 6).

The results show that these two gender groups behaved consistently different towards the two observed compliment topics. Females tended to offer more explicit compliments while more males chose to opt out, or to give implicit compliments or non-compliments regardless of the compliment topics. Both males and females gave twice as many explicit compliments on performance as on appearance. In addition, they used *No Response* and *Non-Compliment* for performance much less often than for appearance. Again, this shows that both males and females compliment on performance more frequently than on appearance.

Table 6: Percentage of distribution of compliment rejoinder types by topic and gender

	APPEARANCE		PERFORMANCE	
	MALE	FEMALE	MALE	FEMALE
No Response	37.0	33.8	13.3	12.0
Non-Compliment	24.8	17.6	9.6	4.2
Implicit Compliment	2.4	0.0	15.1	7.9
Explicit Compliment	35.8	48.6	62.0	75.9

One increase in frequency found in performance is that for *Implicit Compliment*. Male respondents in particular used this strategy much more frequently for performance than they did for appearance. One interpretation could be that men tend to perceive compliments as inherently evaluative, thus they challenge and compete with the action or performance rather than openly acknowledge it immediately.

An examination of the interaction between compliment topic and the gender of participant can provide a clearer picture of gender-specific distribution of compliment rejopinder types. (See Table 7).

Table 7: Percentage of distribution of compliment rejoinder types by interaction between topic and gender of participant

	APPEARANCE				PERFORMANCE			
	M-m	M-f	F-f	F-m	M-m	M-f	F-f	F-m
No Response	29.3	44.6	25.0	42.6	3.6	22.9	17.6	6.5
Non-Compliment	41.5	8.4	2.8	32.4	9.6	9.6	5.6	2.8
Implicit Compliment	1.2	3.6	0.0	0.0	10.8	19.3	9.3	6.5
Explicit Compliment	28.0	43.4	72.2	25.0	75.9	48.2	67.6	84.3

M, F = complimenter; m, f = complimentee

Male and female respondents acted differently on both compliment topics when the complimentee was female. That is, when appearance was the topic, females used *Explicit Compliment* most frequently towards other females (72.2%), while at the same time they used it the least towards males (25%). In the same manner, males used *Explicit Compliment* more to females (43.4%) than to other males (28.0%). As for the topic of performance, females complimented males most frequently among these four types of interactions (84.3%) with males to females the least (48.2%). Furthermore, females gave an approximately equivalent numbers of *Explicit Compliments* to other females on both topics, but they gave almost four times as many to males on performance than on appearance. Similarly, males paid an equal number of *Explicit Compliment* to females, while giving three times as many to other males on performance than on appearance. This reveals that both genders use compliments on performance as the most frequent topic for males and compliments on appearance the most frequent topic for females.

Compliment response type by situation

An examination of compliment response types by situation can reveal the socio-pragmatic source of the speech event of complimenting. Although the data were collected through a designed DCT, the responses show that the respondents were sensitive to the given situations. (See Table 8).

The highest frequency in *No Response* is found in *S5 Sneakers* where nearly half (44.2%) of the respondents chose to avoid paying compliments. In addition, *Non-Compliment* is found to be used slightly higher (29.5%) than *Explicit Compliment* (26.3%). These compliment responses consist mainly of two kinds: a) an inquiry about the price of the sneakers or where they were purchased; or b) whether the new sneakers are physically or situationally appropriate (either comfortable or suitable) for the outing. These are shown in the following examples:

(11) 嘿！多少錢買的？
Hèi! Duōshǎo qián mǎi de?
Hey, how much did you spend on your sneakers?

(12) 不怕把新鞋給毀了？
Bù pà bǎ xīn xié gěi huǐ le?
Aren't you afraid of ruining your new sneakers?

(13) 你穿新鞋走遠路，不怕腳痛嗎？
Nǐ chuān xīn xié zǒu yuǎn lù, bù pà jiǎo tòng ma?
Don't you worry about hurting your feet by walking a long distance with your new sneakers?

Table 8: Percentage of distribution of compliment rejoinder types by situation

	Blouse	Ping Pong	Glasses	Cook	Sneakers	Dress	Dance	Painting
No Response	37.5	7.4	29.5	11.5	44.2	29.5	28.4	3.1
Non-Compliment	5.2	5.3	43.2	6.3	29.5	5.3	8.4	6.3
Implicit Compliment	2.1	8.4	1.1	14.6	0.0	1.1	12.6	8.3
Explicit Compliment	55.2	78.9	26.3	67.7	26.3	64.2	50.5	82.3

The first kind of compliment response as in (11) concerns the newness of the sneakers. Instead of offering compliments, inquiries are made on the place purchased or the price paid. Unlike the response to an implicit compliment, a relevant response to these inquiries is to provide or not to provide the information of a specific place (e.g. the name of the store or the name of the place where the store is) or a specific price of the sneakers. None of the compliment response strategies would be relevant to this kind of inquiry unless used deliberately as a strategy of avoidance. This indicates that "newness" may not necessarily be as highly valued as in the American English compliments (Wolfson & Manes 1981; Manes 1983).

The second kind of compliment response, as in (12) and (13), exhibits particular sensitivity with a specific situation — the outing. Although those rejoinders reflect the speaker's observation of the newness of the sneakers, they question the appropriateness of this newness in such a particular situation. That is, a new pair of sneakers may elicit a compliment, but wearing a new pair of sneakers to go on an outing may not because it is considered inappropriate.

On the contrary, *S8 Painting* is found to have elicited the highest frequency in *Explicit Compliment* (82.3%) and the lowest frequency in *No Response* (3.1%). The fact that one is told about a friend's painting may have already set up a situation for paying a compliment. Moreover, one striking feature in *S8 Painting* is that most of the implicit compliments are phrased with 想不到 *xiǎng bù dào* 'I didn't know/expect...':

(14) 想不到你會畫畫。
Xiǎng bù dào nǐ huì huàhuà.
I didn't know you could paint.

This phrase can be seen as a culture-specific marker of compliments. While this marker conveys a clear meaning of complimenting in Chinese, a non-native speaker might be annoyed by feeling being put down with this kind of phrase.

Implicit Compliment occurs mainly in *S4 Cook* (14.6%) and *S7 Dance* (12.6%). One feature in these utterances is the association of "learning", "teaching", and "teacher":

(15) 有机會請你教我跳舞好嗎？
Yǒu jīhuì qǐng nǐ jiāo wǒ tiàowǔ hǎo ma?
Could you teach me how to dance if you have time?   (*S7 Dance*)

(16) 哎，我跟你學學。
Ai, wǒ gēn nǐ xuéxue.
Hey, let me learn from you.   (*S4 Cook*)

(17) 師傅，收下我這個徒弟吧！
Shīfu, shōuxià wǒ zhège túdì ba!
Master, please take me as your apprentice!   (*S4 Cook*)

Utterances like these are also found in the second sequences following the explicit compliments:

(18) 你舞跳得真好。我要拜你為師。
Nǐ wǔ tiào de zhēn hǎo. Wǒ yào bài nǐ wéi shī.
You dance really well. I'd like to have you as my teacher.
(S7 Dance)

(19) 真能幹，我要向你學習。
Zhēn néng gàn, wǒ yào xiàng nǐ xuéxí.
You are so capable; I should learn from you. (S4 Cook)

This particular association of acknowledging someone as one's teacher or master with compliments is rooted in the Confucian idea of 三人行，必有我師 sān rén xíng, bì yǒu wǒ shī 'walking in a company of three, I will surely find a teacher' (Analects of Confucius, 7/22).

Finally, most of the non-compliments are found in S3 Glasses (43.2%):

(20) 這眼鏡多少錢？
Zhè yǎnjìng duōshǎo qián?
How much does this pair of glasses cost?

(21) 甚麼時候配的？
Shénme shíhòu pèi de?
When did you have them made?

(22) 你的眼鏡是多大度數的？
Nǐ de yǎnjìng shì duō dà dùshu de?
What's the prescription of your glasses?

Rejoinders as in (20), (21), and (22) are inquiries for information concerning the new pair of glasses, not compliments. Interestingly, some compliment rejoinders exhibit sensitivity of the given situation where the interlocutors are students about to have a midterm:

(23) 又准備抄呢，太丑陋了。
Yòu zhǔnbèi chāo ne, tài chǒulòu le.
Are you going to cheat [on the exam] again? That's just too crass.

(24) 知識沒見長，眼鏡戴上了啊。
Zhīshi méi jiànzhǎng, yǎnjìng dài shàng le a.
Knowledge has not increased yet, but the glasses are already on.

(25) 戴新眼鏡，"作弊"夠眼神了！
Dài xīn yǎnjìng, "zuòbì" gòu yǎnshén le!
Your vision is good enough to "cheat" with new glasses on!

(26) 怎麼了？近視度數又加深了？要注意保護眼睛啊！
Zěnme le? Jìnshì dùshù yòu jiāshēn le? Yào zhùyì bǎohù yǎnjing a!
What happened? Is your vision getting worse? You should take care of your eyes.

Again, this shows that specific contexts have an impact on the speaker's interpretation of the nature of a speech event and thus influence the compliment response types.

Compliment response types by situation and gender

Response types are also examined by how each gender group treats each situation (see Table 9).

Both gender groups treat each situation in a similar way, with some difference in *S3 Glasses*, *S7 Dance*, and *S6 Dress*. In *S3 Glasses* most males gave *Non-Compliment* (53.7%), while females used *Non-Compliment* (35.2%) and *No Response* (35.2%) equally frequently. This indicates that most of the male and female respondents did not perceive this situation as a complimenting situation. However, males tended to make comments other than compliments, whereas females either did the same or chose to opt out. With *S7 Dance*, over half of the females gave *Explicit Compliment* (63%) in contrast to only one fourth of the males (34.1%). Males used most of the implicit compliments (19.5%) in this situation whereas famales did so less than half as often (7.4%).

This suggests that males tend to use implicit compliments with females on their performance.

Table 9: Percentage of distribution of compliment rejoinder types by situation and gender

		Blouse	Ping Pong	Glasses	Cook	Sneakers	Dress	Dance	Painting
No Response	M	42.9	4.9	22.0	14.3	36.6	46.3	31.7	2.4
	F	33.3	9.3	35.2	9.3	50.0	16.7	25.9	3.7
Non-Compliment	M	7.1	7.3	53.7	4.8	29.3	9.8	14.6	11.9
	F	3.7	3.7	35.2	7.4	29.6	1.9	3.7	1.9
Implicit Compliment	M	4.8	12.2	2.4	19.0	0.0	2.4	19.5	9.5
	F	0.0	5.6	0.0	11.1	0.0	0.0	7.4	7.4
Explicit Compliment	M	45.2	75.6	22.0	61.9	34.1	41.6	34.1	76.2
	F	63.0	81.5	29.6	72.2	20.4	81.5	63.0	87.0

A major difference is found in S6 *Dress*, where most of the females gave *Explicit compliment* (81.5%), with less than half of the males complimenting explicitly (41.6%). Meanwhile, nearly half of the males chose to opt out (46.3%) while only a few females used the same strategy (16.7%). This situation is shown to be typical; when women compliment each other, it expresses solidarity within the gender group.

Compliment formulas

Compliment formulas are examined in terms of positive semantic carriers and compliment focus. Only the rejoinders in the category of *Explicit Compliment* are examined. Moreover, as the DCT has already pre-conditioned the distributions of the possible positive semantic carriers and compliment focus in each situation,[6] compliment formulas by situation are not analyzed in this section.

Positive semantic carriers

Overall Distributions

Explicit Compliment entails four types of positive semantic carriers, *Adj/Stative Verbs, Adverb, Noun,* and *Verb.* (See Table 10). These results show that the most frequent positive semantic carriers are *Adjectives/Stative Verbs* (54.5%). The major adjectives/stative verbs used are 漂亮 *piàoliang* (pretty) and 不錯 *bùcuò* (not bad):[7]

Table 10: Percentage of overall distribution of positive semantic carriers

Adj/Stative Verb	54.5
Adverb	27.4
Noun	15.8
Verb	2.3

(27) 你這件衣服很漂亮。

Nǐ zhèjiàn yīfu hěn piàoliang.

Your blouse is very pretty. (S1 Blouse)

(28) 你這副眼鏡不錯。

Nǐ zhèfu yǎnjìng bùcuò.

Your glasses are not bad. (S3 Glasses)

Adverbs are ranked second (27.4%). The major two adverbs are found to be 好 *hǎo* (well) and 不錯 *bùcuò*[8] (quite well):

---

[6] Since each situation is designed with a specific compliment topic, the conclusions about distributions of the positive semantic carriers and compliment focus can be drawn from their overall distributions and distributions by topic.

[7] The adjective 不錯 *bùcuò* is one morpheme meaning 'not bad' or 'good' in English.

[8] The adverb 不錯 *bùcuò* is one morpheme meaning 'quite well' in English.

(29) 你打得很好。
    Nǐ dǎ de hěn hǎo.
    You play very well.   (S2 Ping-Pong)

(30) 畫得眞不錯。
    Huà de zhēn bùcuò.
    You paint really (quite) well.   (S8 Painting)

Nouns, which are seldom mentioned in other previous studies of compliments, show a relatively high occurrence in the data (15.8%):

(31) 你很有品味。
    Nǐ hěn yǒu pǐnwèi.
    You really have taste.   (S5 Sneakers)

(32) 你不愧爲舞林高手。
    Nǐ bùkuì wéi wǔlín gāoshǒu.
    You are really a dancer of the highest degree.   (S7 Dance)

The most frequently used nouns are 兩下子 *liǎngxiàzi* 'some know-how' and 手 -*shǒu* '-hand' as in 一把手／好手／一手 *yībǎshǒu/hǎoshǒu/yīshǒu* 'good-hand':

(33) 看不出來，你還有這兩下子。
    Kàn bù chūlái, nǐ hái yǒu zhè liǎngxiàzi.
    I didn't know you had such a skill.   (S4 Cook)

(34) 有兩下子。
    Yǒu liǎngxiàzi.
    You have some know-how.   (S2 Ping-Pong)

(35) 沒想到，你還有這手。
Méi xiǎngdào, nǐ hái yǒu zhè shǒu.
I didn't expect you to have such a talent.   (S8 *Painting*)

Verbs, which are frequently used in different varieties of English compliments (Wolfson and Manes 1981; Holmes 1986; Lee 1990), turn out to be rarely used in the present data, accounting for only 2.3% of the result. Moreover, the only verb found to occur more than twice is 喜歡 *xǐhuan* 'like':

(36) 我很喜歡你的畫。
Wǒ hěn xǐhuan nǐ de huà.
I like your painting very much.   (S8 *Painting*)

In accordance with the low frequency of the use of verbs as positive semantic carriers is the rare occurrence of the speaker's perspective ("I") for compliments, accounting for only 1.2% of *Explicit Compliment.*

Positive Semantic Carriers by Topic

As expected, different kinds of positive semantic carriers are distributed according to different compliment topics. (See Table 11).

Table 11: Percentage of distribution of positive semantic carriers by compliment topic

	APPEARANCE	PERFORMANCE
Adj/Stative Verb	93.3	30.7
Adverb	0.6	43.8
Noun	4.3	22.8
Verb	1.8	2.6

Table 11 shows that the positive semantic carriers used for complimenting appearance are centralized in *Adj/Stative Verb* (93.3%), whereas in complimenting on performance they tend to be more evenly distributed (except verbs), with the highest frequency in *Adverb* (43.8%). The reason can be found in the content of the topic itself. While adjectives or stative verbs are used to describe appearance, adverbs are more likely to be used to describe performed actions.

Another contrast is shown in the distributions of nouns among these two topics, in which nouns are used for compliments on performance over five times more often than compliments on appearance. As nouns are more categorical than continuous — in contrast to adjectives, stative verbs, and adverbs — their relatively high frequencey in the topic of performance suggests that compliments on this topic may be more evaluative than those on appearance.

Positive Semantic Carriers by Gender

The use of positive semantic carriers also reveals some difference in gender-specific distributions (see Table 12).

Table 12: Percentage of distribution of positive semantic carriers by gender

	MALE	FEMALE
Adj/Stative Verb	53.7	55.0
Adverb	19.8	32.0
Noun	24.1	10.8
Verb	2.5	2.2

Male and female respondents are found to use positive semantic carriers differently in adverbs and nouns. Specifically, males used nouns more often than females, while females used more adverbs. Considering adverbs are of the more basic form of compliment markers than nouns,[9] we can conclude that females tend to use the basic formulas for complimenting compared to males who use the culture-specific formulas.

---

[9] The adverbs used for complimenting are un-specific, while nouns are comparatively specific. Moreover, this set of data shows that using nouns as positive semantic carriers involves encoding cultural meanings in the nouns.

Compliment focus

Overall Distributions

The results show that Agent occurs twice as often as Object/Action. (See Table 13). Most of the compliments are directed to either the complimentee's appearance or performance:

Table 13: Percentage of overall distribution of compliment rejoinder types by compliment focus

Agent	68.4
Object/Action	31.6

(37) 你很漂亮呀！
Nǐ hěn piàoliang ya!
You are very pretty! (S6 Dress)

(38) 你真能幹。
Nǐ zhēn nénggàn.
You are very capable. (S4 Cook)

Meanwhile, focus on Object/Action is found to be much less frequently used than on Agent, and it is mostly employed for complimenting performance and sometimes appearance:

(39) 你球打得不錯啊。
Nǐ qiú dǎ de bùcuò a.
You play well. (S2 Ping-Pong)

(40) 你這副眼鏡造型很美。
Nǐ zhèfu yǎnjìng zàoxíng hěn měi.
The frame of your glasses is very beautiful. (S3 Glasses)

The fact that Object/Action occurs less frequently derives from the constraint on performance in compliments where the majority of the focus is on Agent. This is not surprising since the performance is conducted by the agent; while in the case of appearance it is usually the object that creates the complimenting situation.

Compliment Focus by Topic

The examination of compliment focus in relation to compliment topic yields the results illustrated in Table 14:

Table 14: Percentage of distribution of compliment focus by compliment topic

	APPEARANCE	PERFORMANCE
Agent	48.8	80.5
Object/Action	51.2	19.5

Distribution of compliment focus in relation to compliment topic shows that focuses on *Object/Action* (51.2%) and *Agent* (48.8%) are almost evenly distributed in complimenting on appearance; whereas in the case of performance as a topic, focus on *Agent* occurs much more frequently (80.5%) than on *Object/Action* (19.5%). Again, this distributional difference comes more from the difference in topic (where performance is more directly related to the agent's accomplishment) than appearance, where the objects are often the cause of the complimenting situation (with the controlled topic on appearance is basically physical appearance). Therefore, it is more likely that those compliments are focused on the agent rather than on the action.

Compliment Focus by Gender

Male and female respondents are found to display a similar pattern of strategies in selecting the compliment focus (see Table 15).

Table 15: Percentage of distribution of compliment focus by gender

	MALE	FEMALE
Agent	68.5	68.4
Object/Action	31.5	31.6

Both male and female respondents preferred paying compliments with a focus on *Agent*. Moreover, the distributions of compliment focus by these two groups show that males and females act almost exactly the same in terms of their selection of compliment focus. This indicates that compliment formulas are restricted within a narrow range

COMPLIMENT REJOINDERS

As were the results from the analysis of compliments, results from situations S9–S16 are analyzed in terms of overall distribution, compliment topic, situation, and gender-specific distribution.

Overall distributions

765 compliment rejoinders were collected from the DCT. Table 16 presents the overall distribution of compliment response types from the data:

Table 16: Percentage of overall distribution of compliment rejoinder types

No Response	5.9
Acceptance with Amendment	47.2
Acceptance	24.4
Non-acceptance	13.5
Combination	9.0

Unlike the respondents on situations S1–S8, very few respondents chose to opt out or ignore the given situations S9–S16 (5.9%). The distributions of other strategies reveal a regular proportion; when arranged in descending order, the frequency of each strategy is approximately half of the preceding one. The highest frequency occurs in *Acceptance with Amendment*, accounting for almost half of the observed data (47%):

(41) 兩塊錢，便宜！
 Liǎng kuài qián, piányi!
 Only two dollars. Cheap! (S11 Hair)

(42) 馬馬虎虎。
   Mǎmǎ-hūhū.
   Just so-so. (S10 Swimming)

Acceptance, which is the second most common compliment response type, occurs infrequently — approximately half as often (24.3%):

(43) 多謝夸獎。
   Duōxiè kuājiǎng.
   Thank you for your compliment. (S13 Essay)

(44) 我真高興聽你這麼說。
   Wǒ zhēn gāoxìng tīng nǐ zhème shuō.
   I am so glad to hear you say so. (S11 Hair)

Following *Acceptance* is *Non-acceptance* (13.4%):

(45) 不敢當！
   Bùgǎndāng!
   I really don't deserve this! (S16 Presentation)

(46) 還差得遠呢！
   Hái chà de yuǎn ne!
   [I am] far from that! (S13 Essay)

Non-acceptance (13.4%) accounts for half as many responses as of *Acceptance* and 9% of the responses consist of *Combinations* of different strategies:

(47) 燙得好嗎？才花了六塊錢。
   Tàng de hǎo ma? Cái huā le liù kuài qián.
   [Is my hair] done well? I only spent six dollars. (S11 Hair)

(48) 謝謝。我准備了挺長時間。
Xièxie. Wǒ zhǔnbèi le tǐngcháng shíjiān.
Thanks. I prepared a long time.   (S16 Presentation)

The most frequently occuring combined strategy is *Confirmation* plus *Appreciation*, reaching 17% of *Combination*:

(49) 是嗎？蒙承夸獎。
Shì ma? Méngchéng kuājiǎng.
Really? I am honored to be complimented.   (S9 Clothes)

(50) 是嗎？多謝夸獎啦。
Shì ma? Duōxiè kuājiǎng la.
Really? Thanks a lot for complimenting me.   (S10 Swimming)

Contrary to the "normative" response — *Non-acceptance*— prescribed for "standard" Chinese socialization, *Acceptance with Amendment* is found from this study to be the most preferred strategy in actual interaction. This, in a way, though from a different starting point, evidences Pomerantz's (1978) analysis of the "solutions" to the multiple preferences from the interaction among the agreement/disagreement system, the acceptance/rejection system, and self-praise/avoidance system. Specifically, the realization of Chinese compliment responses is actualized in *Acceptance with Amendment*, which deviates from *Non-acceptance* but entails self-praise avoidance. This specific actualization is more clearly seen from the distributions of the sub-categories shown in Table 17.

This table shows that *Downgrade* is the most preferred strategy (17.2%):

(51) 不會游，瞎游。
Bùhuì yóu, xiā yóu.
I can't swim; I just play around.   (S10 Swimming)

(52) 無所謂的，只不過是雙鞋子。
Wú suǒwèi de, zhǐ bùguò shì shuāng xiézi.
No big deal; it's only a pair of shoes.   (S12 Shoes)

Table 17: Percentage of overall distributions of compliment rejoinder types and subcategories

Acceptance with Amendment:		47.2
	Downgrade	17.3
	Comment	9.3
	Confirmation	8.0
	Magnification	6.1
	Transfer	4.7
	Return	1.8
Acceptance:		24.4
	Appreciation	16.4
	Agreement	3.8
	Smile	3.5
	Pleasure	0.7
Non-acceptance:		13.5
	Denial	5.2
	Diverge	4.2
	Qualification	2.2
	Idiom	0.8
	Delay	0.7
	Avoidance	0.4
Combination:		9.0
No Response:		5.9

An interesting strategy is *Magnification* which reaches 6.1% within the categories of *Acceptance with Amendment*. *Magnification* is usually used among social equals, especially when the speaker and the interlocutor are of close social distance:

(53) 那當然啦！
 Nà dāngrán la!
 Of course! (S15 Sweater)

(54) 超水平發揮。
 Chāo shuǐpíng fāhuī.
 It was presented at the superior level. (S16 Presentation)

It should be pointed out that *Magnification* is used in a joking manner and sometimes delivered with sarcasm. However, its joking force may not be cross-culturally transparent, and may create misunderstanding between native and non-native speakers.

Another feature is the use of *Transfer*. The following examples may help to illustrate its use:

(55) 怎麼樣，你也買一雙吧？
 Zěnmeyàng, nǐ yě mǎi yīshuāng ba?
 How about if you get a pair for yourself, too? (S12 Shoes)

(56) 那你就多吃點！
 Nà nǐ jiù duō chī diǎn!
 Then you eat some more! (S14 Cooking)

These rejoinders shift the focus of the compliments. In Holmes (1986) and Herbert's (1988) studies, these kinds of rejoinders were classified as "request interpretations". The Chinese compliment responses from the data show some similarities to this category, except that they are suggestions rather than offers. That is, instead of making an offer entailing the speaker will do something for the hearer, the speaker suggests the hearer do something for him/herself. One possible reason for this is the given topics in the DCT contain a constraint that neither complimenting on appearance nor performance (in contrast to possessions) can readily direct to an offering situation. Nevertheless, those responses still reveal that complimenting on objects may run a risk of being interpreted as an indirect request (Du, this volume; Kasper & Zhang, this volume).10

Despite the fact that *Appreciation* is not regarded as a prescribed norm of compliment response in Chinese, it occurs as the second preferred strategy, reaching 16.4% of the data. Among all the formulas, 謝謝 *xièxie* 'thank you' is the most frequently occurring one under *Appreciation*. In the Chinese tradition, the standard expression for accepting compliments is 承蒙夸獎 *chéngméng kuājiǎng* '[I am] indebted to you for a compliment' or 多謝恭維 *duōxiè gōngwéi* 'many thanks for complimenting me'. These two expressions are considered by the native speakers as polite formulas in which the complimentee expresses gratitude by downgrading him/herself as being granted a compliment. The use of 謝謝 *xièxie* 'thank you' is a more recent compliment response which does not have a connotation of *Downgrade*. This occurrence reflects the cultural contact and social changes happening in the observed speech community, in which the native speakers begin to consider accepting compliments by mere appreciation as socially acceptable.

Nevertheless, *Non-acceptance* is a major culture-specific response strategy reflecting Chinese cultural values. This is particularly demonstrated from *Idiom*:

(57) 慚愧慚愧。
 Cánkuì cánkuì!
 I am really abashed. (S15 Sweater)

(58) 不好意思。
 Bùhǎoyìsi.
 I am embarrassed. (S12 Shoes)

Moreover, most of the rejoinders in *Denial* and *Qualification* are also formulaic in nature:

10In the interviews conducted by Kasper and Zhang (this volume) interviewees mentioned the risk of running into an offering situation when complimenting somebody about something in his/her room in China. Du (this volume) also found similar responses from her Chinese respondents in responding to a complimenting situation.

(59) 哪里。
   Nǎlǐ.
   No way. (S10 Swimming)

(60) 還不行。
   Hái bùxíng.
   Not good enough. (S16 Presentation)

Native speakers of Chinese feel all those rejoinders are normative, and are impressed by non-native speakers who are able to use them (Kasper & Zhang, this volume).[11] However, their frequency of occurrence turns out to be quite low, which shows that this norm is prescriptive rather than descriptive.

Compliment responses by topic

Difference is found in the distributions of compliment responses by topic, illustrated in Table 18.

Table 18: Percentage of distribution of compliment rejoinder types by compliment topic

	APPEARANCE	PERFORMANCE
No Response	8.4	3.4
Acceptance with Amendment	45.0	49.3
Acceptance	28.8	20.1
Non-acceptance	8.1	18.8
Combination	9.7	8.4

Table 18 shows that *Acceptance with Amendment* is preferred for responding to the compliments on both appearance (45%) and performance

---

[11] Kasper and Zhang's (this volume) interviews with the American learners of Chinese found native speakers of Chinese are impressed by the use of these formulas by non-native speakers, and they think having the ability to use these formulas exhibits a high level of language proficiency.

(49.3%). While *Acceptance* appears to be more or less evenly distributed between these two topics (28.8% and 20.1%), *Non-acceptance* shows its tendency as a response to performance (18.8%) rather than appearance (8.1%). This can be examined with the relatively high frequency of compliment focus on *Agent* in performance. That is, since most of the compliments on performance focus on the agent, it is unlikely that the complimentee is ready to accept the compliments from the view of the Modesty Maxim (Leech, 1983; Gu, 1990). The relatively low frequency of *Non-acceptance* for complimenting on appearance, on the other hand, indicates that the evenly distributed complimenting focus on both the object and the agent provides a way to avoid the self-praise constraint (Pomerantz, 1987), and thus opens an easy access to accepting compliments, for it is easier to agree and accept a compliment on an object than on the agent him/herself.

However, the frequency in *No Response* for responding to compliments on appearance (8.4%) is higher than on performance (3.4%). That is, more respondents chose not to respond to the compliments on appearance than to those on performance. This suggests that respondents would rather use avoidance than disagree/reject compliments on appearance.

Relating this finding to the compliment response types to the compliment situations by topic, we can see that Chinese show a tendency towards complimenting on others' performance but they are not ready to accept compliments on their own performance.

Compliment response by gender

The distribution of compliment response shows that male and female respondents adopted different strategies (see Table 19). While *Acceptance with Amendment* still remains as the first preference, males and females show a different tendency in their preference patterns of other strategies. Specifically, male respondents show a slight preference for *Non-acceptance*(18%) to *Acceptance* (15%) whereas female respondents show a much stronger tendency to *Acceptance* (31.7%). Furthermore, more male respondents chose to opt out (7.5%) than the female respondents (4.6%). Statistical analysis shows there is a significant differece between genders using compliment response strategies, χ^2 (4, N = 765) = 31.3, $p < .05$. This finding is consistent with other studies (Holmes, 1988; Herbert, 1990; Miles, 1992), showing that there is a tendency across cultures for men to tend to decline compliments despite the established non-gender-specific cultural norms. On the other hand, it indicates that women may tend to show agreement in form to the previous utterances.

Table 19: Percentage of distribution of compliment rejoinder types by gender

	MALE	FEMALE
No Response	7.5	4.6
Acceptance with Amendment	53.2	42.6
Acceptance	15.0	31.7
Non-acceptance	18.0	10.0
Combination	6.3	11.1

Compliment responses by topic and gender

There are statistically significant differences between males and females in compliment response realizations with appearance, χ_2 (4, N = 382) = 25.8, $p < .05$; and performance, χ_2 (4, N = 382) = 18.0, $p < .05$. (See Table 20). In responding to compliments on appearance, males preferred *Acceptance with Amendment*, whereas females used *Acceptance* and *Acceptance with Amendment* almost equally often. Moreover, males tended to either to use *Non-Acceptance* or *No Response* more often than females.

Table 20: Percentage of distribution of compliment rejoinder types by topic and gender

	APPEARANCE		PERFORMANCE	
	MALE	FEMALE	MALE	FEMALE
No Response	11.4	6.0	3.6	3.2
Acceptance with Amendment	52.4	39.4	53.9	45.8
Acceptance	17.5	37.5	12.6	25.9
Non-acceptance	11.4	5.6	24.6	14.4
Combination	7.2	11.6	5.4	10.6

In responding to compliments on performance, males preferred *Non-acceptance* to *Acceptance*, while females had the opposite preference pattern. However, both gender groups increased their use of *Non-acceptance* by decreasing their frequencies in *Acceptance*. Table 21 gives the percentages between the four gender relationships and the different compliment topics (see Table 21).

Table 21: Percentage of distribution of compliment rejoinder types by interaction between topic and gender of participant

	APPEARANCE				PERFORMANCE			
	MALE		FEMALE		MALE		FEMALE	
	M–m	M–f	F–f	F–m	M–m	M–f	F–f	F–m
No Response	10.7	12.2	8.3	3.7	4.8	2.4	2.8	3.7
Acceptance with Amendment	52.4	52.4	46.3	32.4	53.6	54.2	46.3	45.4
Acceptance	21.4	13.4	29.6	45.4	11.9	13.3	23.1	28.7
Non-acceptance	9.5	13.4	29.6	4.6	21.4	27.7	19.4	9.3
Combination	6.0	8.5	9.3	13.9	8.3	2.4	8.3	13.0

M, F = complimentee; m, f = complimenter

Males used *Acceptance with Amendment* as their first compliment response preference to both males and females, while females used the same strategy among females but *Acceptance* to males. One interesting result is that both males and females used *Acceptance* and *Non-acceptance* evenly when the complimenter was female. Finally, the highest frequency in *No Response* is found in the interaction between males and females. Significant difference is found in the interaction between M–m and F–m. That is, in responding to males as complimenters, males preferred *Acceptance with Amendment* to *Acceptance*. They also preferred *No Response* to *Non-acceptance*. Females, on the contrary, preferred *Acceptance* to *Acceptance with Amendment*; and then *Non-acceptance* to *No Response*. These results also show that males' compliment response pattern is consistent while females' is more dependent on the gender of interlocutors when complimenting on appearance.

When responding to compliments on performance, the four gender interaction categories (F–f, F–m, M–f, M–m) show no major differences. *Acceptance with Amendment* was chosen as the first preference for responding compliments on performance. The only difference between gender is found in that males preferred *Non-Accptance* to *Acceptance*, but females adopted the opposite pattern of preference.

Compliment responses by situation

Responses to different situations, too, show the reaction to contextual features (see Table 22). The highest frequency occurs in *No Response* category is to *S12 Shoes* (13.7%). It seems that a compliment on new shoes does not initiate much interaction. The absence of rejoinders indicates that the complimentee does not want further interaction or may not interpret the previous utterance as a compliment.

Table 22: Percentage of distribution of compliment rejoinder types by situation

	Clothes	Swimming	Hair	Shoes	Essay	Cooking	Sweater	Presentation
No Response	3.1	2.1	6.3	13.7	3.2	3.1	10.4	5.2
Acceptance with Amendment	41.7	53.1	53.7	44.2	46.3	63.5	40.6	34.4
Acceptance	35.4	20.8	24.2	21.1	16.8	12.5	34.4	30.2
Non-acceptance	8.3	17.7	6.3	12.6	28.4	12.5	5.2	16.7
Combination	11.5	6.3	9.5	8.4	5.3	8.3	9.4	13.5

The highest frequency for *Acceptance* category is for the situation *S9 Clothes* (35.4%), followed by *S15 Sweater* (34.4%). This suggests that these two DCT items have the same effect since they are designed to test similar variables (*Appearance, female/male*). The lowest frequency for *Acceptance* is found in *S14 Cooking* (12.5%), which most frequently elicits an *Acceptance with Amendment*:

(61) 湊合吃。
 Còuhe chī.
 Let's just make do with it. (S14 Cooking)

(62) 這是逼出來的。
 Zhè shì bī chūlai de.
 This is the result of being forced to learn. (S14 Cooking)

Complimenting on food or one's cooking skill is one of the most frequently occurring topic in Chinese culture. Although respondents did not accept the compliment, they did not show a tendency to reject it, either. In fact, the result shows that respondents used *Non-acceptance* as often as *Acceptance*.

Meanwhile, the highest frequency for *Non-acceptance* is found in S13 *Essay* (28.4%):

(63) 寫得不好，還需提高。
 Xiě de bù hǎo, hái xū tígāo.
 It is not well written; I need improvement.

(64) 不敢，不敢，還請多多指教。
 Bù gǎn, bù gǎn, hái qǐng duōduō zhǐjiào.
 No, no, I still need lots of advice from you.

Accepting a compliment on one's professional or academic ability seems to be the most face-threatening and the least modest behavior. This can also be observed from its low frequency in *Acceptance* (16.8%).

Compliment response by situation and gender

Gender-specific distributions show some variations in compliment responses in relation to situations. (See Table 23).

Major differences are found in *S10 Swimming*, *S15 Sweater*, and *S16 Presentation*. In *S10 Swimming*, many more of the males (19%) chose *Non-acceptance* in contrast to the females (9%). The majority of the males preferred

Acceptance with Amendment (64.3%), whereas females' reactions were less concentrated in one kind of strategy.

Table 23: Percentage of distribution of compliment rejoinder types by gender and situation

		Clothes	Swimming	Hair	Shoes	Essay	Cooking	Sweater	Presentation
No Response	M	7.1	2.4	9.8	14.6	2.4	4.8	14.3	4.8
	F	0.0	1.9	2.0	13.0	3.7	1.9	7.4	5.6
Acceptance with Amendment	M	50.0	64.3	56.1	48.8	43.9	64.3	54.8	42.9
	F	35.2	44.4	51.9	40.7	48.1	63.0	29.6	27.8
Acceptance	M	21.4	14.3	17.1	9.8	12.2	9.5	21.4	14.3
	F	46.3	25.9	29.6	29.6	20.4	14.8	44.4	42.6
Non-acceptance	M	14.3	19.0	9.8	17.1	36.6	16.7	4.8	26.2
	F	3.7	16.7	3.7	9.3	22.2	9.3	5.6	9.3
Combination	M	7.1	0.0	7.3	9.8	4.9	4.8	4.8	11.9
	F	14.8	11.0	11.1	7.4	5.6	11.1	13.0	14.8

The strategy selection for *S15 Sweater* is more interesting. While males reinfocred with their preference for *Acceptance with Amendment* (54.8%), females preferred *Acceptance* (44.4%). Moreover, males (14.3%) opted out of giving responses twice as often as females (7.4%). Note that in the *S15 Sweater* situation, the given speaker is male making a compliment on appearance. Males seemed to have more difficulty accepting a compliment on appearance by other males while females were happy to do so.

S16 Presentation, too, shows a similar trend in gender-preferential selections. Again, males maintained their preference for *Acceptance with Amendment* (42.9%) whereas females tended to choose *Acceptance* (42.6%). In addition, males tended to decline the compliments by choosing *Non-acceptance*(26.2%), while only a few females (9.3%) chose to do so.

SUMMARY

The empirical analysis has disclosed a basic culture-specific pattern of the speech event of complimenting in Mandarin Chinese. The examination of the distribution of compliments suggests that the frequency of occurrence of Chinese compliments may be relatively low. When this speech event does occur, there are constraints in cross-gender compliments. Compliments on performance are preferred to those on appearance, and *Acceptance with Amendment* is the most preferred compliment response strategy.

DISCUSSION

SOME DISTINCTIVE FEATURES OF COMPLIMENTING IN CHINESE

THE RESULTS OF EMPIRICAL ANALYSIS SHOW that Chinese compliments are formulaic with a limited range of positive semantic carriers. Due to the nature of the language structure, the most frequently used positive semantic carriers are *Adj/Stative Verbs* and *Adverbs*. Moreover, the use of nouns relates the illocutionary force of complimenting to categorization and evaluation; while verbs seldom function as semantic positive carriers in complimenting formulas.

These features in Chinese compliments are worth noticing in both cross-cultural communication and second language acquisition. First of all, adverbial compliments[12] occur ten times more frequently in Chinese than in American English: Chinese adverbial compliments reach 27.4% (cf. Table 3) while their American English counterparts count for only 2.7% (Manes and Wolfson, 1980, p. 120). This contrast results from syntactic differences between the two languages. However, as shown in the data, the most frequently occurring positive semantic carriers for the Chinese adverbs are exactly the same as the most frequently occurring Chinese adjectives/stative verbs: 好 *hǎo* 'good', 'well' and 不错 *bùcuò* 'not bad', 'well'). Their difference lies only on the syntactic level, not the semantic level. From this point of view, it is more appropriate to approach them as markers of compliments than to divide them into different syntactic functions. This approach can make the cross-cultural variables

---

[12] Adverbial compliments refer to the compliments in which adverbs are the positive semantic carriers.

comparable and thus facilitates the study of cross-cultural research on the speech event of complimenting in different languages such as Chinese and English. Through this approach, we can see that the major markers of compliments in Chinese are similar to those in American English.

However, there are some special features in Chinese complimenting. One of them is found in the use of nouns. The use of nouns reflects a process of categorization. By saying 師傅 shīfu 'master', 畫家 huàjiā 'artist', or 舞后, wǔhòu 'dance queen', the complimenter has placed the complimentee into an evaluative category. This demonstrates that the Chinese cultural members' speech behaviors are deeply influenced by the Confucian tradition 名不正，言不順 míng bù zhèng, yán bù shùn 'nothing is perfectly justifiable without being placed into the right categories'.[13] That is, to attack, accuse, or merely make a criticism of a person, first put him/her into a low, negative category.[14] In the same manner, to praise or compliment somebody, first raise him/her up to the top categories. Consequently, the naming of the top categories becomes a compliment marker in the complimenting event implemented by the use of nouns. Accordingly, this compliment strategy easily leads to a denial in response.

Another feature is the low frequency of the use of verbs. This can be observed more clearly in the rare occurrence of its corresponding formula with the speaker's perspective, 我喜歡 wǒ xǐhuan 'I like...'. Several factors are related with this low frequency of occurrence. First, 喜歡 xǐhuan is semantically stronger than 'like'. This can be observed from different distributions of these two words in their respective semantic systems. While "like" can be applied to anything towards which the speaker has a positive feeling or attitude, 喜歡 xǐhuan is relatively restricted to something the speaker evaluates as more than only positive. As a matter of fact, 喜歡 xǐhuan is often used to show the speaker's preference and willingness.

Because of this connotation, the formula 我喜歡 wǒ xǐhuan.... is used for indirect requesting more often than complimenting. By hearing 我喜歡 wǒ xǐhuan ... the hearer would usually interpret the utterance as a request of what follows 喜歡 xǐhuan. This expression is conventionalized though it is not always

---

[13] The literal meaning is "If the name is not correct, the speech cannot be right."
[14] This was typically demonstrated during the Cultural Revolution during 1966-1976, when thousands of innocent people were accused of the crime of attempting to overthrow the government and jailed without a trial, or even assassinated.

meant by the speaker as a request. The following conversation[15] illustrates this point:

(65) A and B were both Chinese female graduate students at the University of Hawai'i. They met in Hamilton Library at the beginning of a new semester.

A: 你的裙子真漂亮。
Nǐ de qúnzi zhēn piàoliang.
Your skirt is very pretty.

B: 謝謝。
Xièxie.
Thanks.

(After a few exchanges, B invited A to her place for a short visit)

A: 真的，我很喜歡你的裙子，pattern 和顏色都很漂亮。
Zhēnde, wǒ hěn xǐhuan nǐde qúnzi, pattern hé yánsè dōu hěn piàoliang.
Really, I like your skirt very much. The pattern and the color are both very pretty.

B: 等我回家時也給你買一條。
Děng wǒ huí jiā shí yě gěi nǐ mǎi yī tiáo.
I'll get one for you when I return home.

---

[15] In order to compare and verify the DCT data, I collected a small amount of data, with the help from my family back in China, through natural observation of native speakers of Chinese from the People's Republic of China in both Hawai'i and in the People's Republic of China.

A: [taken aback, immediately started another topic]

A's first utterance was delivered successfully as a compliment which elicited a rejoinder with an appreciation token (謝謝 *xièxie*). However, when she repeated her compliment it was interpreted as an indirect request that she also wanted a skirt like that. She was taken aback when she heard B's rejoinder as an acceptance of a request. Had she actually wanted a skirt like that, she would have continued the topic by expressing thanks to B and telling B some relevant information, such as the size she wanted, offering to pay in advance, and providing all the other necessary information to make sure she could get the skirt. However, she switched to another topic instead.

Example (65) shows that even though the interlocutors can always feel free to negotiate the meaning of the utterance 我喜歡 *wǒ xǐhuan*...., the hearing of it is often directed to an interpretation of an indirect request by native speakers. Moreover, the hearer feels obliged to make an offer even when he/she does not really think the speaker has any intention of requesting.16

As 我喜歡 *wǒ xǐhuan*.... is frequently used in indirect requesting, its distribution in complimenting is rather low because of the ambiguity created, as found from the DCT data of this study (0.7% of *Explicit Compliment*).

Related to this factor, the speaker's perspective when saying 我喜歡 *wǒ xǐhuan*... is felt to be subjective. The majority (82%) of the compliment formulas yielded in the data are structured with "*Object/Action* + compliment marker" and "*Agent* + compliment marker". These are positive descriptions of the observed appearance and performance. While in the Western tradition the use of "I" is thought to be less evaluative and imposing compared to the use of other perspectives, Chinese perceive the use of 我 'I' as just the opposite. Therefore, in Chinese, saying 你的裙子真漂亮 *nǐde qúnzi zhēn piàoliang* 'your skirt is pretty' sounds objective and highly valued, whereas 我喜歡你的裙子 *wǒ xǐhuan nǐde qúnzi* 'I like your skirt' sounds like a subjective evaluation if it is not heard as an indirect request.

Since the speaker's perspective highlights his/her opinion, it is more plausible in this situation to elicit *Acceptance* as a response. This formula makes

---

16Another level of politeness is involved here, where the hearer uses offering as a politeness strategy to return the compliment. These kinds of offers are conventionalized ritual offers to which substantive refusals are expected in response (also see Chen, Ye, & Zhang, this volume).

it difficult to respond with a denial, though it is not impossible.[17] From this point of view, the rare occurrence of the speaker's perspective may be one of the reasons for the low frequency of *Acceptance* as a compliment response in Chinese.

AN EMIC APPROACH TOWARDS CHINESE COMPLIMENT RESPONSES

The empirical analysis shows that Chinese use *Acceptance with Amendment* most frequently for responding to compliments. This breaks the myth that Chinese use *Non-acceptance* frequently. However, this myth has its source in the prescribed "standard" form of Chinese compliment response which is routinized and ritual in nature.

Routinized and ritual rejoinders

A routinized rejoinder is a fixed utterance or sequence shared in a speech community as a norm to fulfill the communicative function of a speech event. As Saville-Troike (1982) points out, "Perhaps the most important characteristic of routines and rituals is that truth value is largely irrelevant. Their meaning is dependent on shared beliefs and values of the speech community coded into communicative patterns, and they cannot be interpreted apart from social and cultural context" (p. 44).

In different varieties of English, an appreciation token is a routinized rejoinder because it is formulaic and a native speaker of English perceives it as a "correct response" in his/her speech community. "A feature of an appreciation token is that it recognizes the status of the prior as compliment without being semantically fitted to the specifics of that compliment. That is, it does not itself contain a focus upon the referent of the compliment" (Pomerantz, 1978, p. 83). A routinized rejoinder for a Chinese compliment, however, is very different from the one in English, because a denial is preferred over an appreciation token.

The routinized compliment rejoinder in Chinese is ritual in nature. A ritual rejoinder refers to a culturally routinized rejoinder with a distinctive feature of having a paradoxical relationship between the utterance's semantic and pragmatic meanings. Expressions falling into the category *Non-acceptance* in the observed data are basically routinized. A feature shared in those expressions (c.f. the section "Compliment Rejoinders" under "Results") is that

---

[17]*Confirmation* followed by *Downgrade* is the most frequent response to these kinds of formulas of compliment.

the focus of the denial is on the complimentee him/herself, never on the complimenter.[18] The ritual nature of *Non-acceptance* in Chinese can be understood in the Chinese cultural context and can be observed from how native speakers of Chinese interact using this strategy in a ritual manner. First of all, *Non-acceptance* takes a form of disagreement in that it is directed to the proposition of the complimentary utterance, not the illocutionary force of the compliment. That is, *Non-acceptance* carries a pragmatic force of acceptance covered by a semantic form of disagreement. What *Non-acceptance* disagrees with is not the act of complimenting but the content of the compliment. This can be seen in the following example:

(66) A and B were both Chinese graduate students at the University of Hawai'i. A was invited to a party at B's house. B was busy cooking for the party.

A: 你可眞有兩下！
Nǐ kě zhēn yǒu liǎngxià!
You are really good at cooking!

B: 我不行。
Wǒ bùxíng.
I am not.

B's utterance denies the proposition, not the illocutionary force of the compliment. Specifically, B denies her cooking skills, not A's complimenting action.

The ritual rejoinder operates as part of the entire Chinese ritual system of politeness. As Pomerantz (1978) points out, compliments have the status of "supportive" actions (p. 82). One distinctive feature of accepting supportive actions in Chinese, including offers and invitations, is to give ritual rejections as initial rejoinders (Gu, 1990; Mao, 1994; Chen, Ye & Zhang, this volume). The ritual nature of *Non-acceptance* lies in that although the responding utterance takes a form of disagreement with the complimentary utterance, this

---

[18]The subcategories under *Non-acceptance* are basically ritual disagreement, though there is also substantive disagreement, such as in the case of 得了吧 *déle ba*, 'stop it'.

kind of disagreement does not imply a subtansive rejection. Instead of emphasizing an acceptance of the illocution as in the routinized American English compliment rejoinder, the Chinese ritual rejoinder focuses on a disagreement with the proposition of the complimentary utterance. In this way, it avoids rejecting the illocution of the compliment, which is the essential part of the speech event of complimenting, and thus, it encodes politeness in the Chinese speech community. From this perspective, the routinized rejoinder in Chinese does not conflict with the one in English.

The ritual aspect of the Chinese routinized rejoinder can also be observed in Chinese interlanguage pragmatics. Kasper and Zhang's (this volume) interviews of learners of Chinese provide evidence of the ritual nature of Chinese routinized compliment responses. Interviewees expressed their bewilderment about using this strategy when they were in China. One myth they reported was that one should deny the compliment whenever it was given. One highly advanced learner reported that he tried some expressions such as 豈有此理 qǐ-yǒu-cǐ-lǐ 'preposterous' and 亂講 luàn jiǎng 'nonsense', thinking they would be proper denials to compliments yet only to find those responses were rude and meant "nonsense" in Chinese. What he actually did was reject the illocutionary force of the compliment, which was a rude response to the complimenter.

The selection of the sub-strategies of *Non-acceptance* can give a clue to the hearer of the speaker's perception of him/herself, which is illustrated in the following conversation.

(67) In an office at the University of Hawai'i. A, C, and D are native speakers of Chinese, B is a non-native speaker of Chinese whose Chinese is classified at the superior level according to ACTFL Proficiency Scale.

A: 你的中文水平相當可以，都能念詩了。
Nǐde zhōngwén shuǐpíng xiāngdāng kěyǐ, dōu néng niàn shī le.
Your Chinese is pretty good. You can even read poems.

B: 不行。
Bùxíng.
No way.

C: 你怎麼不說"多謝恭維"呀？
Nǐ zěnme bù shuō "duōxiè gōngwéi" ya?
Why don't you say "thanks for the compliment"?

D: 不，應該說"哪里，哪里"。
Bù, yīnggāi shuō "nǎlǐ, nǎlǐ".
No. You should say, "No, no".

B: 對，"哪里，哪里"。
Duì, "nǎlǐ, nǎlǐ".
You're right. "No, no".

C: 你該說："不敢當，不敢當"。
Nǐ gāi shuō: "bù gǎndāng, bù gǎndāng".
You should say, "I really don't deserve this".

The above formulaic expressions reveal the ritual nature of the routinized rejoinder. That is, they are used appropriately when the speaker has reached a certain level of achievement, i.e., language proficiency in this case. 不行 *bùxíng* could be both a real denial and a ritual denial depending on different contexts. One clue to distinguish the difference is in the stressed/unstressedness of the contour. Another clue is that the ritual denial is often followed by an utterance like: 我還要 *wǒ hái yào* ... 'I still need [to improve]'. What C and D were suggesting was that B's Chinese was really good, so a ritual rejoinder might be more appropriate then a flat 不行*bùxíng*. In other words, the complimentee's appearance or performance has to be good enough to decline the given positive evaluation. If a speaker's Chinese level is rather low, and he/she uses 哪里，哪里 *nǎlǐ, nǎlǐ*" as a response in the situation of example (67), he/she is considered to be rather conceited, for, by saying 哪里，哪里 *nǎlǐ, nǎlǐ*", the speaker has already acknowledged that his/her level of language proficiency is rather high. As a result, the speaker is showing arrogance rather than modesty.

Therefore, a ritual rejoinder is delivered with the premise that an acceptance is presupposed, but the preference of the Modesty Maxim over the

Agreement Maxim (Leech, 1983) makes the utterance sound like a rejection. This preference can be seen in the following example, in which native speakers of Chinese do not interpret the ritual denial as a substantive rejection.

> (68) A is a male, 24 years old, student; B, a female, 20 years old, student. They are in a working place in Beijing. A, who was the monitor of the class, requested B to take part in an intelligence contest which was an honor for the participants.
>
> A: 明天你参加智力竞赛！
> *Míngtiān nǐ cānjiā zhìlì jìngsài!*
> You are going to take part in the intelligence contest tomorrow!
>
> B: 不行！
> *Bùxíng!*
> I am not qualified!
>
> A: 别呀，我看你挺聪明的。
> *Bié ya, wǒ kàn nǐ tǐng cōngming de.*
> Don't say that. I think you are quite smart.
>
> B: 哪呀，比你，我可差远了。
> *Nǎ ya, bǐ nǐ, wǒ kě chà yuǎn le.*
> No way. I am far from you.
>
> A: 得了，别谦虚了，就是你参加了。
> *Dé le, Bié qiānxū le, jiùshì nǐ cānjiā le.*
> Stop it. <u>Don't be modest</u> It's settled — you will participate.

Instead of interpreting B's reply as a rejection, A sees B's response as a ritual denial to show politeness and modesty.

This takes us to the concept of modesty in Chinese culture. Modesty is highly valued in this culture but it is also often misunderstood by outsiders as merely denigrating or humbling oneself. One feature that needs emphasizing is the assumption of modesty. That is, modesty is supposed to be applied by people who have acquired status at a high level in the social hierarchy. Modesty arises from the assumption that the higher the social status of a person, the more modesty he/she has to show, since an enlightened person should be aware of his/her ignorance and how much he/she still has to strive.[19] "The exaggerated modesty is not a sign of lack of self-confidence,... The overestimation of one's ability, the exaggeration of one's capacity, designed to elevate one above one's fellows, is frowned upon by society" (Hu, 1944, pp. 48–49).

Returning to the ritual rejoinder in Chinese, we can see that the formulaic denial is not a real denial in the sense of rejecting the compliment. Rather, it has the function of letting the compliment pass. The speaker denies the proposition but accepts the complimenting force, thus emphasizing the value of modesty. This preference is a cultural choice of the Modesty Maxim over the Agreement Maxim (Leech, 1983). As Young (1987) comments on this prescribed norm, "No matter how pleased Chinese people may feel upon hearing a compliment, they must withhold any expressions of gratitude or delight" (p. 26).

It should be pointed out that native speakers of Chinese may not be well aware of the ritual nature of their compliment responses. Their perception of the ritual rejoinder may be different from their speech behaviors. That is, a native speaker of Chinese may not be able to articulate the difference of a denial between the proposition and illocution of the compliment. Nevertheless, the native use of the ritual rejoinder is actualized through his/her behavior, which distinguishes the difference.

Deviation from the norm

Despite the fact that the prescriptive norm of Chinese compliment responses is ritual, this study shows that Chinese do not closely follow this norm in their actual speech event of complimenting. In fact, their strategy deviates from the norm: the strategy of *Acceptance with Amendment* is preferred to *Non-acceptance*. As we have already seen, the result of this preference parallels the one found

---

[19] This only refers to the Confucian ideology that prevails in children's pragmatic development in socialization. However, children do not adhere to this prescribed politeness norm in actual practice, nor do the parents themselves.

for American English compliment responses (Pomerantz, 1987; Herbert, 1988, 1990).

However, that *Downgrade* is chosen as the most preferred subcategory of *Acceptance with Amendment* indicates that the respondents still acknowledge the prescriptive norm.[20] The result is that the Chinese compliment responses are closer to *Non-acceptance* than *Acceptance*. Instead of disagreeing with the proposition of the compliment, the speaker shifts the focus to the weak points of the referent of the compliment. By doing t his, the speaker releases the elements of disagreement contained in the prescriptive norm of compliment response.

There is one feature shared by both Chinese and American preferences of compliment responses: the avoidance of explicit agreement with the compliment propositional utterance. One of the functions of routinized rejoinders is to complete the interaction in the speech event of complimenting. In this way the compliment event is a relatively self-contained system. The selection of compliment response strategies gives the hearer a clue of how much interaction the speaker is willing to engage in. The deviation of the prescriptive norm opens a possibility for the interlocutors to interact further. As *Acceptance with Amendment* mainly provides information about the referent of compliment, it can serve as the opening of a new topic as well as supplying the second part of the adjacency pair of the compliment exchange. Moreover, any deviation from the norm — no matter what cultural norm it is — is a signal of negotiating meaning of the conversational exchanges because it generates new implicatures and furthers interaction.

THE PREFERENCE OF COMPLIMENT TOPIC

The results of the investigation of compliment topic shows a preference of *Performance* over *Appearance*. This is different from the results of the studies of compliments in different varieties of English where these two topics are more or less evenly distributed, with *Appearance* slightly outranking *Performance* (Holmes, 1988; Lee, 1990; Miles, 1992). Young (1987) proposes that the reason for this Chinese preference is "because more emphasis is placed on the virtues of people and qualities of individuals in China, the Chinese people do not consider good looks as [having] great [social] value. Too much attention to

---

[20]Studies in American English compliments show that *Comment* is the most preferred response in the American English speech community (Herbert, 1988; Miles, 1992).

one's appearance would mean less attention to his work or study" (p. 25). Although this explanation is more subjective than objective, it is true that there is a Chinese tradition rooted in the Ru School, which upholds morality, moderation, and modesty among members of the society (Jiang, 1985). Physical appearance is believed to be negatively correlated with one's virtue and ability. Moreover, explicit appreciation of one's physical appearance is considered as uncultivated since implicitness is culturally preferred. Hsu's (1953) contrastive study of Americans and Chinese may offer another reason for this. In his analysis, physical appearance in traditional Chinese cultural contexts has a sexual implication which is a taboo in social interaction. All of these set constraints over appreciation of physical appearance openly, and thus restrict paying compliments explicitly, though this does not mean that physical appearance is neglected or not much valued by individuals.

Moreover, the results show that *Non-acceptance* occurs more frequently in responding to compliments on performance than it does in responding to compliments on appearance. If we relate this to the ritual compliment rejoinder as a prescriptive norm, we can see that complimenting on performance is more conventionalized and concerned with the ritual aspect than that on appearance. That is, a "standard" compliment is "supposed" to be paid on *Performance* and a "standard" rejoinder is "supposed" to decline it. As seen in the results, complimenting on *Appearance* occurs much less frequently, and once it is given it seems more acceptable since this kind of compliment sounds like an objective evaluation with a focus on *Object/Action* that allows the complimentee to agree with it and thus accept it.

CONSTRAINTS FOR COMPLIMENTS ACROSS GENDERS

The gender-specific distribution of compliments is the result of an interaction between social value and the constraints of compliments across gender.

The constraints of compliments across genders are the reflection of the Chinese traditional ethical criteria 男女授受不親 *nánnǔ shòushòu bù qīn* 'no interaction between men and women'.[21] This is particularly shown in the low frequency of the occurrence of compliments in male to females interaction. While by Western customs, paying compliments to women is a courtesy, by Chinese it can be a violation of the social order. Frequent compliments offered

---

[21] The literal translation is "It is improper for men and women to touch each other's hands in passing objects from hand to hand."

having ulterior motives and the complimenter can even run the risk of being accused of harrassment (Jiang, 1985; Chen and Chen, 1990).

FUNCTION OF COMPLIMENTS IN THE CHINESE CULTURAL CONTEXT

The features exhibited in the speech event of complimenting in Chinese suggest that the function of compliments in the Chinese cultural context may be different from those in different varieties of English. However, the Chinese characteristics of this speech event share some commonality with other Asian cultures, such as that of Japan. In Daikuhara's (1986) study of Japanese compliments, she points out the emphasis on modesty in the Japanese responses. According to Daikuhara, one function of the Japanese compliment rejoinder "No, no" or "That's not true" is "not to show explicit disagreement, but simply to avoid self-praise more indirectly. That is, the latter use of 'No, no' seems to mean nothing; it is automatic when one receives a compliment, just as 'Thank you' is in American English" (p. 122). Daikuhara proposes a hypothesis for the use of denial in Japanese responses as a return of politeness, since a compliment is a polite behavior that creates distance between interlocutors. Therefore, "this denial of the compliments serves to sustain harmony between the parties and to emphasize their commonality" (p. 125).

Daikuhara's hypothesis implies an assumption that politeness behavior is a result of a consideration of creating — rather than reducing — social distance between the interlocutors. The finding in this study provides empirical evidence for this claim: the occurrence of compliments is shown to be relatively low in equal relations and the respondents prefer using a compliment response strategy which deviates from the prescriptive politeness norm. Offering compliments and responding with ritual denials to show modesty are applied more to interlocutors of distant social relationships than to those of close relationships. This shows that the speech event of complimenting in the Chinese cultural context may not have the function of solidarity as it does in the speech communities of different varieties of English (Wolfson, 1981; Holmes, 1986; Herbert, 1988).

CONCLUSION

THIS STUDY EXAMINED CHARACTERISTICS of Chinese compliments and compliment responses, including overall strategies, compliment topics, situational factors, and gender-specific distribution. The findings of this study provide an empirical basis for understanding this speech event from the Chinese cultural perspective.

This study is based on data collected through the DCT format. The design facilitated the gathering of a relatively large amount of data in a short period of time, when the analysis had to be performed outside the speech community (i.e., at the University of Hawai'i). The results of the empirical analysis are consistent with the results in previous studies of Chinese compliments based on limited observations (Jiang, 1985; Young, 1987; Zuo, 1988) in regard to compliment topic and gender-specific distributions of compliments, but different in the preferrence pattern of compliment response strategies.

This study only investigates the compliments and compliment responses between interlocutors of equal social status and close relationships. Therefore, its finding may not apply to situations where interlocutors are of unequal social status and distant relationship. It may be possible that native speakers of Chinese are more bound to the prescriptive norm than to the observed descriptive norm when they are in unequal social interactions. Moreover, as the data were collected in the People's Republic of China, the results and analysis are limited to the complimenting event in the observed speech community.

Furthermore, since the DCT format is basically constructed for adjacency pair elicitation, multiple turns of interaction cannot be examined. Therefore, the DCT data cannot provide further information of the hearer's interpretations and reactions of the previous utterances. Consequently, some of the interpretations will have to be empirically verified.

Further studies are needed to investigate complimenting in Chinese. A study of compliment responses to implicit compliments and an analysis of the compliment rejoinder focus in terms of speaker/hearer's focus may provide insight in the culture-specific pattern of the compliment and compliment response strategies. A complementary study could be conducted by collecting data through natural observations, and a study of native speakers' perception of their behavior could also be very helpful to the understanding of this speech event in the Chinese cultural context ◆

APPENDIX A

DISCOURSE COMPLETION TASK FORM
(Pinyin transcription did not appear in the original instrument)

漢語運用咨詢表

Hànyǔ Yùnyòng ZīxúnBiǎo

以下是有關漢語運用的咨詢調查。請您設身處地回答下列問題，並將您在每種情況下可能會說的話逐字逐句寫在"你對他說"，"你對她說"，或者"你說"后面。倘偌您認爲在具體的場合下您不會作任何反應，請選擇B。

Yǐxià shì yǒuguān Hànyǔ yùnyòng de zīxún diàochá. Qǐng nín shèshēnchǔdì de huídá xiàliè wèntí, bìng jiāng nín zài měizhǒng qíngkuàng xia kěnéng huì shuō de huà zhúzì zhújù de xiě zài "Nǐ duì tā shuō", "Nǐ duì tā shuō", huòzhě "Nǐ shuō" hòumian. Tǎngruò nín rènwéi zài jùtǐ de chǎnghé xià ní bùhuì zuò rènhé fǎnyìng, qǐng xuǎnzé B.

1. 你在學校圖書館前遇到同學李曉梅，你注意到她今天穿了件新襯衫。

   Nǐ zài xuéxiào túshūguǎn qián yùdao tóngxué Lǐ Xiǎoméi, nǐ zhùyì dao tā jīntiān chuān le jiàn xīn chènshān.

A. 你對她說：

   Nǐ duì tā shuō: _____

   _____

B. 你甚麼也不說。

   Nǐ shénme yě bù shuō.

2. 你和朋友劉林在打乒乓球。你發現他球打得很不錯。

   Nǐ hé péngyou Liú Lín zài dǎ pīngpāngqiú. Nǐ fāxiàn tā dǎ de hěn bùcuò.

A. 你對他說：

   Nǐ duì tā shuō: _____

   _____

B. 你甚麼也不說。

   Nǐ shénme yě bù shuō.

3. 你去教室找同學王德生複習准備期中考試。你見到他戴了副新眼鏡。

   Nǐ qù jiàoshǐ zhǎo tóngxué Wáng Déshēng fùxí zhǔnbèi qízhōng kǎoshì. Nǐ jiàndao tā dài le fù xīn yǎnjìng.

A. 你對他說：

   Nǐ duì tā shuō: _____

   _____

B. 你甚麼也不說。

   Nǐ shénme yě bù shuō.

4. 你在參加學校的新年晚會，你發現你的同學何秀芳餃子皮扞得又快又好。

   Nǐ zài cānjiā xuéxiào de xīnnián wǎnhuì, nǐ fāxiàn nǐ de tóngxué Hé Xiùfāng jiǎozipír gǎn de yòu kuài yòu hǎo.

   A. 你對她說：

      Nǐ duì tā shuō: _____

   _____

   B. 你甚麼也不說。

      Nǐ shénme yě bù shuō.

5. 你和一些同學去郊遊，看到章民今天穿雙新球鞋。

   Nǐ hé yīxiē tóngxué qù jiāoyóu, kàndao Zhāng Mín jīntiān chuān shuāng xīn qiúxié.

   A. 你對他說：

      Nǐ duì tā shuō: _____

   _____

   B. 你甚麼也不說。

      Nǐ shénme yě bù shuō.

6. 你在校友會上見到丁燕穿了條漂亮的裙子。
   Nǐ zài xiàoyǒuhuì shang jiàndao Dīng Yàn chuān le tiáo piàoliang de qúnzi.

   A. 你對她說：

   Nǐ duì tā shuō: _____

   _____

   B. 你甚麼也不說。
      Nǐ shénme yě bù shuō.

7. 你在學校的舞會上發現你的同學陳丹舞跳得很好。
   Nǐ zài xuéxiào de wǔhuì shang fāxiàn nǐ de tóngxué Chén Dān wǔ tiào de hěn hǎo.

   A. 你對她說：

   Nǐ duì tā shuō: _____

   _____

   B. 你甚麼也不說。
      Nǐ shénme yě bù shuō.

8. 你去朋友宋浩家玩兒，見到牆上有一幅很好的山水畫兒。他告訴你這是他自己畫的畫兒。

   Nǐ qù péngyou Sòng Hào jiā wánr, jiàndao qiángshang yǒu yīfú hěn hǎo de shānshuǐhuàr. Tā gàosu nǐ zhèshi tā zìjǐ huà de huàr.

   A. 你對他說：

   Nǐ duì tā shuō: _____

   _____

   B. 你甚麼也不說。
   Nǐ shénme yě bù shuō.

9. 你今天穿了件新衣服，在學校門前遇到同學陸志成。他對你說："嘿，今天真精神！"

   Nǐ jīntiān chuān le jiàn xīn yīfu, zài xuéxiào mén qián yùdao tóngxué Lù Zhìchéng.

   Tā duì nǐ shuō: "Hei, jīntiān zhēn jīngshen!"

   A. 你對他說：

   Nǐ duì tā shuō: _____

   _____

   B. 你不說話。
   Nǐ bù shuōhuà.

10. 你在游泳時遇到朋友陸雁雁。
    她對你說："你游得眞不錯！"

    Nǐ zài yóuyǒng shí yùdao péngyou Lù Yànyan.

    Tā duì nǐ shuō: "Nǐ yóu de zhēn bùcuò!"

    A. 你對她說：

    Nǐ duì tā shuō: _____

    _____

    _____

    B. 你不說話。
    Nǐ bù shuōhuà.

11. 你剛剛做了頭髮。回家的路上遇到鄰居鄧茵。她對你說："燙頭啦，眞精神！"

    Nǐ gānggāng zuò le tóufa. Huíjiā de lùshang yùdao línju Dèng Yīn.

    Tā duì nǐ shuō: "Tàngtóu la, zhēn jīngshen!"

    A. 你對她說：

    Nǐ duì tā shuō: _____

    _____

    _____

    B. 你不說話。
    Nǐ bù shuōhuà.

12. 你今天穿了雙新鞋去學校。
    班上的章晶對你說："穿新鞋啦，眞神氣呀！"
    Nǐ jīntiān chuān le shuāng xīn xié qù xuéxiào.
    Bānshang de Zhāng Jīng duì nǐ shuō: "Chuān xīn xié la, zhēn shénqì ya!"

A. 你對她說：
    Nǐ duì tā shuō: _____
    _____

B. 你不說話。
    Nǐ bù shuōhuà.

13. 你的同學方雯雯把你的論文還給你。
    她對你說："你的文筆眞不錯。"
    Nǐ de tóngxué Fāng Wénwen bǎ nǐ de lùnwén huán gei nǐ.
    Tā duì nǐ shuō: "Nǐ de wénbǐ zhēn bùcuò".

A. 你對她說：
    Nǐ duì tā shuō: _____
    _____

B. 你不說話。
    Nǐ bù shuōhuà.

14. 你邀請了一些朋友來你家玩兒。你現在正忙著給他們做吃的。
    你的朋友彭龍對你說："你做飯真有兩下子。"

    Nǐ yāoqǐng le yīxiē péngyou lái nǐ jiā wánr. Nǐ xiànzài zhèng máng zhe gěi tāmen zuò chī de.

    Nǐ de péngyou Péng Lóng duì nǐ shuō: "Nǐ zuò fàn zhēn yǒu liǎngxiàzi".

    A. 你對他說：

    Nǐ duì tā shuō: _____
    _____
    _____

    B. 你不說話。
    Nǐ bù shuōhuà.

15. 你穿了件新毛衣去參加新年晚會。
    你的同學畢勇銘對你說："新毛衣，真精神！"

    Nǐ chuān le jiàn xīn máoyī qù cānjiā xīnnián wǎnhuì.

    Nǐ de tóngxué Bì Yǒngmíng duì nǐ shuō: "Xīn máoyī, zhēn jīngshen!"

    A. 你對他說：

    Nǐ duì tā shuō: _____
    _____
    _____

    B. 你不說話。
    Nǐ bù shuōhuà.

16. 你剛剛在課上作了發言。
    下課后同學王衡對你說："你的發言真精采。"
    Nǐ gānggāng zài kèshang zuò le fāyán.
    Xiàkè hòu tóngxué Wáng Héng duì nǐ shuō: "Nǐ de fāyán zhēn jīngcǎi".

    A. 你對他說：

    Nǐ duì tā shuō: _____

    _____
    _____

    B. 你不說話。
       Nǐ bù shuōhuà.

請回答下列有關問題：
Qǐng huídá xiàliè yǒuguān wèntí:

年齡：_____
Niánlíng

文化程度：_____
Wénhuà chéngdù

職業：_____
Zhíyè

普通話是否您的母語？   A. 是_____   B. 否_____
Pǔtōnghuà shì fǒu nín de mǔyǔ?   A. Shì   B. Fǒu

如果您選擇B.，請列出您講的方言：＿＿＿＿＿＿＿＿＿＿＿＿＿＿
Rúguǒ nǐ xuǎnzé B., qǐng lièchū nín jiǎng de fāngyán:

外國語學習情況：
Wàiguóyǔ xuéxí qíngkuàng:

語種	最初學習年齡	學習年限	程度
Yǔzhǒng	Zuìchū xuéxí niánlíng	Xuéxí niánxiàn	Chéngdù

您是否出過國？　　　　　　　　A. 是＿＿＿＿　B. 否＿＿＿＿
Nǐ shì fǒu chū guo guó?　　　　　A. Shì　　　　B. Fǒu

如果您選擇A.，請接著回答下列問題：
Rúguǒ nín xuǎnzé A., qǐng jiēzhe huídá xiàliè wèntí:

國家	逗留時間（年，月）
Guójiā	Dòuliú shíjiān (nián, yuè)

感謝您的合作！
Gǎnxiè Nín de Hézuò!

APPENDIX B

ENGLISH TRANSLATION OF DISCOURSE COMPLETION TASK FORM

The following information is being gathered for a research project on Mandarin Chinese language use. Please provide the information, based as much as possible on your actual use in everyday life.

Imagine yourself in the following situations in Mainland China. All relationships noted are between acquaintances. Please note your response down **exactly what you would say** in the space provided either by writing your response or by circling option **B**.

1. You meet your classmate *Lǐ Xiǎoméi* in front of the library and notice that she is wearing a new blouse today.

A. YOU: _____

_____

_____

B. YOU DO NOT SAY ANYTHING.

2. You are playing Ping-pong with your friend *Liǔ Lín*. You notice that he is a good player.

A. YOU: _____
_____
_____

B. YOU DO NOT SAY ANYTHING.

3. You are meeting your classmate *Wáng Déshēng* in a classroom to prepare for the mid-term exam. You notice he is wearing a new pair of glasses today.

A. YOU: _____
_____
_____

B. YOU DO NOT SAY ANYTHING.

4. You are at a New Year's Party at campus. You notice your schoolmate *Hé Xiùfāng* is good at making dumpling wrappers.

A. YOU: _____
_____
_____

B. YOU DO NOT SAY ANYTHING.

5. You are on an outing with a group of students. You notice your classmate *Zhāng Mín* is wearing a new pair of tennis shoes today.

   A. YOU: _____
   _____
   _____

   B. YOU DO NOT SAY ANYTHING.

6. You meet your old classmate *Dīng Yàn* at a party and notice that she is wearing a new pretty dress.

   A. YOU: _____
   _____
   _____

   B. YOU DO NOT SAY ANYTHING.

7. You are at the school dance ball and notice that your classmate *Chén Dān* is a good dancer.

   A. YOU: _____
   _____
   _____

   B. YOU DO NOT SAY ANYTHING.

8. You are visiting your friend *Sòng Hào*. You see a nice Chinese painting on the wall. Sòng Hào you that he himself is the painter.

A. YOU: _____
_____

B. YOU DO NOT SAY ANYTHING.

9. You wear a new dress today. Your meet your classmate *Lù Zhìchéng* at the school gate.
   Lù: "Hi, You look great today!"

A. YOU: _____
_____

B. YOU DO NOT RESPOND.

10. You meet with your friend *Lǚ Yànyàn* when you are swimming.
    Lù: "You are a good swimmer".

A. YOU: _____
_____

B. YOU DO NOT RESPOND.

11. You just had your hair done. You meet your neighbor *Dèng Yín* on your way home.
    Dèng: "You look great with your hair done".

    A. YOU: _____

    _____

    _____

    B. YOU DO NOT RESPOND.

12. You wear a new pair of shoes to the school
    Zhāng Jīng in your class: "You look good in these new shoes!"

    A. YOU: _____

    _____

    _____

    B. YOU DO NOT RESPOND.

13. Your classmate *Fāng Wénwén* is returning your essay to you.
    Fāng Wénwén: "Well written".

    A. YOU: _____

    _____

    _____

    B. YOU DO NOT RESPOND.

14. You have invited some friends to your home. Now you are busy preparing dinner for them.
    Your friend *Péng Lóng*: "You are a good cook!"

A. YOU: _____
    _____
    _____

B. YOU DO NOT RESPOND.

15. You are wearing a new sweater at the New Year's Party.
    Your friend *Bì Yǒngmíng*: "New sweater. You look great!"

A. YOU: _____
    _____
    _____

B. YOU DO NOT RESPOND.

16. You have just given a presentation on your project in the class.
    After class, your classmate *Wáng Héng*: "Your presentation was really good!"

A. YOU: _____
    _____
    _____

B. YOU DO NOT RESPOND.

The following questions are optional. They provide information concerning research. Please check the appropriate information:

1. Age _____

2. Highest level of education completed _____

3. Present occupation _____

4. Do you speak any other Chinese dialects than Mandarin Chinese?
   Yes ___   No ___
   If yes, what dialects do you speak _____

5. Foreign language study

Language	Years studied	Starting age	Level

6. Please list the countries you have visited

Countries	Length of stay (months/years)

REFERENCES

Beebe, L., & Cummings, (in press). *Speech act performance: A function of the data clollection procedures?* Paper presented at TESOL Convention, New York.

Beebe, L., Takahashi, T., & Uliss-Weltz, R. (1990). Pragmatic transfer in ESL refusals. In R. Scarcella, E. Anderson, & S. Krashen (Eds.), *On the development of communicative competence in a second language* (pp. 55–73). Cambridge, MA: Newbury House.

Bilmes, J. (1988). The concept of preference in conversation analysis. In *Language in Society, 17*, 161–181.

Blum-Kulka, S. (1987). Indirectness and politeness in requests: Same or different? *Journal of Pragmatics, 11*, 131–146.

Blum-Kulka, S. (1989). Playing it safe: The role of conventionality in indirectness. In S. Blum-Kulka, J. House, & G. Kasper (Eds.), *Cross-cultural pragmatics: Requests and apologies* (pp. 37–70). Norwood, NJ: Ablex.

Blum-Kulka, S. (1990). You don't touch lettuce with your fingers. *Journal of Pragmatics, 14*, 259–288.

Blum-Kulka, S., Danet, B., & Gerson, R. (1985). The language of requesting in Israeli society. In J. Forgas (Ed.), *Language and social situation* (pp. 113–141). New York, NY: Springer Verlag.

Blum-Kulka, S., & House, J. (1989). Cross-cultural and situational variation in requestive behavior. In S. Blum-Kulka, J. House, & G. Kasper (Eds.), *Cross-cultural pragmatics: Requests and apologies* (pp. 123–154). Norwood, NJ: Ablex.

Blum-Kulka, S., House, J., & Kasper, G. (Eds.). (1989). *Cross-cultural pragmatics: Requests and apologies.* Norwood, NJ: Ablex.

Brown, P., & Levinson, S. (1987). *Politeness: Some universals in language usage.* Cambridge, MA: Cambridge University Press.

Brown, R., & Gilman, A. (1989). Politeness theory and Shakespeare's four major tragedies. *Language in Society, 18,* 159–212.

Chao, Y. (1968). *A grammar of spoken Chinese.* Berkeley, CA: University of California Press.

Chen, X. (1992). *A study of the speech act of refusal: Chinese vs. American.* Unpublished scholarly paper, University of Hawai'i at Mānoa, Honolulu, HI.

Chen, Z., & Chen, J. (1990). Sociolinguistics research based on Chinese reality. *International Journal of the Sociology of Language, 81,* 21–41.

Cottrill, L. (1990). Face, politeness and indirectness. *International Pragmatics Association,* 1–16.

Daikuhara, M. (1986). A study of compliments from a cross-cultural perspective: Japanese vs. American English. *Penn Working Papers in Educational Linguistics, 2* (2), 103–134.

Du, J. (1992). *Chinese, Japanese and American face-threatening acts realizations.* M.A. thesis, Department of English As Second Language, University of Hawai'i at Mānoa, Honolulu, HI.

Faerch, C., & Kasper, G. (1989). Internal and external modification in interlanguage request realization. In S. Blum-Kulka, J. House, & G. Kasper (Eds.), *Cross-cultural pragmatics: Requests and apologies* (pp. 221–247). Norwood, NJ: Ablex.

Fraser, B. (1978). Acquiring social competence in a second language. *RELC Journal, 9,* 1–21.

Fraser, B. (1990). Perspectives on politeness. *Journal of Pragmatics, 14,* 219–236.

Fraser, B., Rintell, E., & Walters, J. (1980). An approach to conducting research on the acquisition of pragmatic competence in a second language. In D. Larsen-Freeman (Ed.), *Discourse analysis in second language research* (pp. 75–91). Rowley, MA: Newbury House.

Goffman, E. (1967). *Interaction ritual: Essays on face-to-face behavior.* New York, NY: Anchor Books.

Gordon, D., & Lakoff, G. (1975). Conversational postulates. In P. Cole & J. Morgan (Eds.), *Syntax and semantics, vol. 3: Speech acts* (pp. 83–105). New York, NY: Academic Press.

Grice, P. (1975). Logic and conversation. In P. Cole & J. Morgan (Eds.), *Syntax and semantics, vol. 3: Speech acts* (pp. 41–58). New York, NY: Academic Press.

Gu, Y. (1990). Politeness phenomena in modern Chinese. *Journal of Pragmatics, 14*, 237–257.

Hancher, M. (1979). The classification of cooperative illocutionary acts. In *Language in Society, 8* (1), 1–14.

Herbert, R. (1988). The ethnography of English compliments and compliment responses: A contrastive sketch. In W. Oleksy (Ed), *Contrastive pragmatics*. Amsterdam: John Benjamins.

Herbert, R. (1990). Sex-based differences in compliment behavior. In *Language in Society, 19*, 201–224.

Herbert, R. (1991). The sociology of compliment work: An ethnocontrastive study of Polish and English compliments. In *Multilingua, 10* (4), 381–402.

Herbert, R. &. Straight, H. (1989). Compliment-rejection versus compliment-avoidance: Listener-based versus speaker-based pragmatic strategies. *Language and Communication, 9* (1), 35–47.

Holmes, J. (1986). Compliments and compliment responses in New Zealand English. *Anthropological Linguistics, 28*, 485–508.

Holmes, J. (1988). Paying compliments: A sex-preferential politeness strategies. *Journal of Pragmatics, 12*, 445–465.

Holmes, J. & Brown, D. F. (1987). Teachers and students learning about compliments. *TESOL Quarterly, 21* (3), 523–546.

House, J. (1989). Politeness in English and German: The functions of "please" and "bitte". In S. Blum-Kulka, J. House, & G. Kasper (Eds.), *Cross-cultural pragmatics: Requests and apologies* (pp. 96–119). Norwood, NJ: Ablex.

House, J. (1986). Cross-cultural pragmatics and foreign language teaching. In K. Bausch, F. Konigs, & R. Kogelheide (Eds.), *Probleme und Perspektiven der Sprachlehrforschung* (pp. 281–295). Frankfurt: Scriptor.

House, J., & Kasper, G. (1987). Interlanguage pragmatics: Requesting in a foreign language. In W. Lorscher & R. Schulze (Eds.), *Perspectives on language in performance: Festschrift for Werner Hullen on the occasion of his 60th birthday* (pp. 1250–1228). Tubingen: Narr.

Hsu, F. L. (1953). *American and Chinese*. Honolulu, HI: University of Hawai'i Press.

Hu, H. C. (1944). The Chinese concept of "face". *American Anthropologist*, 46, 45–65.

Jiang, X. (1985). *Chinese compliments: A socio-linguistics perspective.* Unpublished paper, American University.

Ju, Z. (1991). The 'depreciation' and 'appreciation' of some address terms in China. *Language in Society*, 20, 387–390.

Kasper, G. (1989). Variation in interlanguage speech act realization. In S. Gass, C. Madden, D. Preston, & S. Selinker (Eds.), *Variation in second language acquisition: Discourse and pragmatics* (pp. 37–58). Clevedon, U.K.: Multilingual Matters.

Kasper, G. (1990). Linguistic politeness: Current research issues. *Journal of Pragmatics*, 14, 193–218.

Kasper, G. (1992). Pragmatic transfer. *Second Language Research*, 8, 203–231.

Kirkpatrick, A. (1991). Information sequencing in Mandarin in letters of request. *Anthropological Linguistics*, 33, (2), 183–203.

Knapp, M., Happer, R., & Bell, R. (1984). Compliments: A descriptive taxanomy. *Journal of Communication*, 34, 12–31.

Lau, D. C. (1983). Confucius: The analects. *Chinese classics: Chinese–English series*. Hong Kong: The Chinese University Press.

Lee, C. (1990). Cute yaw haiya-nah! Hawai'i Creole English compliments and their responses: Implications for cross-cultural pragmatic failure. *University of Hawai'i Working Paper in ESL*, 9 (1), 115–161.

Leech, G. (1983). *Principles of pragmatics*. London and New York, NY: Longman.

Lewandowska-Tomaszczyk, B. (1989). Prasing and complimenting. In W. Oleksy (Ed.), *Contrastive pragmatics* (pp. 73–100). Amsterdam: John Benjamins.

Li, Jinxi, & Liu, Shiru. (1955). *Zhongguo yufa jiaocai [Materials on Chinese grammar]*. Wushi Niandai Chubanshe.

Lin, Yuwen. (1983). *Pianzheng fuju [Complex sentences with subordinate clauses]*. Shanghai: Shanghai Jiaoyu Chubanshe.

Manes, J. (1983). Compliments: A mirror of cultural values. In N. Wolfson & E. Judd (Eds.), *Sociolinguistics and language acquisition* (pp. 96–102). Rowley, MA: Newbury House.

Mao, L. (1994). Beyond politeness theory: 'Face' revisited and renewed. *Journal of Pragmatics*, 21, (5).

Matsumoto, Y. (1988). A sort of speech act qualification in Japanese: *Chotto*. *Journal of Asian Culture*, 9, 143–159.

Miles, P. (1992). *Complimenting behavior in two American communities*. M.A. scholarly paper, Department of English As Second Language, University of Hawai'i at Mānoa, Honolulu, HI.

Olshtain, E., & Weinbach, L. (1993). Interlanguage features of the speech act of complaining. In S. Blum-Kulka & G. Kasper (Eds.), *Interlanguage Pragmatics* (pp. 108–122). New York, NY: Oxford University Press.

Pomerantz, A. (1978). Compliment responses: Notes on the co-operation of multiple constraints. In J. Schenkein (Ed.), *Studies in the organization of conversational interaction* (pp. 79–112). New York, NY: Academic Press.

Rintell, Ellen. (1981). Sociolinguistic variation and pragmatic ability: A look at learners. *International Journal of the Society of Languages*, 27, 11–34.

Saville-Troike, M. (1982). *The ethnography of communication*. Baltimore, MD: University Park Press.

Scarcella, R. (1983). Discourse accent in second language performance. In S. Gass, & L. Selinker (Eds.), *Language transfer in language learning* (pp. 306–326). Rowley, MA: Newbury House.

Scollon, R., & Wong-Scollon, S. (1991). Topic confusion in English-Asian discourse. *World Englishes*, 9, 113–123.

Searle, J. (1975). Indirect speech acts. In P. Cole and J. Morgan (Eds.), *Syntax and semantics, Vol. 3: Speech acts* (pp. 59–82). New York, NY: Academic Press.

Takahashi, S. (1990). Exploring the comprehension process of non-literal utterances and some implications for automaticity. *University of Hawai'i Working Papers in ESL*, 9 (2), 67–97.

Takahashi, T. &. Beebe, L. M. (1993). Cross-linguistic influence in the speech act of correction. In G. Kasper & S. Blum-Kulka (Eds.), *Interlanguage pragmatics* (pp. 138–157). New York, NY: Oxford University Press.

Tao, H., & Thompson, S. (1991). English backchannels in Mandarin conversations: A case study of superstratum pragmatic 'interference.' *Journal of Pragmatics*, 16, 209–223.

Thomas, J. (1983). Cross-cultural pragmatic failure. *Applied Linguistics*, 4, 91–112.

Weizman, E. (1989). Requestive hints. In S. Blum-Kulka, J. House, & G. Kasper (Eds.), *Cross-cultural pragmatics: Requests and apologies* (pp. 71–95). Norwood, NJ: Ablex.

Weizman, E. (1993). Interlanguage requestive hints. In G. Kasper & S. Blum-Kulka (Eds.), *Interlanguage pragmatics* (pp. 123–137). New York, NY: Oxford University Press.

Wierzbicka, A. (1985). Different cultures, different languages, different speech acts: Polish vs. English. *Journal of Pragmatics, 9*, 145–178.

Wierzbicka, A. (1991). *Cross cultural pragmatics*. Berlin: Mouton de Gruyter.

Wolfson, N. (1981). Compliments in cross-cultural perspective. *TESOL Quarterly, 15* (2), 117–124.

Wolfson, N. (1989). *Perspectives: Sociolinguistics and TESOL*. Cambridge, MA: Newbury House.

Wolfson, N. &. Manes, J. (1981). The compliment formula. In F. Coulmas (Ed.), *Conversational routine* (pp. 115–132). The Hague: Mouton.

Ye, L. (1991). *A study of IL request realization of Chinese learners of English*. Unpublished manuscript, Department of English As Second Language, University of Hawai'i at Mānoa, Honolulu, HI.

Yeh, J., & Shih, A. (1993). *A study of pragmatic transfer in Taiwan English learners' interlanguage discourse behavior*. Unpublished paper, University of Hawai'i at Mānoa, Honolulu, HI.

Young, S. (1987). A comparison between Chinese and American cultures in forms of address, greetings, farewells, and compliments. *Cross Currents, 13*, 13–28.

Young, W. L. (1982). Inscrutability revisited. In J. Gumperz (Ed.), *Language and social identity* (pp. 72–84). New York, NY: Cambridge University Press.

Zhang, Y. (1990). *The requestive behavior of Chinese learners of English*. Unpublished manuscript, Department of English As Second Language, University of Hawai'i at Mānoa, Honolulu, HI.

Zhang, Y. (1991). *Politeness and indirectness: A cross cultural investigation*. Unpublished manuscript, Department of English As Second Language, University of Hawai'i at Mānoa, Honolulu, HI.

Zuo, H. (1988). Verbal interactions of compliment in American English and Chinese. In W. Hu (Ed.), *Intercultural communication: What it means to Chinese learners of English* (pp. 117–136). Shanghai: Shanghai Translation.

www.ingramcontent.com/pod-product-compliance
Lightning Source LLC
Chambersburg PA
CBHW032034150426
43194CB00006B/275